Adventures of a
Young Rifleman

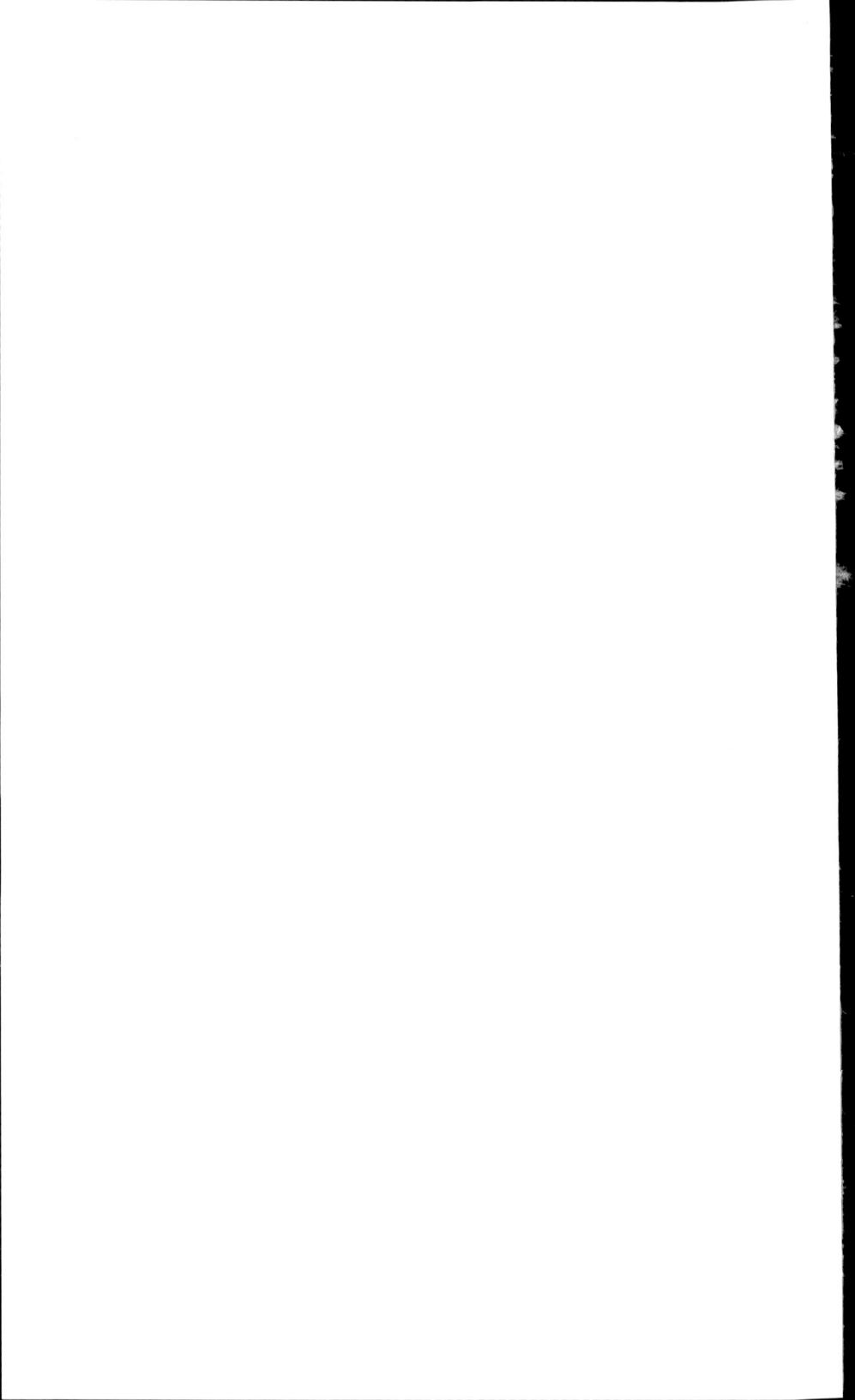

Adventures of a Young Rifleman

The Experiences of a Saxon in
the French & British Armies
During the Napoleonic Wars

Johann Christian Maempel

LEONAUR

Adventures of a Young Rifleman: the Experiences of a Saxon in the French & British Armies During the Napoleonic Wars
by Johann Christian Maempel

Originally published in 1826 under the title
*Adventures of a Young Rifleman, in the French and English Armies,
During the War in Spain and Portugal, from 1806 to 1816*

Published by Leonaur Ltd

ISBN: 978-1-84677-508-6 (hardcover)
ISBN: 978-1-84677-507-9 (softcover)

http://www.leonaur.com

Publisher's Notes

The opinions expressed in this book are those of the author
and are not necessarily those of the publisher.

Contents

Preface

In whatever degree we strive to become acquainted with things past, and occupy ourselves with history in general, yet we find at last that we gain most information from the personal narratives of individuals, and the relation of particular occurrences. On this account, therefore, memoirs, auto-biographies, original letters, and documents of this nature, are particularly sought after.

Memorials of this kind may differ in value with respect to the persons, times, or occurrences treated of, yet no such writings are wholly to be disregarded. The occurrences in the lives of men residing together, vary but little in general; and what happens to one may be considered as a type of thousands. The following memoir appears, therefore, well worthy of attention.

Our young soldier is naturally of a good disposition; he accommodates himself to everything he meets with; he is obedient, brave, hardy, good-tempered, and honst—with the exception of a slight propensity to plundering—which, however, he always manages to palliate, under the plea of pressing necessity. In short, were we thrown into this course of life, he is just the companion we should wish for.

His military career was entered upon without consideration—it was passed through without care: and thus we find the occurrences easily and pleasantly narrated. Want and plenty, good fortune and ill fortune, death and life, flow equally from the pen; and the book makes a very enduring impression. There is something peculiarly interesting in the adventures of an individual wandering, without any will or purpose of his own, wherever he may be directed by the orders of his superiors, or by stern necessity. We see the gain of one moment lost in the next; and in the back-ground, opposed to very trifling advantages, labours, wounds, sickness, imprisonment, starvation, and death!

The description of this ever-varying career, is also rendered particularly interesting on this account: that the commonest soldier, seeking his home wherever he goes, is, by means of his billets, as if led by the hand of Asmodeus, introduced into every house, and into the deepest recesses of domestic privacy. Of revelations of this nature there is no scarcity in the volume before us,

There is not a more pleasing method of recalling the past, than by the contemplation of individual realities. The particular circumstances of events, slightly and perhaps erroneously made known to us by means-of the newspapers, are only historically and evidently brought before our view, when an unimportant and uninterested individual gives us a description of scenes witnessed by him, not intentionally or out of curiosity, but because compelled by necessity.

Our friend was also taken by the button, and spoken to by Napoleon, at a review of the troops at Valladolid—he entered Madrid under the command of Murat—he plundered and slew there during the insurrection of the 2nd of May, 1808—he was quartered in Aranjuez, in the ruined palace of the Prince of the Peace—suffered from the Guerillas—languished in sickness under the hands of self-interested attendants—and almost lost his life in a cruel imprisonment. For these sufferings he was, however, compensated, in having the good fortune to assist in the destruction of the prison of the Inquisition, and to see the accursed building in flames, not without suspicion of having, along with his comrades, caused the conflagration.

May his work, therefore, spread itself abroad, and, along with many others, afford an agreeable amusement, and perhaps, here and there, an opportunity for useful reflection.

Goëthe

8

Introduction

The Emperor Napoleon, intent upon excluding the English from the trade of the Continent, considered it necessary to occupy Portugal, which, owing to situation and particular circumstances, had hitherto continued in connexion with England. The Prince Regent was declared to have forfeited his right to the throne, because he had not allowed the confiscation of English merchandise. To prevent any uneasiness in Spain respecting the occupation of the neighbouring kingdom, a treaty was concluded with the king; but Napoleon, even at that time, appears, by means of secret intrigues, to have meditated the downfall of the Spanish Royal Family.

Charles IV. on a sudden, placed his son, the Crown Prince, in confinement, under the plea of his being engaged in a conspiracy against him, his father and king. Before the Spanish public had recovered from the surprise occasioned by this event, a second royal proclamation was issued, declaring that the Crown Prince had penitently confessed his crime, and that his father had forgiven him. Napoleon was, in all probability, the promoter of this discord between father and son, by deceiving both with the promise of his assistance.

The Prince of Portugal quitted his country, which he was unable to defend against a superior force, and fled to the Brazils. The French now occupied the country, but thought no more of the agreements contained in the treaty with Spain; reports were even prevalent, that Napoleon meant to incorporate the whole of Spain, as far as the Ebro, with his large dominions, which at that time would have been easy, as he had a large force in Spain, destined to go to Portugal. The Spanish people now first began to be aware of their dangerous neighbours; an enraged multitude repaired to Aranjuez, destroyed the palace of the all-powerful minister, the Prince of the Peace, and declared him an enemy and a traitor to his country.

The following day, Charles IV. issued a proclamation, declaring that on account of ill health, he abdicated the throne in favour of his son, Ferdinand VII. The populace considered that by the downfall of the minister, and the accession of Ferdinand, satisfaction had been given them, and that they were secured from the pretensions of the French. Murat, duly weighing the importance of these changes in the Government, advanced quickly to Madrid, with an army apparently destined to go to Portugal, secretly made arrangements by means of skilful agents, both with the abdicated and the new monarchs; the former shortly issued a protest against his forced abdication: the latter, Murat persuaded to go in person to Napoleon, who had already crossed the frontiers of Spain, in order to request the Emperor's acknowledgement of his right to the throne. This inconsiderate step the new King took, in opposition to the advice of his ministers, and the wishes of the people, who, in every town he passed through, surrounded his carriage, and begged of him to remain. He went as far as Bayonne; and in a few days his father, the Queen, the Princes, and the Prince of the Peace arrived. Here Ferdinand was compelled to abdicate the throne, because his father declared, that he himself had been compelled to surrender his crown, and to him the Emperor left the choice of death or abdication: he chose the latter, abdicated in favour of Napoleon, who immediately declared his brother Joseph King of Spain.

The Spanish people, enraged at the idea of a king being forced upon them by a foreign power, rose unanimously, and displayed a power which the Emperor had never given them credit for, not conceiving it possible that such a feeling for their religion, their country, and their legitimate rulers, could exist. Among a people so far behind the rest of Europe in education and industry. The clergy, whose power over the people yet remained unshaken, feared to experience the fate of their brethren in France, and excited still more the nation already thirsting for revenge; the overbearing conduct of the French troops, and the assistance afforded by the English, were also powerful excitements to a general rising, which occasioned the capture of General Dupont in the Sierra Morena, by the Spanish army, and Marshal Junot in Portugal, by the English, upon which the French army retreated behind the Ebro.

The Emperor, now conceiving that his presence would suffice to quench the flames of rebellion, advanced with the large army returned from Germany, defeated the forces opposed to him, and without quelling the insurrection in the least, entered Madrid. Here he abolished a number of institutions, which were not consistent, certainly, with the advanced State of civilization, and only operated as a check upon improvement; but by the indiscriminate abolition of religious houses, the inquisition, and the privileges of the nobility, he exasperated the higher orders and the clergy still more against him, without gaining the good opinion of the populace. He soon perceived the almost insurmountable difficulties of this truly national war; and, in order to save his life and his personal reputation, quitted Spain never again to return.

His generals continued the war with alternate success; King Joseph could only call himself master of the country wherever French troops were stationed. The contest became every day more bloody, and raged in all the provinces. Only large detachments could traverse the country, and the communication between France and the separate corps was, with the utmost difficulty, kept open. Lives without number were lost, less in open battle than by assassinations, sickness, and hunger, until at last the yet unstained reputation of the French armies sank before the obstinacy of the Spanish people, and the valour of the English army under Wellington.

This short introduction may serve to give the reader an idea of the state of things at the period to which my narrative refers, and which is closely connected with the proceedings of the French armies.

CHAPTER 1

I Enlist in the French Army

My father was a poor but upright country clergyman, whom I unfortunately lost a few weeks after my birth; and thus the care of bringing me up fell upon my good mother alone. My wild disposition, which paternal authority could alone have suppressed, soon discovered itself. My mother's exhortations were not wanting; but my careless spirit soon forgot her well-meant instructions. I soon became the leader of my companions in all their plots; and whenever any mischief was perpetrated, it was laid to the charge of the parson's orphan, on whom all eyes were directed.

A spirit of adventure, which afterwards decided the course of my life, soon showed itself. Nothing gave me greater pleasure than passing a night with my companions in a barn, or a summer-house; nothing on earth could have dissuaded me from this enjoyment, and kept me quiet in my bed. If a fire broke out in the neighbourhood, I was sure, if possible, to be one of the first there.

One afternoon, as we were bathing in the river, at some distance from our homes, the alarm gun gave notice of the breaking out of a fire. Without asking the leave of our parents, or troubling ourselves about the distance, we all agreed to set off. A village was in flames. Without knowing the way, we ran thither, guided by the light. At last we reached it; but being too young and inexperienced to afford any assistance, we found out the folly of our adventure; and as we were unknown in the place, which was several miles from our home, we soon began to experience both hunger and thirst. The last was easily quenched: water was every where to be found; but the cravings of the stomach, at that time not accustomed to fasting, were not so easily satisfied. Money none of us possessed. We were ashamed to beg, and our hunger every moment increased. In vain we consulted together, in vain were all our pockets ransacked; at last a penny was found in mine, the sight of which gave us fresh courage. We had long been enviously watching a peasant, who was sitting in charge of a pile of furniture saved from the flames, and was now and then paying his respects to a large loaf. In possession of money and compelled by hunger, we now approached the man boldly; as owner of the coin, I was of course the speaker, and the following conversation took place between us:—

"Pray, Sir, will you be so good as give me a pennyworth of bread?"

"A pennyworth? that will be a great deal! Where do you come from? and are those your companions standing there?"

"Yes, they are."

"And are they all hungry?"

"Yes, my good Sir, they all are."

"Keep your penny; there is a piece for you, and there is some for your companions, a piece for each; and now get away with you: but first tell me what did you want here?"

I answered without consideration: "Oh, we only wished for once to see a village in flames!" This was just the answer to stir up the ire of our benefactor:

"You good-for-nothing young rascals, let me find a stick?" We did not wait for the end of his speech, or to see his intentions fulfilled, but ran away with our bread, as fast as we could, and did not get home until late at night. Being closely questioned by my mother, I acknowledged the truth, and my back smarted for it, but her lecture and advice were forgotten with the pain.

I could relate a thousand such tricks, but I should only tire my readers; and this example may suffice to show my thirst after adventures, even in my youth. All my errors sprang from this source; I was never vicious, this I can still conscientiously say.

As I increased in years, my mother became desirous that I

should embrace the profession of my father. I received instructions, and my tutors soon discovered that I possessed natural talents and capabilities, which only required care and attention to be made available. To this they daily exhorted me. I followed their instructions, and was advancing in my studies, when in my fifteenth year I lost my mother, after a short illness. I lost in her my only support, and my only hope of being able to prosecute my studies with success.

The little property which was left to me and my brothers and sisters, fell into the hands of a greedy relation, who was more intent upon his own gains than the preservation of our small inheritance. Study was now out of the question: it became necessary for me to think of some employment, and I made choice of one nearly allied to the learned professions, the trade of barber-surgeon. Although this was entirely my own choice, yet I soon repented of it. On further acquaintance, my dislike even amounted to abhorrence.

This was chiefly caused by a circumstance which often occurs in a surgeon's business, but which wholly deterred me from it.

In the first three months of my apprenticeship, my master had the body of an old woman for dissection: it was summer time; the corpse had lain upwards of twenty-four hours, and the smell was abominable. I was present, I suppressed my abhorrence for some time; but at the opening of the body, and the sight of the entrails, I could no longer contain myself, and my stomach emptied itself of its contents. I soon recovered, and when the operation was completed, returned home. Dinner was just ready, and as ill-luck would have it, a dish of calf's liver, with brown sauce, was placed upon the table; the instant I perceived this, all the circumstances of the dissection rushed upon my mind; I turned pale as ashes, and going out of the room, a violent vomiting deprived me entirely of strength, and completed my dislike to my trade.

In this manner an unfortunate dish influenced my future destiny, and drove me to seek my fortune far from home.

A gloomy period was now approaching for my country. The French armies entered the north of Germany for the first time, and wherever they came spread terror and dismay. The battle which decided the fate of Prussia, was fought in the vicinity of my abode, and all the evils attendant upon war fell to our lot. For myself, I had plenty to do, beards to shave, and still oftener, wounds to bind up.

Here I was first witness to the unspeakable misery occasioned by war. Many a blooming young man, whose health promised a long course of years, I saw brought wounded from the fight, and expire in misery and torture; and these horrid scenes made the occupation of a soldier, brilliant as it is in outward appearance, hateful to me.

After the battle, the French army entered our town, and all discipline among the troops was soon at an end. Thirsting for plunder, they broke into every house. My master and my-self were in one of the churches, occupied in attending to the wounded; but as the balls, which were fired upon the flying Prussians, flew thickly over the town, and damaged many of the houses, almost all the Prussian army-surgeons, as well as those belonging to the town, took to flight. We made the best of our way to our house, which we found occupied by French soldiers, ransacking for booty.

By way of precaution some loaves had been hidden under the stairs; these were afterwards discovered, and carried off. But before this the following circumstance occurred:—A person came to require the attendance of my master to some wounded persons, lying in the house of a *traiteur*; I went there direct-ly. Whether my master ever came I know not to this day. The house was already filled with soldiers of French light cavalry, who each seized two or three bottles of wine, leaped on their horses, and rode off; but these were instantly replaced by fresh arrivals. In this manner the supply of wine, which was in readi-ness, soon disappeared. The cry was now "Wine, instantly!" ac-companied by blows, of which I received my share, patiently. The landlord begged of me to help his people to fetch wine from the cellars, to satisfy these stormy enquiries. As there was no means of escape at hand, I consented to this: I had made six or seven journeys to the cellar, when an opportunity offered itself. In an instant I was out of the house, and with a bottle in each hand, aided by the darkness of the night, I reached home without molestation.

On arrival I found our house as full of French soldiers as the one I had left, and, therefore, did not think it advisable to enter, but hid myself near a well, at the back of it. Here I found an unhappy Prussian fusilier, severely wounded with a shot through the arm, and a stab in the breast. He groaned bitterly, and complained of hunger, having eaten nothing for twenty-four hours. I took compassion on him, gave him the bottles, and in spite of danger, crept into the houses took one of the loaves from under the stairs, and brought it to the Prussian, and saw with pleasure, how much the poor fellow enjoyed his meal. When he was satisfied, and had heartily thanked me, I resolved to take him to the hospital, as the night was very cold; and had got about half-way when we were surrounded by the French, one of whom, on seeing the Prussian, exclaimed:—"A Prussian! O your rascal of a king!" I had got, without being aware of it, the second bottle of wine in my hand; this was soon snatched away and tasted. I was now ordered to procure more, but how was I able to do this? After giving me a few blows, they contented themselves with searching me; but they were disappointed, as I had little, or nothing about me. After this they gave me a kick, and sent me about my business. I turned once more towards home, for the Prussian had disappeared in the scuffle; and besides, I had no particular wish to accompany him any farther, for at this time self-preservation overcame all other feelings.

On reaching home, not without danger, I found everything in still greater disorder than before; either purposely, or by chance, some houses near our's had taken fire, and every one was occupied in removing his property. We hastened to save what, in this scene of tumult, it was possible to save, although we were obliged to show every thing over and over again to the French, who, when they saw anything which pleased them, saved us the trouble of carrying it off, although it was, perhaps, in the next minute, thrown away for something which pleased them better. What little we did save, we placed in a cart, and, leaving the house entirely, went into a neighbouring street, not so much resorted to by these gentlemen, where we remained the whole night in the open air. The prisoners, in the House of Correction, had obtained their liberty, and at daybreak, we found several of them near us, who were busied in freeing themselves from their chains, and then disappeared. We did not think it advisable to remain any longer here, being fearful of visits from prowling marauders, but escaped to a house where there was a guard posted for our safety; here we remained until the Saturday, by which time order was pretty well restored. We found the houses almost emptied; and what remained, so much damaged as to be rendered nearly useless; and yet the troops now arriving, and which were quartered upon the inhabitants, were to be well provided for.

The soldiers to whom gain was so easy, and possession so uncertain, were so little sparing of their money, that I was never in want. This superfluity led me into several scrapes, which the wife of my master, well-intentioned, no doubt, sharply lectured me for. Her severity, coupled with the dislike I had taken to my business since the dissection, induced me one morning to pack up my bundle, and without taking leave, to quit my master's house.

But where was I to go? Among the soldiers! This operated like a clap of thunder to me. What road should I take? What course should I pursue? Deeply engaged in these reflections, which occurred for the first time when I found myself at liberty. I went on, and almost without knowing it, found myself at the gates of the fortress of Erfurth, which was occupied by a French garrison.

I was entering the gates, and was ordered to halt. "Where are you going, young man, have you a pass?"

At these words I trembled like an aspen leaf, and answered, "No!" The officer on guard ordered me to be taken to the commandant, and I was immediately led there by a soldier. I had to wait a long while: at last the dreaded warrior appeared, and asked me a number of questions, among others, whether I should not like to serve the Emperor of France; and added, in a friendly manner, that by so doing, I might make something of myself.

During these words be played carelessly with his order, to draw my attention to it, and said: "if such an ornament was hanging at your breast, you would be proud of it, and justly so? Come, enlist; be a brave man, and you will arrive at distinction."

In this manner I was persuaded to make choice of an occupation I so much dreaded; I fancied a few days would procure me a decoration such as the officer's; but notwithstanding all my exertions, I never received it, although I was never the last in battle.

I was now quartered upon a citizen in easy circumstances, who received orders to take good care of me. I went early to bed, but as may easily be imagined, I slept but little; the most opposite thoughts passed through my mind. I thought on my home and on my friends, then on my future destiny, and the troubles of my new occupation; then I saw in idea the well-deserved cross of honour on my breast; in short, I never closed my eyes. As soon as daylight appeared, I left my bed, and went into the apartment of my landlord, whom I found engaged in his business; he was a butcher.

"Hey!" exclaimed my good-natured host, "what up already, my lad?"

"Ah! I have not slept the whole night."

"And why not?" asked the old man, a little disturbed; "many have slept in that bed, and have never complained of it."

"Ah! my friend," replied I "the bed is a very good one, and I have rested well in it, but it is my thoughts which have kept me waking."

"Why, you surely have committed no crime?" said mine host, "you look too honest and too young for that."

In this manner we conversed together during breakfast, until eight o'clock, when the muster-hour approached. As the clock struck, the same corporal who had conducted me to my quarters, came into the room to bring me to the place where my new comrades were collected.

I was then, together with some more recruits, presented to the captain of the detachment, who spoke in a very friendly manner to me, and gave a most agreeable description of my new trade.

"You are but a young lad" said he, "but you have done wisely and bravely to become a soldier; in the military life alone, can a man now do any good for himself. You will soon find that no one on earth lives better than a soldier; you have nothing to care for, you may enjoy yourself every day; the Emperor finds you food, and gives you money besides; the citizens and peasants provide every thing else you want; and all this for nothing, and without daring to refuse!" (soon enough I found how little truth there was in all this.) "Now, my son, go, in God's name, to the surgeon, and let him examine you."

I and my comrades followed the corporal to the surgeon, where we were obliged to strip ourselves. He felt all our limbs, and last of all looked into our mouths; the inspection of our teeth concluded the examination, which appeared very strange to me, and we were dismissed with the military command, "March!"

From hence we were taken to the depôt for clothing; here I tried on one after the other, coats and trousers, shoes and stockings, gaiters; schakos, and foraging caps: nothing would fit me; and it appeared as if the tailor had never reckoned upon such a customer as me.

At last I collected an equipment which fitted tolerably well. What was wanting was immediately put in order by the tailor,

Immediately on receiving my clothing, I was prohibited, on pain of arrest, from selling any part of my dress, and ordered never again to show myself in plain clothes. I promised punctually to obey these commands, and now received my first five days' pay, amounting to twelve *groschen*.

I was accompanied on my way home by a crowd of pedlars, who were numerous in this place, driving a trade, for them at least advantageous, with the new clothed recruits. In less than a quarter of an hour my whole barber's wardrobe was in their hands; and in mine—but very little money.

On my arrival at my quarters, my landlord surveyed me from head to foot. The worthy old man shook his head sorrowfully, and said: "Young man, it is a good thing just now to be a soldier, as you want for nothing, and are not in distress; but other days will come when you will remember what old Kerbs has said to you." My new equipment, however, had given me fresh courage; and the young runaway of sixteen years of age thought little of the future, and the warnings of the old man. I even thought it becoming and soldier-like now to behave myself in a free and overbearing manner. The conduct and way of thinking of my new acquaintances were not the most upright, and had not the best influence upon my actions; instead of setting me right, they encouraged me in my follies, and thus I was certainly not following the most virtuous path.

In a few days I received musket, sabre, pouch, and my new portmanteau, the knapsack. Now my work began. How often have I worked at the cleaning of my accoutrements, until they were dirty again; and many an hour was I obliged to work hard before I succeeded in getting them in order. The daily drill of four hours, namely, two hours in the morning, and two in the afternoon, afforded me likewise no great pleasure; and many a time would I rather have, shaved a few beards than received instructions in the art of war.

The first time I mounted guard was on the Cyriaxburg. We had scarcely entered the guard-room, when my comrades began to tell the most horrible ghost-stories, and even showed me some boards in the room which they told me had been broken by an evil demon, who nightly walked and played all sorts of antics in this apartment: upon these boards they compelled me to take up my resting place. I could not close my eyes; the dreadful spectre who had prepared my couch was always present to my imagination; at last it struck eleven, and with a heavy heart and downcast courage I rose up to go upon guard.

As ill luck would have it, I was posted in an old tower, where there was a bell, upon which the soldier on guard was obliged to strike the hour after the sounding of the clock. In this lonely place was I obliged to stand sentry in the hour when spirits are abroad. I gazed steadfastly upon the darkness of the night; my heated fancy conjured up a thousand phantoms before me. I began to find myself feverish and excited, when on a sudden something pulling at my cloak, raised my apprehensions to the highest pitch. I screamed out like a madman, and was within a little of pulling the bell and raising an alarm. The whole guard ran to see what had occasioned the noise, and what was the matter with me. On examination, it was discovered that some wag had tied a string to the back of my great coat; this he had pulled at from the guard-room, and thus excited in me the idea that a demon had seized me with his claws. The sub-officer on guard made strict enquiries after the perpetrator of this action, but of course everyone had good reason to protest his own innocence. This discovery convinced me that my comrades had been joking at my expense, and that all they had before related was false. My purse was the object they aimed at, for everyone of my comrades had offered to take my post; for this indeed a compliment beyond my means would have been required, and I therefore declined the proposal. When they found, in spite of all their endeavours they could not gain their ends, they took this method to frighten me, and thus deter me for the future from mounting guard on this spot.

When I was relieved, my comrades all ridiculed and laughed at me, and called me a coward I troubled myself very little about their jokes, but learned this lesson from the occurrence, not to believe everything which was told me, particularly ghost-stories.

As they had not succeeded in this way, in making me pay for mounting guard, they left me in peace; and though I afterwards often stood sentry in the same place, I never experienced any annoyance. About three months after my enlistment, our detachment received orders to march; this time had been just sufficient to initiate me in the duties of a soldier.

After my disappearance from the house of my master, my relations had used all the means in their power to discover the place of my abode, but they could learn no tidings of me. I took care to give them no intelligence, and thus departed from the neighbourhood, leaving them in the greatest uncertainty respecting my fate.

The regiment to which I belonged, was formed from the wrecks of the Prussian army, after the unfortunate campaign of 1806, and had often changed its head quarters; it had been in garrison at Fulda, Brunswick, Paderborn, and Minden; but as in the German territories it had rather diminished than increased, it was thought proper to remove it, and it was placed at Boulogne, to which place we were now to follow it.

On the morning of the march I took a hearty farewell of my worthy hosts, who wished me luck and happiness, and set out cheerfully on my way. The whole march from Erfurth to Mentz was very agreeable. The day's journeys were very easy, the towns lying at short distances from each other. Our poor countrymen were obliged to subsist us, and to find whatever we required, get it where they could, and we led altogether a very pleasant life.

In Gelnhausen I was most comfortably billeted in the house of a linen-weaver, who regaled me with cyder. This liquor, new to me, I found excellent; my host did not let me want for it, and I drank to my heart's content, even more than I could bear. In the morning, after my debauch, I found myself so unwell that I was not able to walk, and was carried like a sick man, in a cart.

Those of my comrades, who for the first time in their lives were in a wine country, found the juice of the grape at Höchst so enticing, that the captain in command of the detachment, found it necessary to engage the market boat, which goes daily from Frankfort to Mentz, and stops here about noon.

We were now, not without some difficulty, embarked, and went pleasantly enough down the Maine. Upon reaching the Rhine, my thoughts once more turned upon my native country, my relations, and friends; repentance, and an eager longing after them reigned in my breast, and were beginning to have the ascendancy; but the wild merriment of my comrades, and a false sense of honour, which whispered in my ear, "If you now return to your home, you will be scoffed at and despised," repressed my feelings of contrition, and I resigned myself patiently to my lot. Some of my comrades, whom the wine at Höchst had inspired with mirth, began now to sing the well known national melody: "*Auf, auf, ihr*

Brüder und seid stark." When they came to the verse:"*An Deutsch-lands Gränze füllen wir mit Erde unsre hand*," I could contain myself no longer, and floods of tears rolled down my cheeks.

An old corporal came up to me, and said—"What are you crying for, foolish boy! there, drink; you will soon be better." But it was not in my power to drink and to be merry; the remembrance of my forsaken friends, and the feelings excited by the song, lay heavy on my heart.

When we reached the French territory, we found a multitude of spectators assembled, who had evidently expected guests of a different sort, by the boat; for on perceiving us land, they went off with evident uneasiness in their looks.

With our billets we received orders not to require the least thing from our hosts, for in the French territory they were bound to furnish us with nothing but lodging and food. This order we did not much relish; we were now upon a different footing from the other side of the Rhine, where the unfortunate Germans were obliged to furnish every thing we asked for. I, with some others, was quartered upon a baker, who, notwithstanding his handsome and well filled shop, gave us nothing. In the evening, soup was set before us, without bread; and upon further examination, we found hairs and other things in it, which deprived us of all appetite, and we sent it back to our landlord, without having touched it. Had any of our poor countrymen in Germany set such a dish before us, they would have suffered for it; but we were now in France, and were obliged to put up with it without complaining.

The next morning I received; for the first time, bread, furnished by the commissariat; this I did not at all relish, and I afterwards learned that the contractors at Mentz did not pride themselves on furnishing it of the best quality. In the afternoon I went with some of my comrades to one of the wine-houses, and there soon forgot all my troubles, I had no sooner drank a bottle of the delightful Rhenish, than I became merry and joyful, and thought neither on the past or the future.

On the following day we went down the Rheingau, as far as

Bingen. How much was I delighted with the splendid scenery. On the opposite side of the river, beautifully varied, were seen mountains with ruined castles, handsome country-houses, pleasant towns, green valleys, with lively-looking villages, and the whole landscape interspersed with vineyards. The banks on this side, steeper and more woody, afforded a less pleasing but more imposing picture. At Bingen we saw the Bingerloch, the well known Mausethurm, built, according to the old legend, by Bishop Hatto, and the chapel of St. Roch, on a high mountain. We marched always on the left bank of the Rhine, through Boppart, Oberwesel, Coblentz, and passed the ancient town of Andernach, the houses in which, to judge from the style of building, must have stood for centuries.

At Cologne we quitted the river, and, turning to the left towards the Netherlands, parched through Juliers to Aix-la-Chapelle. Here we rested for one day, which I made use of to look around the town, and to visit the noted warm baths at Burschied, which are in the vicinity, We then went on to Maestricht, a strongly fortified town on the Maese, to Louvaine, where the well-arranged hospital for invalid soldiers, who, in reward for their services, are here provided for, particularly interested me. From thence we proceeded to Brussels, where the Hotel de Ville, above everything else, drew my attention.

In a journey like this, it is impossible to obtain more than a very superficial view of the interesting objects in the different towns; but as far as laid in my power, I have always endeavoured to get a sight of whatever was worthy of attention.

We next marched through Brabant, by way of Ghent, Lisle, and St. Omers; and at last joined our regiment at Boulogne. Here a new scene burst upon my view; for the first time in my life I beheld the sea—what an imposing sight! The ocean lay before me, enlivened by large vessels, whose weight appeared enormous; I could scarcely be convinced that such enormous machines could be borne upon the waves. The novelty and splendour of this sight so forcibly drew my attention, that for several days I was not weary of gazing on it.

At Boulogne I saw the large camp, which had been occupied by the French troops, destined for the invasion of England; this numerous and well-disciplined army would have given the English occupation enough, if by means of their gold they had not induced Austria to declare war. Thus began the war of 1805. The troops; which were for the most part embarked, were despatched in full haste from Boulogne, to give the Emperor of Austria a lesson which he did not soon forget.

Here the arms we had brought with us were exchanged for new. Soon after our arrival, the whole regiment was marched to Mechlin, where we were placed in garrison. Now began the drills again, and I came in for many a memorial not at all to my taste; but what signified that? a soldier must obey, and even if he is unjustly treated, he dares not murmur against his superiors. A subaltern officer, named Rehm, gave me one day such a blow on the foot, that my shoe was immediately filled with blood. I was laid up for a fortnight, and my friend Rehm was under arrest for the same time. Another circumstance, however, afforded me more satisfaction: an officer of our company, named Vigelius, took a fancy to me; and chose me for his servant; he was well versed in science, and took much pains in instructing me.

CHAPTER 2

The March to Iberia

Thus passed the time tolerably enough, until I, with several of my comrades, was taken ill of fever, and was compelled to go into the hospital. Being here, in a;very miserable condition, necessity got the better of my false sense of honour, and I wrote to my sister to beg for a little money.

Scarcely fourteen days after the departure of my letter, our colonel, whose name was Schenck, came into the hospital and desired to see me. When I heard this I was terribly frightened, although conscious of no crime. He asked me—"Had I written for any money?"

"Yes," answered I, trembling.

"Come, then, don't be uneasy, my lad; here is a letter for you, and a *ducat* with it, and here is also a dollar for you besides."

Who was now more joyful than I, at finding myself so rich. I was now worth three dollars, and believed myself in possession of all France. In my joy, however, I did not forget to thank this good man, who, in addition, advised me for the future to direct my money to be sent to his wife, at Fulda, in order to save the postage.

I was very economical with my treasure, only allowing myself what was absolutely necessary, and I found the benefit of my frugality afterwards; as when my sickness left me, being very much weakened, I was enabled daily to procure myself a couple of measures of the capital beer brewed in Mechlin, in order to recruit my strength, which I found everyday returning.

I now thought it necessary to thank my good relations for their present, and wrote the following letter, which, on my return to my native country, I found still in the possession of my sister:

Mechlin, in Brabant
26th Oct. 1807
Dear Sister,
I have received your letter, with the money, but was obliged to pay two Dutch *guilders* postage for it. I am thankful for the love you have shown me; and as long as I live I shall not forget it. I am now servant to our first lieutenant, Vigelius, and thus exempted from all service, from drills and guards; my master has also promised, if I behave well, to get me made corporal. We shall never come back to Germany during our lives; for I understand we, and the 31st Yager Regiment, are to remain in garrison at Mechlin. Every thing is very dear here, the basket of potatoes cost seven *schillings*, that is the third part of a dollar. Farewell now, my dear sister, as my master is inquiring for me.
I remain your affectionate, and for your love, ever thankful brother—
P. S. When you write again, address your letter to the wife of Colonel Von Schenck, in Fulda.

Very soon after my recovery, an unexpected order arrived to select all the young men of the regiment to form a first battalion, which it was said was destined to form the guard of Jerome, King of Westphalia. An order for our march to Paris arrived at the same time, where we were to receive our colours, and when this ceremony was over, to be sent into Germany.

Our destination, already at that time, was Spain, but it was kept secret, and we were deceived in this manner, that we might not be tempted to desert, while we were so near the Dutch frontiers. The intelligence pleased most of us, and we rejoiced at the thoughts of returning to Germany; many, however, were suspicious, and took themselves off in time, and these acted the wisest.

The day of our departure arrived; the first battalion, in which

I was, took the road to France; the second remained behind, and some days afterwards was; marched to Magdeburg. I was thus separated from my master, Lieutenant Vigelius, and I never saw him after.

Our first quarter for the night was at Brussels; from thence we marched by way of Mons, Valenciennes, and Cambray, to Versailles, where we were lodged in the barracks. I should gladly have taken some rambles in the environs, and in the fine park belonging to the Imperial palace, if sufficient time had been spared us.

We remained still in the belief, that in a few days we were to receive our colours, and then immediately to be marched back into Germany. There were some whispers about Spain, but these, our officers contradicted, and assured us, that at the utmost, we should only, be sent into cantonments at Orleans, about five days' march from Paris, until a Prince of the blood could present us with our colours, and receive the oath of fidelity.

Strengthened, by these representations, in our error, we marched in good spirits to Orleans, where we rested; I was quartered upon a cutler, who found my presence disagreeable, and offered me six *francs* if I would quit his house, and provide for myself. The money made an impression upon me: six *francs*, thought I, is a handsome sum; for this I can procure many a breakfast, instead of as now, making a hungry march in the morning. In short, I took the money, went back boldly to the quartermaster, and assured him that I had lost my billet. I received another without any hesitation, and rejoicing in my fortunate speculation, went in search of my second quarters. This was a lucky day for me, as I came to a baker, who had passed some time in Germany, and understood a little of the language. "German man good man," were his first words; "come in, eat, drink, and sleep;" in this manner I was received. This reception pleased me much, and the six *francs* not less. Altogether, I was very comfortable in Orleans, and lived for that day, like a Prince; but, alas! it did not last long, and I was the worse off afterwards. But thus the world goes round, pain follows pleasure, as sunshine follows rain.

With a well-furnished knapsack I quitted Orleans; my land-lord was not contented with having fed me well during my stay, but gave me shirts, stockings, a large white loaf, and three *francs* in money; to these he added, the most hearty good wishes. I was now rich, and well provided with necessaries; on the first day's march we halted about half-way, and those who possessed a breakfast took the opportunity of eating it. I took out my large loaf, and cut deeply into it; this excited the appetite of my comrades, and as I always gave away willingly, it soon disappeared. I comforted myself with my store of cash; for nine *francs*, thought I, I shall be able to buy plenty of bread.

Towards evening we reached a small town, which could scarcely afford. accommodation for two companies; the one to which I belonged, was detached, and went some distance further, to a village on the main road. Here, with a comrade, named Vogel, I was billeted upon a farmer. It was customary, in France, for the soldier to receive either his meat raw, or money to procure it for himself; the last was now the case, and we sent out our landlord to procure us some. He was obliged to furnish vegetables, salt, &c., but more we could not require. We went to the tavern, but first gave directions to get every thing ready for us, and to take care that our supper was on table when we returned. Having drank a bottle of wine, we liked it so well that we had a second; both together cost twelve *liards*. We were not accustomed to such good wine, were merry, and returned, somewhat heated, to our quarters, where, civilly asking our landlord for our supper; "there it stands," said he, roughly. He was desired to lay the cloth, but he refused, and we did it ourselves; but on our application for plates, he brought us some dirty ones, saying, at the same time:—

"*C'est assez bon pour vous, cochons d'Allemagne*," (they are good enough for you German hogs), I answered him immediately, we were not hogs; and accompanied the words with a smart blow.

My comrade, who was more heated with wine than myself, cried out—"What does the rascal say? *cochons allemands!* Stop, I'll pay him for this." Upon which he drew his sabre, and struck our host a couple of blows, which almost knocked him down. My comrade was not satisfied with this correction, but seized him by the throat, threw him down, and took up a knife to stab him. Seeing the peasant in this dangerous situation. I exerted all my powers to master my enraged companion, and at last succeeded in wresting the knife from him, and thus saving the peasant, who, as soon as he found himself at liberty, got up and ran away, leaving us masters of the field. We now got our meat, sat down quietly at the house-door, and ate our supper. The peasant came back, and it being autumn, and rather cold, we enquired for our beds. Showing us the way to an apartment, which was entered by means of a ladder, he said—"Here you may lay down and sleep, and cover yourselves with your great coats." We did not choose to put up with such accommodations, and insisted upon a better bed; but it was of no use; he continued to refuse us in a very insulting way. We now lost all patience, and though I had spared him before, I now paid him off with interest.

When we had thrashed him till we were tired, we let him alone, took some bed-clothes to cover ourselves with, and went up to our apartment, drawing the ladder after us to secure us from any attack. Tired with our march, and our exercise upon the peasant, we were soon sound asleep, but our sleep was of short duration; we were awakened by a violent noise, and heard our names called. We quickly jumped up, and found that our host had lodged a complaint against us, and had procured two *gendarmes* and a patrol of our regiment, from the town. We related the circumstance as it had happened, endeavoured to set the behaviour of the peasant in its true light, and succeeded in convincing the *gendarmes* of our innocence. They even undertook our defence, and described the peasant as a man whose bad behaviour they were no strangers to. The corporal of the guard, however, an ill-tempered man, in spite of all our arguments, put us under arrest. We were obliged to dress ourselves, give up our bayonets and sabres, unscrew the flints from our muskets, and march back into the town. In the morning, our punishment was made known; it consisted in five days' arrest. We were obliged to march with the rear guard, and sleep at night in the guard-room; this punishment we found very supportable, as we had always companions in trouble.

The corporal, Ludwig, whose obstinacy had placed us under arrest, joined us on the following afternoon, on account of having been drunk and insulting the officer on duty. When he had slept off the effects of the liquor, we reproached him for his unkind behaviour towards us, and told him that what had happened was a judgement upon him; convinced of his guilt, he was silent, and made no attempt at reply.

When the five days were over, and the adjutant did not make his appearance, we applied to the colonel to set us at liberty, which he immediately did; but we were obliged to show ourselves at his quarters, where he was at dinner with the other officers. He read us a lecture upon our conduct, and threatened us with a severer punishment in case of a repetition of the offence; we thanked him for his kindness, and promised the best behaviour for the future. As we were going out, the colonel called us back, and presented us with a few *francs*; this example was followed by the other officers, so that we made money by our arrest. Thus, this little accident ended better for me than I had expected; and in my new quarters I found my landlord, who was a Pole by birth, a good-tempered friendly man.

We were approaching every day nearer to the south of France, and it was now openly said, that sooner or later, that is, as soon as we had received our colours, the regiment would march into Spain. In the mean while we went into cantonments in the neighbourhood of Bourdeaux; the staff and the grenadier company, were quartered in a town named Villefranche; the other companies were dispersed some distance around.

My company was posted in the village of St Martin, and I was billeted upon a poor tailor, who had not much to eat himself; the best part of his store was dried fruit, which I diligently helped him to consume.

A few days afterwards we were removed from this place to make room for the first company, and went to the small village of St. Miar, where we arrived so late in the evening, that it was quite dark when we received our billets. I asked the first person I met, the way to the house in which I was to be lodged; he answered: "*trois quarts de lieue d'ici,*" (three quarters of a league from hence). In addition to this, it was very dirty, and threatened every moment to rain. I begged of the man to go with me; and he agreed to go so far that I could no longer mistake the road. Upon making some inquiries of him respecting my host, I was informed, that it was an old widow lady, of good family, living upon her own estate; that she was a very good woman, but a Huguenot. This was all which he could say against her, and this was what pleased me the most, as I should thus be quartered among people of my own persuasion. When he had put me in the right road, he left me, and I went on as well as I could. At last, reaching a large house, which proved to be my quarters, I knocked at the door, and was asked from within, "Who is there?"

Upon my answering, "A soldier," the door was opened. A neat looking maid-servant appeared, and inquired what I wanted. I showed my billet, which was acknowledged to be right, and I was invited in. I was then shown into a handsome room, where were seated the lady of the house and her son, a young man about four-and-twenty.

"*Eh bien! vous êtes Allemand?*"—

"*Oui, Madame.*"

"*De quel pays?*"

"*Saxony, Madame.*"

In this manner the conversation began, and the old lady was never weary with asking questions. "You are very young to be a soldier, and so far from your country too, and now you are going into Spain; Oh! the Spaniards are bad people, with long knives, with which they cut the throats of all who come near them." I looked anxiously round to see if there was not already a Spaniard with a, long knife behind me, but to my great satisfaction I saw no one but the pretty maid-servant, busily employed in covering the table with several inviting-looking dishes. I had no idea that I was to have the honour of supping with the lady, but at her express desire, I sat down with her and her son, to a very handsome supper.

I had not for a length of time been so sumptuously entertained, and never before in France, and felt perfectly contented with my lot.

We had a good deal of conversation during supper, and among other things my landlady questioned me about my religion, whether I was Lutheran or Catholic; she was pleased when I told her I belonged to the Lutheran Church.

"I am not Lutheran," said she, "but reformed, and our two creeds much nearer resemble each other than the Catholic belief." Afterwards, she wished to know my name, and as she found it very difficult to pronounce, she gave me that of Christian.

After supper I was shown into a very comfortable sleeping-apartment, and the servant was directed to clean my shoes and clothes, and in the morning to get all my dirty linen washed.

In this manner I lived every day, and I cannot describe the kindness of this excellent old lady towards me; I was placed exactly upon the same footing with her son, who was a well educated and agreeable young man, and called me always *mon petit frere.* Madame de Correge usually called me *mon bon petit fils.* I generally slept till nine o'clock, and every one in the house took care not to disturb me until Monsieur Correge himself came to call me. "Get up," he used to say; "*allons paresseux, le dejeuné est pret,*"

I then used to get up and dress myself, and sit down to breakfast, like a great man. When this was over, we usually went out, either shooting, according to the custom of the country, in wooden shoes, or riding, or amused ourselves in one way or other; sometimes we read French books, of which, indeed, I understood but little, but it served, as Monsieur de Correge said, *pour faire passer le tems.*

One day I was out shooting, and had taken, contrary to the advice of my young companion, a double-barrelled gun, which had been a long time loaded. Near the village we put up a covey of partridges; I fired, but instead of the birds falling, I fell myself backwards, into a muddy ditch. The recoil of the gun had completely stunned me, but the cold water in the ditch soon brought me to my senses. My cheek swelled very much, and the blood ran from my mouth and nose. In this condition, and covered with mud from head to foot, I returned home. Madame de Correge met me at the door. On seeing me, she cried out in alarm, "O Christian! what is the matter with you! where have you been? My God, what a swelled face!"

"Don't be uneasy," said I, "there is nothing the matter."

"Nothing the matter, indeed," said she, in a melancholy tone, "but change your clothes immediately, or rather go into bed."

I really felt a great deal of pain, but made myself out better than I was, in order to quiet her, and went and changed my dress. When I came down again, and sat myself by the fire, she began to remind me how heedless youth was, and how many accidents had been occasioned by the improper usage of firearms, &c, &c.

Upon all occasions she showed herself equally well disposed towards me. By degrees, she had learned my whole history, and felt much pity for my fate; she gave me the best of advice, which was not without effect. During the six weeks I remained here, I was always in the best society; saw but little of my comrades, and, encouraged by good example and friendly advice, laid aside many follies contracted during my military career.

Besides this, the young gentleman instructed me in French; and in return, I taught him several German waltzes, which he played upon his flute.

To render my abode here still more agreeable, I became, by degrees, more intimate with the pretty chambermaid. I plainly, discovered that I was not indifferent to her; she looked upon me so tenderly with her fine black eyes, that I must have been made of stone to have remained unmoved. In short, I could not have wished for a more agreeable residence; but alas! this happiness lasted only six weeks, for news was suddenly brought from head quarters, that the colours were arrived, and the day appointed for the presentation. They had not been brought us by a prince of the blood; but an order had arrived for the regiment to march immediately after into Spain.

The colours were consecrated with the greatest pomp in Villefranche. The regiment appeared in full dress, (*en grande tenue*) and. formed a square, the colours being in the centre, and the officers standing around. The colonel made a speech, in which he informed us to what intent the colours had been presented; how shameful it would be for a soldier to forsake them, and what was the punishment attendant upon this crime. At the conclusion of this speech, we presented arms; the colonel slowly and solemnly recited the oath of fidelity, and we all repeated it after him.

After this ceremony was concluded, the whole regiment, officers and soldiers, sat down to table together, in huts constructed for the occasion, of branches of trees, each company in one. Officers and privates, indiscriminately mixed, sat down at the same table: a cask of wine stood at the entrance of each hut, and all this was furnished at the Emperor's expense. The healths of the members of the Imperial family were drank, and during the meal, our own Sovereign, was not forgotten. At table, in spite of the quantity of wine drank, all passed off tolerably peaceable and orderly; but when, at the conclusion of the feast, the band struck up a dance, pouches, schakos, and sabres, were hung up in an instant on our piles of muskets, and the uproar began. The wine had heated many; some were drunk, and but few sober; officers, soldiers, and spectators of both sexes, danced together in indiscriminate mixture, and many a bearded warrior clasped his fair partner closely in his arms, without offence being taken at the liberty.

This merriment lasted till the evening, and no-one cast a thought upon the future. We all enjoyed, like true soldiers, the pleasures of the present moment, without reflecting upon our approaching dangers. He who was able to walk to his quarters, now departed; he, who could not stand, remained in Villefranche; for on an occasion like this, military discipline was relaxed. Many attempted to reach their homes, but the wine was too much for them: the equilibrium was lost, and they slept where they fell, for scarcely a single soldier was to be found capable of assisting his comrade.

Madame de Correge, who was always so careful of me, had foreseen the consequences of this festival, and had sent a carriage and servant into the town to fetch me; this I luckily fell in with in the evening. In this manner I reached home safe, although a little overcome with wine. They naturally enough wanted me to describe what had occurred, but this I begged them to defer till morning, as I was not sufficiently master of myself to give any rational account. I slept sound all night, and in the morning found myself quite well. Those of my comrades who had slept all night in the open air, felt the effect of their debauch for some time afterwards.

I remained a fortnight longer in these pleasant quarters, and passed such days of happiness in the house of this excellent lady, as I never enjoyed since, and certainly never shall again.

The orders for our departure came at last, and with tears in my eyes, I went into the room of my worthy hostess, whose goodness had also provided for my future comfort; my stock of linen had been increased, and put into the best order, and when I kissed her hand for the last time, she put a paper of money into mine, and said—"Take this trifle, my worthy young man, it may serve for a short time to protect you from want; until necessity has accustomed you to self-denial."

I was too much moved to find words to thank her—besides, tears choked my utterance; she, herself, could scarcely refrain from weeping. Wishing me health and happiness, she gave me a mother's blessing, and retired quickly to her own apartment, to hide her emotions. May God reward this excellent woman a thousand fold, for the kindness she showed to me!

I endeavoured to recover myself, and with a heavy heart, quitted a family to which I was so much indebted.

Castillon was the mustering place of the battalion; from thence we marched, the same day, to Sauveterre, along a road intersected by several streams, which we crossed in boats. In a few days we reached the small town of St, Maria, Here I was billeted in a lonely house, a quarter of an hour's distance from the town.

When I went into the room, four oxen with large horns stared me in the face; before them stood a female, employed in giving one of them, from time to time, a handful of the dried leaves of maize. I was astonished, and stood gazing on this novel spectacle, until all the oxen had been fed in their turn. My landlord informed me that there was a great scarcity of forage in the country, and that they were obliged to feed the cattle in this manner, to prevent waste. Gascony is certainly not one of the most fertile provinces of France, as it contains so many sandy plains and morasses, which are only to be passed on stilts. It seemed always a comical sight to us, to meet a Gascon coming into town, with his load on his back, and stalking along upon high stilts.

Though the dress of the country people of this provinces much resembles that of the Spaniards, whom I afterwards saw, yet their character is essentially different. The Gascon is friendly, officious, and talkative; the Spaniard, on the contrary, is proud, serious, and reserved.

The next day, upon halting about half way, we were overtaken by a heavy storm; by good luck we were in a village, and the whole battalion took shelter in the houses. When the drums beat to march, the greater part of us turned a deaf ear, and remained in our places of shelter. The colonel was very angry at this delay, and swore that we should be bivouacked that night. He kept his word, for on arriving in the evening at Mont de Marsan, he tore up our billets, and marched us some distance farther, to a large heath; here he ordered us to quarter for the night. He remained with us, but the next morning he must have repented being so severe, as it cost him dear; the night being cold, we were obliged to make fires to warm ourselves, and procured the fuel from the neighbouring gardens and villages. Complaints poured in of this, and the colonel had a long bill to pay for stolen straw and wood, and for trees which we had cut down.

This was my first bivouack; I did not find it very agreeable, and was glad when, at three o'clock in the morning, we were once more on our march. By seven o'clock we had reached

Paul de Dax, our appointed halting place for the night, where I got very good quarters, at least an excellent bed, which I took possession of without delay. Before I laid myself down, I ordered my landlord to get something ready for me to eat, but upon no account to wake me. He did as I desired, and I slept till six o'clock in the evening, when I got up and ate my dinner and supper together. When I had finished my meal, I went out to look round the town, in which there is an old palace, strongly fortified, and near it some hot springs. After this I went to bed again, and slept till five o'clock in the morning, so that I rested myself pretty well.

From Dax to Bayonne is about five and thirty miles, which we were to march in one day. At first, I got on very well, but when we had got about half way I began to feel weary. I was yet weak, scarcely seventeen years old, and my feet, owing to our former marches, were quite sore. Alone, in the rear of the battalion, I crept along the road, which it must not be supposed was like the German paved roads, to which, at that time, at least, it bore no resemblance; this was nothing more than a broad path, in which at every step we were up to our ankles in sand. It got darker and darker. I fancied myself still distant from the town, when on a sudden a cannon was fired: this terrified me excessively; I trembled all over, I thought a battle was at hand, and this the signal for attack. For a moment I did not dare to stir, (from this my courage, at that time, may be judged of); but as every thing remained quiet I went on, and soon reached the suburbs of Bayonne, where I learned the gun had been, fired from the citadel.

To the great vexation of my comrades, but to my joy, the regiment had been waiting upwards of two hours for billets, so that I arrived before they were served out, otherwise I should, probably, have been obliged to sleep under the canopy of the heavens. For my bodily refreshment I immediately provided,. as there was a French-woman among us crying out, without ceasing—"*qui veut 'oire la goutte et aussi la croute?*" I purchased of her a glass of brandy, and a piece of *polenta*, or bread, made of Indian corn, which looked as inviting as the nicest cake, but which tasted very disagreeably. At last we received our billets, and were allowed two days rest, during which time, we were furnished with every thing necessary for service in the field.

When, the two resting days were over, we began our march towards the frontiers of Spain. We had only one night more to pass upon the French territory; the magnificent Pyrenees already rose before us, with their summits covered with snow, and reaching to the clouds.

CHAPTER 3

Campaigning in Spain

On the 13th of January, 1808 we entered the Spanish territory, which is only separated from the French by a small rivulet, bounded on each side by the Custom-houses of the respective nations. Our first night's quarters seemed, at a distance, to belie the unfavourable description which had been given us in France, of Spain; the white houses appeared so inviting, that each man promised himself at least a good lodging; and this is what the tired soldier always most fervently, wishes for: he would rather be without eating and drinking than without a good bed.

We were now very anxious to become acquainted with the nation, which had been depicted to us in such black colours. On entering the town; we found the inhabitants assembled in considerable numbers, and thus we had an opportunity of mutually surveying each other.

We were not able, at the first glance, to discover whether they were so proud, revengeful and lazy, as they had been described; but the attitudes in which they stood, always without thinking of any occupation, with a cigar in the mouth, appeared; at any rate, to indicate proud and idle beings.

Upon reaching the great square, before the delivery of our billets, our colonel made us a long speech respecting our conduct towards the inhabitants. I received a billet for myself only, upon *Don* Manuel Garcia (this man interested me so much, that I shall never forget his name). Full of joy at my good luck, I set off, in order to seek out the residence of my illustrious landlord.

I flattered myself upon obtaining most excellent quarters, for I had read in so many romances, that *Don* was a title only borne by persons of rank. Upwards of a quarter of an hour I wandered about the town to no purpose; no one would give me any information; at last a good-natured boy showed me the way.

On arrival, how was I astonished, when, instead of the palace, or handsome house, at least, which I had expected, I stood before a miserable half-ruined hut; my heart misgave me, the boy knocked, but the door was fastened, that is, a log of wood was placed against the inside; a rough voice called out, "Who's there?"

"A French soldier," answered the boy.

The man refused to open the door; but at last, induced by the arguments of the boy, still more by the blows of my musket, he drew away the log, and I saw my worthy *Don* face to face. A man of middling stature, rather advanced in years, appeared before me, his head covered with a three-cornered cap, a ragged cloak, which, I afterwards learned, had covered a long line of ancestors, hung over his shoulders, and gave no very favourable promise of the state of his under garments. His lady was just then busied in preparing supper with her own hands; and for want of bellows, was lying on the ground blowing the fire with her breath.[1] All this did not by any means contribute to raise my spirits; my quarters more resembled a robber's cave than a decent dwelling-house; and to mend the matter, we could not understand a word of each other's language. I laid down my knapsack and musket, and looked round for a chair; but alas! my hosts did not appear to have any accommodation for visitors; the only two chairs in the room, if chairs they could be called, were occupied by this worthy pair, and they did not appear disposed to part with one of them for my use. At last, I insisted upon having a seat and my landlord was hospitable enough to give up his.

Now, at least I was seated, but it was cold, the winter being as severe in the Pyrenees as with us in Germany, and I would willingly have placed myself by the stove; but unluckily this comfort

---

1. Bellows, such as are in use with us, are not to be found in all Spain; in the place of these, are used fans, made of asparto, and old gun barrels.

is unknown in Spain, and the fire on the hearth burned so sparingly, that I could not obtain the least warmth from it. It began to grow late, and I saw no preparations making for my supper; in France I always made a hearty meal from the half-pound of meat allowed me, to which my landlord was always obliged to furnish vegetables: my stomach had become accustomed to this, and now reminded me of my want. We had received no rations; and, upon inquiry, I found that the pound of meat cost five reals, a price much too high for the purse of a private soldier. Compelled by hunger, I had recourse by means of words and signs, to my hostess; and she asked me in the same manner, if I had any bread, for of this article there did not appear any superfluity in the house. Upon my answering in the affirmative, she mixed some garlic, Spanish pepper, and olive oil together; to this she added some boiling water, and poured it upon my bread, which I had sliced in the mean time. I made myself as comfortable as I could over this frugal meal; but although I had a pretty good appetite, I could not relish it, in spite of her praises. In aftertimes I have often thankfully recalled Donna Garcia to my recollection, for having taught me to make this broth; I have often relished it, and it has kept me in health. When I had finished my supper, I looked about to see where I was to sleep, and look about I might, for I could discover no place for me. The bed, which stood in the room, and was formed of three boards and a sack of straw, was scarcely enough for the pair which occupied it, and that they would give it up to me I had not the slightest idea; besides, I had made up my mind to refuse the offer, for the suspicious motions of the *Don*, during the whole evening, gave evidence of a numerous population; and I wished to keep myself as free as possible from such unwelcome guests.

Upon my landlord remarking that sleep began to weigh heavy upon my eye-lids, he gave me to understand, contrary to my expectations, that the bed, with all its appurtenances, was to be given up to me. I explained to him, as well as I could, by signs, that I would not, upon any account, deprive him of it, and I should be perfectly satisfied with a little clean straw; but in spite of all my representations, I was forced to accept it, and the *Don* and his lady lay quietly down in a corner upon a little straw and a kind of coverlet. Tired with the march, I soon fell into a sound sleep, but this was of short duration. I had scarcely slept an hour, when I was awakened by an indescribable kind of tickling all over my body. I was frightened, but soon became convinced that my suspicions were well-grounded, and that this unpleasant sensation was caused by lice, of which there are quantities all over Spain, and from which my landlord was not free. These little insects had spread themselves all over their new guest, and were feasting upon my blood. I endeavoured to rid myself of them, but in vain, their number was legion. After having at least avenged myself upon a few of the offenders, I sprang impatiently from the bed, and seated myself by the fire.

This afforded me no relief, and my torment still continued. I got a light, made up the fire, and resolved in this manner to wait the break of day. My landlord, disturbed by my movements, waked, and asked what was the matter. I could, of course, give him no distinct answer, but muttered a few German and French oaths. He gave me in reply, a few hard words, which probably were Spanish curses, turned himself round, and went to sleep again.

These troublesome guests, and the cold, annoyed me a good deal; luckily I had a pipe and tobacco, with which I managed to pass the time. Sleep at last overcame me; upon the bed I would not again trust myself, and remained sitting in my chair. In my sleep I leaned forward, lost my balance, and fell down at the feet of the sleeping couple. A tremendous storm now burst forth among us. Explaining matters was quite out of the question; we raged and swore in all languages, and the *Don* seemed to have an idea, that I had some attempt upon the chastity of his lady in view, and was in readiness to repel any attack. I had recovered myself as quickly as I could, and had taken up a defensive position, in order to be secure from any hostilities; but in a short time this all passed off, and peace was restored; I now firmly resolved to keep myself awake, to prevent the, recurrence of such scenes, and fortunately soon after the daylight dawned, and found me, in consequence of my nocturnal adventures, nearly as much fatigued as when I had laid down; however, the tediousness of the night was past, and, as I thought, nothing worse could happen to me, at least on that morning; but later time brought days a thousand fold worse than that which, inexperienced as I then was, I thought scarcely to be borne. The soldier always lives in hopes; frequently, in his dangerous career, hope alone remains, the worst occurs too often. When we were assembled in the morning, I began to complain to some of my comrades, but I soon found we were all companions in misery, all were infested with these disagreeable Spanish insects. When I discovered this, I became more contented, with my lot, and bore my cross patiently.

The worst circumstance attending this march was the lateness of the season; scarcity reigned wherever we came; few provisions were to be had; bread and wine were all we could procure, and these we were often obliged to take by force. The Spaniards were particularly mistrustful, and would seldom allow us to eat our breakfasts in the houses. Bread and wine, which we paid for, they gave us at the doors, and in the worst weather, we were often obliged to remain in the open air; even if we halted in a town, we were lucky if we could obtain shelter under a shed. In addition to our troubles, we had nothing but French money, which, the Spaniards either would not take at all, or would give but little for, so that our few *francs* were gone before we knew where we were.

Upon quitting the Pyrenees, and advancing towards the interior of the country, we found provisions (bread, wine, fish, &c.) cheap, and very good; but tobacco, an article indispensable to a soldier, bore an extraordinary price—the pound cost forty-eight *reals*, or a *ducat*; according to our money; this we could not possibly pay, and were obliged to use all kinds of substitutes. Many smoked rose-leaves moistened with wine; others, the dried bark of the vine, mixed with a little tobacco; and if these substitutes would but smoke, we were as happy as if our pipes were filled with the best canaster. The Spaniards, accustomed to the high price, have a very saving method of smoking, namely, five or six persons smoke the same cigar, of which they make from twenty to thirty out of an ounce; the first takes two or three puffs, keeps the smoke in his mouth, and after handing the cigar to his neighbour, puffs it out through his nose—in this manner the cigar goes round.

The whole of the second day we marched over mountains and through valleys, until we reached Villa Real, a small and poor town, where, for the first time, we were not quartered upon the inhabitants, but lodged in the churches and chapels. Our rations consisted of one pound and half of bread, half a pound of meat, and a pint of wine; our victuals were very badly dressed, for at that time we were quite inexperienced in field-cookery; many ate their bread and drank their wine, and left the hard pease, the still harder meat, and the tasteless broth, to their comrades. I did not belong to this number—I swallowed my hard pease, chewed the tough meat, and drank the broth, to which, by mixing a little wine with it, I had given a better taste, to my great joy I perceived that it did me good. On the following day I found myself more healthy and cheerful than those who had despised the frugal fare.

Montdragon was our third resting place, but no better than our former ones. A thousand of us were lodged in one house: our number was indicated by a sign over the door, upon which was painted, in large letters— *"Logement pour 1000 hommes."*

The French troops, which had passed this way before us, accustomed to rapine, had not been able to restrain their propensity, but before reaching Vittoria had begun to plunder. The peasants had sounded the tocsin in order to defend their property against the intruders, but were obliged to submit to superior forte, and on our arrival, We could only drive away the stragglers who were robbing the houses. Our colonel behaved upon this, as upon fill similar occasions, very honourably; but what had been stolen, it was out of his power to restore.

In Vittoria we came in for our usual Spanish quarters. We were lodged in an old convent, which swarmed with fleas, lice, and bugs; altogether we were here so badly off, that numbers of soldiers fell sick, and several died. In these delightful quarters, we remained upwards of a week, during which time we were several times reviewed by Prince Murat. The army increased by degrees; every day fresh troops arrived, and we, with several other regiments, were marched forward, in order to make room for others.

Our cantonment was in a Franciscan monastery, near a small town, about seven leagues from Vittoria. The cloisters, which surrounded the court, were fixed upon for our quarters. Here we were obliged to lay like cattle, upon straw, on the ground; and this pleasant life lasted three weeks. At this time another disease crept into the regiment—the itch, with which I and several others, and, by degrees, full two-thirds of us, were seized. We were placed in a separate part of the building, and the doctor, who was a Spaniard, endeavoured, by a most abominable method of cure, to relieve us, namely, by means of hunger. We received nothing but a little broth, and our ration of bread; but, in spite of this diet, the disorder kept its ground. Suddenly arrived an order for our march; and, although considerably weakened by this pleasant method of cure, we were obliged to; make the same long marches as those in perfect health.

Already on the first day I was obliged to exert my utmost strength to follow the regiment, and it was with the greatest difficulty that I reached, along with the others, the town of Miranda, on the Ebro. We saw everywhere traces of devastation; in the church, where we were lodged, benches and chairs had been burned: this example we were obliged to follow, as the fuel allowed us was scarcely sufficient to cook our victuals, and it was very cold. At this time, many a saint who had formerly suffered martyrdom on the cross, or in any other manner, was obliged to undergo the ceremony of being burnt in effigy, without our consciences being troubled in the least about it.

We marched next to Briviesca. Before reaching this place, I was seized with such a weakness, that I thought I must have sunk down on the road. However, I roused myself and crept on; but on the following morning I could scarcely march out with the regiment; I crept rather than walked, and before I had got half way, I lost sight of the regiment, which on that day entered Burgos, and then marched by way of Aranda to Madrid.

Fortunately, I was not alone; several invalids, whom the Spanish doctor had treated in the same manner as myself, kept me company. Upon reaching Burgos, we presented ourselves before the commandant, and entreated to be taken into the hospital. This he would not listen to, on account of the number of sick already there, and insisted that we should, on the following morning, march forward to follow the regiment to Madrid. Quarters were found for us in some old barracks, where we met with a detachment of troops of all arms, among which were some with long fingers, for in the morning I found all my cartridges had been stolen.

I set off early on my way; but my strength was so much exhausted, that I was obliged to sit down before I had walked half an hour. Two of my comrades, Hugo and Turno, both natives of Munster, were in the same state as myself, and remained with me. We agreed, upon no account whatever, to separate, but to keep together; for, singly, we had no chance for our lives. After we had rested about an hour, and were a little encouraged by this resolution, we proceeded on our way. The detachment we had long lost sight of, and had now only to trust to ourselves, and to Providence. We had passed on the road several houses, which had been plundered by the French, and abandoned by their inhabitants, but saw not a living being who could have directed us on the right way, all the inhabitants having left the main road, and fled into the interior of the country. For several miles we passed over a level plain, apparently well cultivated, but not a soul was to be seen. Fortunately, the weather was fine, and although in the middle of February, the air was as soft as it usually is in the southern parts of Europe. At last we reached a village, and joyfully marched in; but, to our astonishment, the inhabitants rushed upon us as if they meant to murder us. This fate we should not have escaped, for we were too weak to offer any resistance, if luckily the *alcalde* had not been present, and restored order, by taking a small staff from under his cloak, which commanded so much respect from the peasants; that they immediately desisted, and all took off their caps with much reverence. We were astonished to find a staff possessed of such magic powers; but our protector now explained this to us: every *alcalde*, he told us, had such a staff, which he either received from his precursor in office, or from the government at Madrid: whenever there was any occasion to restore order, or to arrest any persons, he had only to show this and to say—"in the king's name, I command order;" or "in the king's name, you are my prisoners"—and his commands were immediately obeyed.

This good man carried us to a tavern, but the landlord, in spite of all our entreaties, would give us nothing, until the *alcalde*, taking compassion upon our empty stomachs, said: "Michael, give these poor fellows bread and wine directly, without more ado, or"—upon this he showed his staff,—"I command you, in the king's name," The effect of the staff was so powerful, that in an instant bread, cheese, and wine, were placed before us, and we began to think of the fairy tales we had heard when children. We now also learned the reason of the enmity of the peasants: our comrades had feasted handsomely in this village, and had paid for nothing; not contented with this, they had broken into the houses to plunder; this shameful behaviour had naturally enraged the peasants, and they sought revenge upon us who were innocent.

We had now ate and drank and refreshed ourselves, but our pockets were empty; for since entering the Spanish territory, we had received no pay. The money which the good Madame de Correge had given me was spent, and the landlord would take no French moneys the good *alcalde*, however, came once more to our assistance, and paid our score out of his own purse, for which we gave him our hearty thanks, as well as we were able to express them. The priest of the place, a worthy servant of God, as he proved by his actions, soon after we came in. He endeavoured to enter into conversation, but as we were ignorant of each other's language, this was rather difficult, until at last I spoke a few words of Latin, which I had learned at school, and now began a discourse, in which I related to him our misfortunes. When he heard that my comrades were Catholics, and of course I passed for one too, he took more interest about us, and at last gave us an invitation to his house, which we did not refuse. When we arrived there, he set before us all his kitchen would afford, and added to this some excellent wine. Upon seeing what a lamentable condition we were in, and that we were not able to proceed any farther, he asked us to remain in his house for the night. We did net require much pressing, put our muskets and knapsacks aside, and made ourselves very comfortable.

In this manner we pleasantly ended a day, in the course of which we had been threatened with ill treatment and death. How worthy of a Christian pastor was the humanity of this priest, and how different was his behaviour from the rage of the peasants, who would have made us suffer for the guilt of others.

A good night's rest refreshed us so much, that in the morning we found ourselves strong enough to be able to march a few miles. With tears in our eyes, we thanked our worthy host for his friendly reception; he and the *alcalde* accompanied us part of the way, and we then separated with thanks on our side, and with good wishes for our safety on theirs.

May the Almighty, to whom these good deeds are not unknown, reward these honest men for what they did for us.

We went forward upon the road they had conducted us to, which was not the high road to Madrid, but a by-way, intersected by so many others, that we were at a loss which to choose. We had no other resource but to adopt one, and trust for our further direction to those whom we might meet, but all the Spaniards of whom we inquired, whether any French soldiers had passed that way, either would not, or could not understand us, and we could gain no information. At last we reached a small town which had not been visited by the French this we easily guessed by the curiosity of the inhabitants, who crowded around us, and teased us with a thousand questions, to which we could give no answer, because we did not understand them. However, at last, a well-dressed man approached, and asked us, in the French language, where we were going. We replied, that we were following our regiment, and inquired if a detachment of French troops had not passed through the place. He told us, in reply to this, that the military road did not pass through this town, but that we had come much too far to the left. We requested of him to take us to the *corregidor*, and to ask in our names for a night's lodging. He agreed to this, and persuaded the *corregidor*, after some hesitation, to grant our request.

The name of this town was Padrosa; it is situated in a chain of mountains, reaching a considerable distance, and called the Sierra Occa. Here we were very fortunate, the people being much more friendly than the inhabitants of the Pyrenees. We were comfortably entertained without any payment being required; in short, these were the best quarters we had as yet met with in Spain. It was very disagreeable that we were obliged to carry guests about with us which are nowhere welcome; but with all our endeavours we could not rid ourselves of them. We took the utmost care to conceal the presence of these vermin, and suffered the greatest pain, rather than betray it by scratching. In the morning, when we got up, we found our beds covered with these insects: we thus found our precautions had been unnecessary, and we could part from our kind entertainers without the consciousness of having left them any disagreeable remembrances of this nature.

To free ourselves from these hateful and tormenting insects, we tried all the means we could think of. Some rubbed the seams of their shirts and clothes with fat; but the best and most effectual method was, what was called the Hungarian washing, which was performed in the following manner:—A fire was made of straw or dry wood, and the shirt, being tied up at one end, was held over it; the smoke caused it to open like a balloon, and the insects, disturbed by the heat, loosened their hold upon the linen, and fell into the flames; this was repeated several times, and thus, for a little while, we could manage to free ourselves from these vermin. During our halts for the night, officers and soldiers were constantly seen employed in this manner, and this occupation frequently gave rise to tragi-comical scenes; for many a one, unaccustomed to this manner of washing, paid for his experience by the loss of perhaps his only shirt; others, who had perhaps saved half, were subjected to all manner of jokes from their comrades, while putting on what remains. It may appear incredible to many, but I am firmly convinced that no-one can have been in Spain without being tormented by these vermin.

After we had made a hearty breakfast, we begged of our landlord to show us the way to Aranda; he took us out of the town, and pointed out a road to us, with these words: "That is the road to Aranda; go, in God's name!" but he either directed us wrong, or we mistook our way without perceiving it, for we got farther into the mountains, where we only met a few sheep and goatherds, who willingly gave us what little they could spare from their stock of provisions, but were too ignorant of the country to be able to afford us any information.

We afterwards passed through several tolerable villages; and to our inquiries respecting the road to Aranda, always received for answer—"straight forward." In this manner we travelled on till evening, when we found ourselves in the centre of the mountains; not a village or a house was to be seen; at every step we sunk up to our knees in snow and mud: we were tormented with hunger and thirst, without any prospect of obtaining anything in this inhospitable region. Every one must acknowledge, that our situation was truly pitiable, had there been any one present capable of commiserating and relieving us. When it became dark, we consulted what was to be done; it was proposed to kindle a fire, and pass the night in the wood. This scheme was rejected; and it was resolved to make another attempt, and to go on.

We came first to a rivulet, and afterwards to a mill; but unfortunately this was shut up, for in Spain the mills are almost always at a distance from the towns, and not inhabited. However, this raised our spirits, and we were in hopes of finding a village not far off. We followed the course of the stream for about half an hour, and at last heard the barking of a dog in the distance. This was to our ears more acceptable than the sound of the finest instrument. Following the noise, we soon reached the village: all were buried in sleep, the dogs alone were awake, and made a tremendous uproar. We knocked at several doors, but no one opened; at last we found a good Samaritan, who asked us what we wanted. "*Alcalde logiamento*" was all that we could say.

The man saw how we were situated, and was kind enough to bring us to the *alcalde*, who surveyed us from head to foot, and at last said—"I cannot find you quarters, but if you will sleep in the poor-house I will let you in, there you will find hay and straw." As there was no remedy we accepted the offer, and begged for something to eat: this we received, together with a good glass of wine. When we were satisfied, the *alcalde* took us to the poor-house, wished us a good night, and shut the door. Each one made himself up a nest for the night in the hay, and my two comrades, more hardened to fatigue than myself, were asleep and snoring in a few moments, but my feet were so sore from walking, that I could not close my eyes. In this manner I had probably lain about an hour, occupied with reflections upon my situation, when I was roused by a violent outcry and knocking at the door. The word *matar*, so closely resembling the Latin *mactare*, and which has the same signification, sounded like a dagger in my ears. I felt already the numberless stabs the Spaniards were about to give me.

The moment before, I was shuddering with cold and pain: I now perspired, and felt nothing whatever. Without knowing what I was about, I kept working deeper into the hay; at last I could no longer breathe, and the horrible cry still sounded in my ears. Fortunately, for our safety, the door was strongly fastened, and, in spite of the endeavours of our enemies, it would not give way; although, if our besiegers had continued their work much longer, it would probably, at last, have been forced. The blows were still continued, when I distinguished several voices which appeared to be in animated conversation; the noise increased, but soon became more distant, and at last ceased altogether.

I laid long with a heavy heart, in my corner, before my eyes were closed in wished-for sleep. When I awoke it was broad day, and the *alcalde* was just come to open the door. Upon my inquiries respecting the occurrences of the night, he gave me to understand, that some peasants, who had beep drinking in the taverns, wished to murder us; but that, luckily for us, he had heard their cries, and had come in time to save us.

In this manner the staff of an *alcalde* again preserved us. My comrades were now first made acquainted with the danger which had threatened us during the night, and warned by this adventure, we saw clearly how unsafe our situation was, and loaded our pieces, in order, in case of necessity, to be able to defend ourselves. The *alcalde* brought us a good breakfast, after which we left him, with many thanks, and pursued our way. We wandered for several days more about the country, without being able to obtain any correct information respecting our route; at last, on the sixth day, when we were become heartily weary of our laborious occupation, we perceived, at a distance, a town, with several steeples: we took this for a fortified place, and were in hopes of falling in with a French garrison. We hastened towards it; but before we had reached the gate, a Spanish soldier met us on the bridge, and asked for our passports. Upon our making it known that we had none, he would have arrested us; but as we were the strongest, he got a few blows for his officiousness, and went off with a long face. The town was not fortified, as we had imagined, but only surrounded by a high wall; upon going in, we were, as usual, surrounded by a crowd of inquisitive idlers, who pestered us with a multitude of foolish questions, which we, unacquainted with the Spanish language, were unable to answer.

An old soldier at last took us to the town-hall, to the *corregidor*, who spoke very good French, and examined us very closely. I being the only one who had learned a little French, answered his questions. After he had conversed a short time with me, a Spanish officer came in, who asked us what countrymen we were, how we came into the French service, and whether we had any inclination to enter the Spanish. This question offended us a good deal, as we were neither prisoners nor deserters, who might be compelled by any means to enlist. We gave a decided refusal, therefore, and requested of the *corregidor* to furnish us with quarters for the night, and a guide for the following day. Owing to our having no marching orders, or any thing else to explain the reason of our being here, we were really taken for deserters; and before we could look round us, four bandit-like looking fellows came in, followed by a fifth, having the appearance of a hangman, and in that instant, not expecting any attack, we were disarmed.

We were chained, hands and feet, and put into a dungeon, secured by double iron doors, and fit only for the vilest criminals; altogether I have not seen such horrible prisons as those in Spain. This treatment came so unexpected, that we remained sitting in our prison full a quarter of an hour before we could recollect ourselves. The jailor, the man with the physiognomy of a hangman, came in to bring us some bread and water: we overwhelmed him with questions, to which he appeared to have neither inclination nor time to reply, and went grumbling out again.

I had now leisure enough to reflect upon my fate; and when I considered, that only ten months before, I had been living comfortably in my native town, and that now several hundred miles distant, I was confined in a dungeon filled with vermin, in the power of rough and revengeful men, I was almost in despair, and no one who can conceive my situation, will find fault with this avowal.

Happily for us, on the following day, we had some companions. Several young persons belonging to the town, (which we now found out was named Soria) on account of some crime, were confined with us. They provided us abundantly with provisions, and told us, that if we were to hang a little bag, or any thing of the kind, at the window, we might be assured that the charitably disposed among the inhabitants would not suffer us to want. This good advice we immediately followed; a foraging cap was made into a bag, tied with the cords of a schako, and in this manner we went to work. The first day's success far surpassed our expectations, and confirmed what our fellow prisoners had told us, Bread, meat, wine, cheese, stockfish, onions, garlic, and money, were the fruits of our speculation; and the produce of our cap served, in some degree, to reconcile us to our unhappy fate.

Our condition at night was the worst; we had nothing to lie on but some short half-decayed straw, swarming with vermin: to escape this torment, we endeavoured to sleep upon the ground, but it was too cold; we crept as close as we could to each other, and when we could not sleep, we told stories.

We were often visited by the towns-people; among the inhabitants were some Germans: O how we were rejoiced when, for the first time, we heard once again the sound of our native language! To circumstances of this kind we attach no value, until we find ourselves destitute and deserted, in a foreign country—then we first feel what a happiness it is to meet with a countryman. These good people never left the prison without making us some present, for which they had our heartfelt thanks.

Every morning mass was performed in the chapel of the prison, and as there was no doubt of our being Catholics, we took part in it, without however quitting our prison—there was merely a large shutter opened, and through the aperture we could see into the chapel.

By degrees our receipts began to fall off; the visits became fewer, and at last ceased altogether, and we were reduced, as at first, to bread and water. The before-mentioned Spanish officer now once more made his appearance, and asked us again if we would enter the Spanish service. Upon our refusal, he used all sorts of threats, in order to induce us to comply, and told us that we should be delivered over to the French authorities as deserters; we should then see what would become of us; and should repent, when too late, of having refused to accept his offers. We laughed at these threats, and he left us in a rage.

A few days might have passed after this visit, when one morning, earlier than usual,. our prison-door was opened, and we saw, with astonishment, five fellows enter, followed by the jailor; they had brought ropes with them, in order to bind us. Not accustomed to such treatment, we foamed with rage, and protested loudly against it; we were, however, too weak to resist: all our struggles were useless, and power got the better of justice. One of the men seized me and turned me round, while another tied my hands behind my back. My comrades were treated in precisely the same manner. Our rage now broke out in tears and curses. All the oaths we could muster in any sort of language, were here vented—but they only laughed at our powerless fury, and this enraged us the more.

When the operation was completed with each of us, we were fastened together like dogs; our arms and knapsacks put upon our backs, and we were marched off. A crowd of the populace followed us to the gates of the town, some cursing, and others pitying us.

As soon as we had quitted Soria, our escort appeared more friendlily disposed towards us, notwithstanding their former barbarous treatment. They were now humane. In every place which we passed through, they procured us some refreshment, and all along did not suffer us to want for any thing to eat or drink; they even, when they found we did not wish to escape, unbound us, and laughed and talked with us, so that, as far as circumstances permitted, we had a very pleasant journey.

The first night we passed in a village, where we were placed in the *Casa Ordinacia;* it was by no means so miserable a place as the prison at Soria, but our feet was shut up in the stocks. This instrument consists of two parallel pieces of wood, with round holes fitting to each other, into which the feet are placed. In this machine there was a quantity of bugs; these insects did as they pleased with our feet, without our being able to hinder it. We were forced to lie all night on our backs, upon a little straw.

One night, after being placed in one of these machines, we had in addition, a chain, weighing at least thirty pounds, fastened to our feet, with a lock of such a size as I had never before seen.

At Elburgo, we saw a Spanish dragoon-regiment enter the

town, which drew our attention by the singularity of its equip-
ments; the men, for instance, wore leather gaiters instead of
boots, and the manes and tails of the horses were ornamented
with showy coloured ribbons, so that the whole presented more
the appearance of a wedding cavalcade than a regiment of dragoons. They vented their warlike feelings upon us, and abused
us in every possible manner. It was at first proposed to have put
us into the custody of these gentlemen, in which case we should
not have been very well off; but, fortunately, we were taken to
a monastery in the large square. The inhabitants treated us very
well here, and did all they could to alleviate our distresses.

It was, to our great joy, only two days' journey from, hence to
Aranda; we looked forward, therefore, to the termination of the
ill-treatment we had so long suffered. In this place was a French
garrison, and when we at last reached it, we thought all our troubles at an end, little suspecting that a still harder fate awaited us.

Our escort took us immediately to the commandant of the
place, a captain in the 100th Regiment of French infantry, and
presented their order. Upon reading this, he told us that he sin-
cerely pitied us, but, as the order expressly mentioned that we
were delivered up as captured deserters, he could do no less than
send us under arrest to the regiment, where it would give him
great pleasure to find that what we had told him was true. We
were then sent under a guard to the military prison. From hence
we were to be sent forward the following day, under an escort of
gendarmes, to Madrid, where the regiment was stationed.

Our new lodging was as like to that at Soria as one egg is to
another, only that there was no straw in it, and that it was much
more damp, owing to the river flowing dose under the windows.
Vermin we cared little about, as we were already so completely
covered, that we had no apprehensions about any increase. We
here found a number of companions in misery, of different sorts;
there were deserters, thieves, murderers, a madman, and in short,
such a mixture as I never in my life met with before. Our scanty
supply of provisions were given us through a trap-door, and if
these were not immediately devoured, they became the prey

either of the rats, or of some member of the company, who, on such occasions, usually made a boast of his roguery. If any of us dared to make complaints of this behaviour, we were subjected to the most brutal treatment.

The madman (who probably only acted the part in order to escape punishment,) had stolen, a gold watch, and was condemned for five years to the galleys. He was an object of horror dining his paroxysms; he turned up his eyes, ran his head against the wall; scratched the stones till the blood ran down his fingers, and roared like a lion. We were subjected to all kinds of annoyance from this man, without our daring to make any opposition; for as soon as we made any attempt to drive him from us by force, all the others took his part. We repeatedly begged. the jailor, in the most pressing manner, to take us out of this horrible dungeon, but in vain; he paid no attention either to prayers or threats, and closed the trap-door with a growl. Five days were we kept here; five days, therefore, were we compelled, without being guilty of any crime, to take up our abode among beings a disgrace to humanity.

At last, on the sixth day, the hour of our delivery approached; the *gendarmes* came to fetch us, and according to the custom of the country, we were once more coupled together, to be conveyed to Madrid. This sorrowful journey, however, did not last long, for on the following day, about noon, we unexpectedly fell in with our battalion, which was in cantonments, at a village some distance from Madrid. Who could be more joyful than we were, when the sight of the white coats made known to us the vicinity of our comrades. The *gendarmes* brought us immediately to the colonel, Schenck; the provost master of the company was sent for, and questioned concerning us, when, without any hesitation, he confirmed our assertions, by which it was made evident that we were not deserters, and we immediately received our long-wished-for liberty.

The colonel sent for us to his quarters, and ordered us to give him a circumstantial account of all that had befallen us. He pitied us very much, ordered some food and wine to be set before us to recruit our exhausted frames, and then gave orders that we should be fresh clothed. What a joyful day this was for us! I can still remember my feelings upon putting on my new clothes, and thus freeing myself from the Spanish vermin: this joy, however, was but of short duration.

Soon after our return, the whole column received orders to break up and march to Madrid; at this we were all heartily rejoiced, for our battalion had been in very bad quarters: the troops were very much crowded, together, and the damp cold weather, which reigns during the winter in the interior provinces; had occasioned a great deal of sickness. We reached Madrid without any occurrence worthy, of remark. We made our entry on the 21st of March, 1808, under the command of Prince Murat, and were tolerably well received by the inhabitants. The infantry was quartered in the convents, where we found blankets, sheets, and sacks of straw in readiness, all quite new. The cavalry and artillery took possession of the vacant cavalry barracks, and only the staff-officers and generals were quartered upon the inhabitants.

Madrid, the capital of Spain, is situated in the centre of Castile, and is a considerable, though not generally well built city. It abounds with handsome churches and splendid palaces. The Royal palace is situated at one end of the city, and ranges with the walls; it is distinguished by its massive and antique style of architecture, and not a little, resembles a castle or fort. El Buen Retiro is a beautiful country palace, belonging to the king, in the environs of Madrid. At that time it had been fortified by the French, and more resembled a fortress than a palace; the French arsenal was placed there, and it served, at the same time, for barracks.

The palace of the Prince of the Peace, Godoy, had been nearly destroyed by the rage of the populace before our arrival, and it was now used as barracks, for the French troops. I have myself several times been quartered there; there was a very fine garden belonging to it, which was then partly run wild and partly destroyed; for, owing to the want of fuel, the soldiers had cut down the finest trees, and had trodden under foot the most beautiful plantations, and burnt and destroyed the hot-houses.

Here I remarked in how little estimation the Spanish soldier is held by his countrymen. In the court-yard of this palace, there was a magazine belonging to the Spanish troops, over which Spanish sentries of the Walloon guards were posted.

One day, happening by chance to be near this post, there came by two half-drunk citizens of the lowest order, who ridiculed, and afterwards began grossly to abuse the sentries, and at last went so far as to make water upon the sentry-boxes, without the soldiers making the slightest attempt to resent the outrage. As the Walloon guards consist chiefly of Germans, we asked the soldiers why they had not knocked down these brutes with the ends of their muskets? "Yes" replied they, "in that case they would either have murdered us on the spot, or have lodged a complaint against us, and we should have been put in irons for a few years."

The Prado is a long and spacious walk, in which there are several handsome fountains. Here, and at the Puerta del Sol, during fine weather, the *beau monde* of Madrid is every day to be seen. Antique and modern equipages, horsemen of all sorts, monks, ladies of quality on foot, and riding upon mules, are here to be met with. In the midst of this motley assemblage, the water carriers and fruit-sellers, with their shrill voices, carry on their various occupations, and almost force their wares upon the passengers. The sellers of water recommend their fluid as the coolest which is to be found in the whole world, although it has perhaps not ten minutes before been taken from the nearest fountain, and is so warm as not to be drinkable. However, when once poured out it must be paid for; the price, is, indeed, but a trifle, more resembling an alms than a payment; an *ochavo*, the quarter of a *dreyer*, being the whole amount.

The insolent overbearing behaviour of the French military soon began to show itself; and this the proud revengeful Spaniards did not so quietly put up with as our patient countrymen. Scarcely a fortnight had passed, before the inhabitants and the troops came to blows, and several on both sides were wounded. The Spaniards began to be less civil, and to express more openly the hostile feelings which they had long secretly cherished, and assassinations began to be frequent among the French soldiery. At this time the demands of our commanders became higher, and they wished to have the remaining members of the Royal Family in their power; and us the mass is usually affected by the consequences of individual actions, so the hatred, which should properly have only fallen upon the Emperor for his extravagant pretensions, fell upon us individuals, who were only instruments in his hands. Complaints were every where made of quarrels between the two nations; the guards, and sentries were insulted and pelted with stones, and several, even who were not sufficiently upon their guard, were murdered during the night.

The mutual exasperation increasing, we were now, in order to ensure our safety, and likewise in case of any insurrection, to be in larger bodies together, removed out of the city and encamped in the Royal gardens. The Imperial guard and the cavalry alone remained in Madrid, and the necessary guards were furnished from the camp.

We found ourselves here very comfortable; our tents were in good condition; our bedding we had brought with us out of the city; and as we had but little to do, we amused ourselves with ornamenting our camp: we built arbours, turf-seats, and various things of this sort, for which the Royal gardens afforded us abundant materials. Prince Murat visited us every day, and was much pleased with our rural abode.

At last, on the 2nd of May, 1808, the hatred of the Spaniards, which had so long been smothering, burst out into aflame, which we had some difficulty in extinguishing. The infantry and artillery were, at the moment the alarm-gun was fired, occupied in receiving their rations, from the large magazine which was established at the entrance of our camp. The troops all hastened back to the encampment, and seized their weapons. The *generale* was beat through the whole camp, and in a few minutes every regiment was under arms. We were marched off in brigades, the light troops in advance, and in this manner we reached the Porta Legoria, where we were ordered to halt. Inhabitants and soldiers were seen rushing out of the gate—shot after shot was heard in the city—but we remained quiet, having as yet received no orders to enter. At last the word was given to march: we charged into the city by half companies, with fixed bayonets, where we found the inhabitants in open insurrection: we pressed on—overthrew every thing which was in our way, but the citizens were not idle; they, threw down from the windows and roofs of the houses every thing which they could reach, and killed and wounded a great number of our men.

Our cavalry charged into all parts of the city: we marched through the streets by whole companies, and every person we met, or saw at the windows, was shot without mercy, so that in a short time several streets were covered with dead, among which were several women. This murderous scene lasted for some hours, until the inhabitants, were obliged to submit to our superior force, and to beg for mercy; we, however, had had work enough to do, and not satisfied with the amicable feelings of they now displayed, looked for a more substantial reward for our trouble, and on this occasion our brigade was not the worst off. We were stationed in the Plaza Major, where there was a number of large shops for the sale of eatables of all kinds: these were all eagerly ransacked, and chance threw a small casket in my way, filled with coins of different sorts. Without troubling myself about the value of my prize, I thrust the casket into my half-empty knapsack, and my comrades used all their endeavours to enrich themselves as much as they could, without considering whether it was just or not.

In times like these, when the danger is over, the soldier thinks little about morality—he has saved his life, and seeks to enjoy it by procuring the means by which enjoyment is to be obtained.

To ensure the safety of the French troops, strong picquets were posted, parties of cavalry and infantry patrolled the streets incessantly. The troops not required in the city were bivouacked close on the outside of the gates; and by these measures all inclination to tumult on the part of the inhabitants was dissipated.

Desertion was become very frequent among the Spanish

troops: in our regiment alone, we had more than five hundred deserters, mostly Germans, who had been in the Spanish service, in the Swiss and Walloon regiments. They seized the opportunity, in hopes, by entering the French service, to come nearer to their native land, and then, sooner or later, to escape to their homes, which, on account of the great distance, would have been difficult from Spain. These numerous desertions afforded the Spaniards a favourable pretence for withdrawing the national troops, as well as the foreign regiments, from Madrid, and by that means from our vicinity. At first they were in cantonments in the villages round the city; but they soon withdrew farther into the interior, and with the assistance of the militia, formed several columns, which, a month afterwards, were in the field and acting against us. They were under the command of *Don* Ventura de Caro, a general, distinguished by personal courage, but too inexperienced to command an army against such well disciplined troops as the French. The first division of our army, under General Moncey, was in June, 1808, ordered to disperse these forces.

CHAPTER 4

Battles & Guerillas

Our first night's halt, after leaving Madrid, was at Aranjuez, where there is a splendid Royal palace. Nature has so abundantly supplied this city with every thing necessary for the enjoyment of life, that the inhabitants must certainly have but few wants. The palace of the Prince of the Peace, which the populace of Madrid, in their blind fury, had almost destroyed, was appointed for our quarters, and we laid upon bad straw in the empty rooms, which, but a short time before, had dazzled the sight with their magnificence, and had only been entered by persons of the highest rank.

On the second day we marched through Akam, noted for a fine aqueduct, built by the Romans, to Santa Cruz, a small place about twenty miles farther, where we expected to find the advanced guard of the Spanish army. It had actually been lying here, but, upon, receiving intelligence of our advance, had hastily retreated, leaving behind a contribution of twenty thousand rations, which fell into our hands. A similar magazine of provisions we likewise found at Saragossa, and this booty proved very acceptable to the commissaries.

We next marched to Cuenca—but this town was also deserted by the enemy, who had retreated into the mountains.

We remained here six days; after which we quitted the main road to pursue the enemy's forces into the mountains, and, if possible, to disperse them. We had brought with us from Madrid a very considerable convoy of warlike necessaries of all kinds;

but as in the country we were about to traverse, there were no roads passable for carriages, we were here obliged to leave them behind us, together with the military hospital, and only took with us, upon mules, what was absolutely necessary, the provisions being divided among the soldiers. Among all those whom we left behind us in Cuenca, not one was ever again seen; for, shortly after our departure, the place was surprised by a corps of guerillas; and as the protecting force was too weak to make any effectual resistance, nearly the whole were inhumanly murdered, and but very few were kept as prisoners.

The march into the mountains, which we were now undertaking, was a most difficult one. We were very heavily loaded, the heat was almost intolerable, and the roads scarcely passable, so that we were not able to advance more than from six to eight miles a day. We were frequently obliged to carry the guns from one rock to another; the cavalry often under the necessity of walking for miles together, and leading their horses along the narrow paths. The nights were intensely cold, so that at night we were nearly frozen, while in the day we could scarcely bear the heat.

In this manner the army advanced several days, without any particular occurrence. After a toilsome march, we one evening reached a few houses, which were immediately taken possession of by the staff. The troops encamped, but there was here such a scarcity of water, that many a soldier could not procure a drop during the whole night; and provisions were out of the question: the valley was notwithstanding the privations we suffered, remarkably beautiful, surrounded on all sides as if with a wall, by the mountains, and coveted with fine trees. The blazing watch-fires on the heights, presented a magnificent spectacle; the full moon shone particularly clear, and nothing broke the silence of the night but the voices of the sentinels. This lasted until the *reveilleé* announced the approach of day, and gave notice for our departure. But before the column was put in motion, the knapsacks of every regiment were opened; the men were only allowed to retain what was absolutely necessary, and the remainder was thrown away, in order to be able to march with more expedition.

Water, which we expected to find plentiful in this mountainous region, often failed us; inhabitants were nowhere to be met with; the men were in the field against us, and the women, through fear, had fled. As by this means, we found ourselves sole masters of the villages, things were frequently not left in the state they should have been; a soldier is a bad economist, he often wastes today what he feels the want of tomorrow.

For several days we wandered in this manner in the mountains, without getting a sight of the enemy; forsaken encampments, torn clothing, &c., betrayed the places where they had lately been; but we never succeeded in reaching them, and began to suspect that the Spaniards never meant to make a stand, when quite unexpectedly we fell in with a corps of upwards of five thousand men. Without discipline, but full of courage, they attacked us, and succeeded in causing some little disorder; soon, however, order was restored, and the enemy received such a well-directed fire, as deprived them of all inclination for a second attack. They quitted the field in confusion, and many prisoners were made; but upon their promise to return home, and live peaceably, they were set at liberty. As readily as these prisoners made this promise, as little did they intend to perform it, and only waited our departure, to return again to their comrades. From this time there were daily and hourly skirmishes; the light-armed Spaniards, who understood the art of mountain-warfare much better than we had expected, annoyed us incessantly on all sides; but they never made a stand against us in masses, as they well knew our superiority in the field. The prisoners which they took from us were put to death in torments: we often found these unfortunate beings mangled in a shocking manner. We met with some of our comrades, whose hands and feet they had not chopped off, but had actually separated them at the joints with their knives; others had their tongues cut out; others had been hung up to the trees by the feet, and roasted to death; and others mutilated in a manner too horrible to describe.

These spectacles inflamed the rage of our soldiers; they thought themselves justified, and even bound to retaliate: and in this manner, ferocity increased on both sides, although, perhaps, forbearance on our parts, would have tended to humanize our opponents. The Spaniards were certainly, in the first instance, oppressed by the French; and thus considered themselves justified in their cruelties, an opinion arising entirely from the revengeful nature of the Spaniards; for at first, the French had not conducted themselves worse than in Germany, and yet such scenes were never heard of there.

At last, at a short distance from Valencia, we came to a general engagement. The position of the Spaniards was extremely advantageous, as we had several well defended passes to force before we reached their line, the flanks of which rested upon the mountains, and the plain in their front was intersected by ditches, rising ground, and obstacles of various kinds. The enemy was far superior in numbers to us, having more than twenty thousand, while we had scarcely fourteen thousand men, among which were a number of sick, and a corps of cavalry, which, owing to the nature of the ground, was unable to act; besides which, we were obliged to leave a detachment in reserve to protect the baggage.

A single attack sufficed to put us in possession of the defiles; the guns were taken, and the occupiers driven before us. I must allow, however, that we lost a number of men, and had a great many wounded. These unfortunates were most to be pitied, for they all perished either through mortification, occasioned by the great heat and want of proper attendance, or a still more horrible fate awaited them at the hands of our cruel enemies; for as we had no means of conveyance, we were obliged to leave them behind us.

Upon reaching the main body, the attack on both sides was impetuous; the Spaniards shouted as if they were mad, but we advanced in silence: the resistance was more obstinate than we, from our former experience, had anticipated; it was long before we forced them to give way, and much blood was shed on both sides. At last their whole line gave way, and they fled in the utmost disorder to the mountains, where we were unable to follow them; we, however, came up with a good many, whose slowness cost them their lives. Their artillery fell into our hands, together with their encampment, filled with provisions of all kinds; we found the kettles with meat still hanging on the fire, and. these were very acceptable to us, as, after such a hard day's work, we stood in need of refreshment. Unfortunately we could only make use of the provisions for the moment; as we had no means of conveying them, each soldier provided himself with as much as he could carry of the rice, stockfish, wine, meat, bread, &c., which we found. There were no provisions daily served out; and, during the whole march, every soldier was obliged to provide for himself, and therefore took what he could find. The cannons, which were mostly of very large calibre, we could not possibly take with us; they were therefore spiked, rendered useless, and then buried.

We now marched direct upon Valencia; and from this time no house was spared, the property of the owners remained nowhere unmolested—even the churches were plundered, although a strict order to the contrary was issued, and several soldiers, taken in the fact, were shot. The utmost severity proved of no avail; the thirst after money overcame all fear of punishment among the French soldiery. Numbers separated themselves from the corps, and ravaged the vicinity upon their own account; stole mules, and loaded them with the plunder; others, who could find no mules, returned, bending under the weight of the burdens they carried upon their backs. Of course all soldiers did not act in this way, though many did, and these usually kept themselves between the rear guard and the main body, where they could plunder safely and undisturbed; for at this time there was no leisure to arrest them; some who suffered themselves to be caught, were punished, but these were not many. The officers themselves took advantage of any good opportunity, without thinking it any disgrace: the surgeons in particular, were not to be surpassed in this trade: instead of attending to the sick and wounded, they were intent only upon filling their own pockets.

Upon entering the houses, the first operation was always to break open the wine-cellars: holes were shot in the casks; but after each man had taken what he wanted, they were never stopped again. If one sort was not approved of, two, three, and very often all the casks in the cellar were tried. In a cellar belonging to a convent, containing at least fifty hogsheads, I once saw some soldiers belonging to the 34th Regiment, fire into every cask, and the wine ran out so abundantly, that some drunken *gendarmes* were actually swimming in it. This mischief was not always done wantonly, but frequently occasioned by carelessness and want of thought. The immoderate use of strong wine, and meat without any bread, gave rise to dangerous disorders, which carried off numbers of the men. Although I drank as much wine as the rest, I continued always healthy, and this may probably be attributed to the bread which I made for myself; I always endeavoured to procure flour, of which I made pancakes, baked in oil. Ten or twenty of such cakes I always carried in my knapsack.

The nearer we approached Valencia, the more beautiful the country became; lemons, oranges, and figs we here found in abundance; and whoever has experienced the heat in the months of July and August, on the coasts of the Mediterranean, well knows what a refreshment a glass of water, mixed with lemon-juice, affords; just as refreshing too is the fruit of the cactus, which were here in such quantities that the supply was inexhaustible. The St. John's bread-tree also grows here, the fruit of which we ate with our pork instead of bread.

A few miles to the southward of Valencia, there is a small town situated on a canal, and here the Spaniards were posted to receive us. We were placed in a wood of olives, which was fired upon by the Spaniards, and many of our men were wounded, both by their shots and the falling of the branches. Our general had no intention of attacking, he was in hopes that the enemy would make an attempt to drive us out of the wood; but as their position was very advantageous, they took care not to leave it, and waited patiently for us: at last our commander gave the order for attack. It was necessary, first of all, to force the bridge over the canal, which was strongly fortified, planted with cannon, and well defended: the Spanish artillery kept up an incessant fire, the guns were mostly served by monks, who showed us that they understood as well how to use the match and ramrod as the rosary and book and stretched many a German and Frenchman in the dust. As the ground was level, there was an opportunity here for the cavalry to act; but in spite of all our endeavours we were repulsed in several attacks: at last, some old grenadier companies succeeded in forcing a passage. As soon as these had opened a way, the remaining troops pressed forward; the cavalry charged in, and the enemy fled in confusion to Valencia. Our day's work was now finished; we halted, and a flag of truce was sent in to requite the surrender of the city, and in case of refusal, to threaten it with bombardment The flag of truce soon returned, with the answer, that we should be allowed to enter Valencia as soon as we had laid down our arms. After this reply, there; remained nothing for us to do but to attack the place (26th and 27th July, 1808).

The fields in the neighbourhood of the city were covered with hemp, growing to a great height: in this, a number of Spaniards were hidden, who fired upon us without ceasing, and after every shot, changed their places, in order not to be remarked.

About midday I was sitting with one of my comrades at a little distance from the regiment, and we were very quietly eating our pork, when a musket-ball passed between us. This unwelcome visitation disturbed us a little; but, without being much alarmed, we moved farther on, and were sitting down again, when a second ball came, which passed through my schako and my companion's head. This was too much for me, and I was terribly frightened: this may be excused in a young man, only seventeen years of age, making his first campaign. Quite confounded, I left this dangerous place, and made all the haste I could back to the main body, where, however, I was not a jot more safe than in my former situation.

The artillery was brought up—but this amounted to nothing, as we had no battering-train, but only twelve-pounders, and no more ammunition in reserve than was sufficient to fill the tumbrils belonging to the guns. The infantry was advanced within musket shot; the light troops, to which I belonged, pressed forward to the charge; the Spanish cavalry, which lined the road, was overthrown, and we reached as far as the gates. Here we were received by a tremendous fire of musketry and artillery, and the grenades made terrible havoc. The soldier in front of me, a Brunswicker, named Görz, received a ball through his head, and I was obliged to supply his place. What my feelings were, can only be imagined by those who have been in a similar situation. As we were able to effect nothing, we turned about at double quick time, and at every step we took, had to pass over the bodies of the dead and dying; the cries and entreaties of the wounded were heart-rending, and every moment, death acquired fresh victims—for the Spaniards could not miss, if they fired upon the main body: those who had the misfortune to be precipitated out of the road into the ditches by the retreating crowd, were all massacred by the Spanish cavalry which pursued us.

In this retreat our regiment came to a stand, behind a church in the suburbs. As soon as this was perceived in the city, the heavy artillery was directed at the tower; but as the church towers in Spain are built of large stones, and not covered with slate, this served to protect us, and the enemy did us no mischief.

From our place of shelter we could plainly see the people on the wall, for we were not above fifty paces distant. This was a most singular sight: there were mixed together, half-naked inhabitants of the lowest classes; peasants, citizens, people of rank, soldiers, and friars—even the women brought up ammunition, and carried away the wounded; and priests were seen passing to and fro' through the ranks with the crucifix in their hands, encouraging them to resistance.

Amidst a shower of balls, Marshal Brune came galloping up to give some verbal orders to our colonel. While they were speaking, he desired a soldier, Faupel, from Erfurth, who had an empty grenade-case hanging at his side for a drinking-cup, to fill it for him, at a small brook which was close by. While Faupel was in the act of doing this, a ball struck the vessel out of his hand, and wounded his fingers; another ball struck the general's horse.

Our artillery was not idle, and the howitzers set the city, on fire in several places. Owing to want of ammunition, we were not able to keep up a sufficient fire to make any considerable impression. The houses were all built of stone, and contained but little wood, so that the fire did not do much damage. We remained a considerable time at our post; small detachments were sent out from time to time, to see if the enemy showed himself upon any other point, in order to disturb, or take us in the rear. But these detachments always sustained more or less loss, and never returned with their full complement.

At last night came on, and hostilities ceased on both sides; we quitted our position, and rejoined the brigade.

The next morning the fire of artillery was warmly kept up, but we made no further attempt to storm the city.

In the evening, all the wagons taken in our advance, which could be spared, were destroyed: several hundred asses, mules and horses were shot; a number of guns, for want of artillery men, were spiked and buried. All the provisions were served out among the troops, and as soon as it was dark, the watch and bivouack fires were kindled, and the army commenced their retreat. A party from each regiment remained behind to keep up the fires, that the Spaniard, might continue as long as possible in ignorance of our retreat. Among those who remained behind, I was one—not to my great joy, for, with an enemy so near, it is always better to be with the main body than in a small detachment.

At midnight, we set off and hastened to overtake the column; this we had good reason for, for as soon as the Spaniards perceived our departure, they were at our heels.[1]

Near the first village, one of my best friends received a shot through his leg, so that he was unable to proceed any farther. We did not like to leave him behind us—he himself was terrified at the idea of the fate which usually awaited the prisoners; this

1. The assertion in *Posselt's Annals* is utterly false—that Valencia was taken by storm on the 30th of June, 1808. As an eye witness, I trust, I may be believed. It is true, that upon the capture of the city, every man was promised a gratification of eighty *francs*: but, at that time, no Frenchman, with arms in his hands, got a sight of the interior of Valencia.

fear made him forget his pain, and gave him strength, with our assistance, to reach the village. In spite of the haste with which we were obliged to retreat, as the enemy was in pursuit of us, we went into the first house in which we thought a mule might be found: luckily we discovered one standing in a stable. The owner was compelled by threats to harness the handsome but wild animal, to a cart. Happy at having gained our point, we thanked the peasant, put a little straw into the cart, and placed our comrade upon it. In this manner, heartily rejoiced at having saved him, we hastened after the column, not without fear of being captured by the enemy. As the mules are very sure footed, we were enabled to proceed as fast as the beast would go, and in about half an hour overtook the detachment without the slightest loss; we were fired upon, but the balls all passed over our heads.

Soon afterwards we reached the rear guard of the column, and in a short time our own regiment. The cart, occasioning disorder among the men, was not allowed to remain; and therefore was sent, under my care, to the baggage. After proceeding a few miles, the cart was unfortunately overturned: the mule, which was naturally wild, was rendered more shy, and entangled the harness in such a manner that I was not able to put it in order again. While occupied in this manner, a hussar rode by upon a mule, which was a much quieter, although a worse one, than mine; he offered to make an exchange, and I, in order to save my companion, agreed. Upon raising up the cart, I found it was so much damaged as to be of no farther service. I now scarcely knew what to do; but, as there was no time to lose, took my great coat, and that of my comrade, bound them upon the mule, placed my wounded friend upon it, and hastened forward as quickly as possible; for this accident had detained us above half an hour: this time also we reached the column in safety.

A few days' march from Valencia, we had to cross the Xucas, a not inconsiderable river; but before reaching it, our road passed through a village, almost entirely deserted by the inhabitants: some of our grenadiers began to plunder, and were seized in the act by General Brune himself; they underwent no trial, but were shot without ceremony, half an hour afterwards. We had scarcely reached the banks of the river, when we saw all the ferryboats in flames, and the heights on all sides covered with Spaniards. There being no other road to take, we were forced to wade through the river, which was pretty deep, and reached the opposite side under a heavy fire, when our cavalry, the ground being tolerably level, made tremendous havoc among our opponents: what remained, saved themselves quickly by flight, which was easy to them, as they were so lightly clothed, namely, with linen trowsers, a shirt, sandals, and a red cap, A long fowling-piece, which they well knew the use of, was the only weapon they carried; the cartridges they usually kept in a scarf, tied round their waists, or in their shirts.

Here I was foolish enough to step out, when volunteers were required to remain on this side of the river, to keep the Spaniards in check until the baggage should have passed over: I came off safe, although the chief part of my companions were either killed or wounded. The wounded were nearly all left to their fate, for we were so far from the main body that no attention was paid to them.

This retreat occasioned much sickness, principally through the heat. The men were nearly fainting on the road: and as we did not return by the way we came, but by the high road from Valencia to Madrid, we found no fruit to quench our thirst. When we came to a well, the crowd was so great that men were frequently pushed in. When even a single drop of water fell upon our sleeves, it was greedily sucked, in order to cool our tongues. Wine we had in abundance; but this only heated us the more, and did not in the least serve to quench our thirst. At one time I was so tormented by thirst, that I took a lump of clay, wrapped it in a silk handkerchief; and sucked it, in order to keep my mouth a little cool. In spite of all this I continued (thanks to Providence!) always in good health, and marched cheerfully forward along with the main body, which was pursued by the Spaniards in just the same manner as we had formerly pursued them. They did not, however, check our march; once only a detachment opposed us, but half a dozen cannon-shot sufficed to disperse them. This was fortunate for us, as we had scarcely any ammunition remaining; many men had not more than half, others not more than a third of their number of cartridges, and the artillery also had but little remaining.

We retreated, in this manner, as far as St. Clemente, where we fell in with a division of the corps of Dupont; nearly the whole of which had been taken prisoners at Baylen, near Cordova.

This division had fortunately cut its way through, and was on the road to Madrid; it consisted chiefly of cavalry, of which we were in want; and on this account the meeting was very agreeable. It was resolved to rest here, to get the army together as well as possible, and to await the enemy. The Spaniards, however, took care not to come too near us, and halted likewise about fifteen miles in our rear.

By degrees came in all the stragglers, who had been plundering in all directions, but kept out of the way when fighting was going on; these received their well-deserved punishment: the plunder was taken from them; several were put under arrest upon bread and water, and others were shot. Among these last, I well recollect a handsome young farrier, who, convicted of robbing a church, was executed without mercy.

After having rested a few days, and collected together, we went on to Madrid. Here all were in the utmost consternation, for the army of Junot had also been obliged to capitulate at Lisbon, and was embarked in English transports, in order to be conveyed to France upon their parole of honour, not to serve against England during the war.[2]

Our regiment was quartered in the palace of the Prince of the Peace; the magazine of stores which were there, was cleared out and thrown into the basin in the garden, in order that they might not afterwards fall into the enemies' hands.

On the day before our retreat, the 30th of July, 1808, a detachment was sent into the city to receive some clothing for

---

2. Notwithstanding this, about six or eight months afterwards, they were again opposed to the English at Oporto.

the regiment. I was one, and resolved for once to be merry in Madrid before our march, and went into a wine-house, in order to drown all recollection of the hardships I had suffered, in good Spanish wine. After I and some of my companions had handsomely regaled ourselves, we bade *adieu* to our civil host, and hastened to find out the detachment; but the night was dark, and we were a little in liquor. After wandering about for some time, we came to a barrack, in which we found the 43rd Regiment; here we took up our quarters for the night.

When we awoke in the morning, we found our comrades had marched, and, together with all the remaining troops, left Madrid. We had nothing else to do but to follow: when we came out at the door, we were received by the populace, who had assembled to plunder the stores left behind by the French army, with such friendly expressions as these: "Kill the rascally Frenchmen, the dogs, the robbers" &c. &c. We made off as quickly as we could, to prevent these threats from being put in execution; stones indeed flew after us, but hit no-one. Our death, notwithstanding, would have been unavoidable, if a patrol of cuirassiers had not luckily passed through the street and conveyed us in safety to the gate, at the moment when the last division of our army, which had been encamped near the Ponte Toledo, was passing by.

As we were passing the Prado, we saw a number of soldiers busied about a wagon; we went up, and found it was a treasure-wagon, which had been left. The casks were broken open, and the five-*franc* pieces were being divided. We seized our share of this rich booty, and in a few moments each of us had packed a few hundred dollars in his knapsack. Pleased with the turn our fortune had taken, we hastened forward to reach our regiment. Yesterday, however, we had come into the city without musket and cartridge-box, and arrived only with our sabres; and in the hurry, this morning, it was impossible to fetch them. We were thus obliged to look about, in order to procure arms, as without them we should not have met with a pleasant reception at the regiment: luckily we fell in with several soldiers, lying exhausted in the road, who were glad to make an exchange with us, and for four five-*franc* pieces, each of us possessed himself of a musket and accoutrements.

Now, provided with all necessaries, and money in abundance, we marched cheerfully after our regiment, and found it in camp, about fifteen miles from Madrid. We were sharply reproved by our captain, for staying behind; but our five-*franc* pieces consoled us, and I enjoyed, in anticipation, the pleasant days my money would procure me in France, whither I had no doubt we were marching.

On this retreat from Madrid, our army more resembled a band of robbers, than disciplined troops: all the towns we passed through, were obliged to furnish heavy contributions; the villages where we slept were generally set on fire in the morning; all the cattle, whether necessary for our subsistence or not, were slaughtered; in short, every thing was destroyed and laid waste, even the corn ricks, standing in the fields, were burned.

As the Spaniards did not pursue us farther than Madrid, we halted for a few days in Burgos, there, also, contributions were levied; the magazines were opened, and the stores divided among the soldiers. No-one, during this time, was better off than the camp followers, who accompanied the army, with two or three wagons each; they enriched themselves with stolen goods, and sold the provisions and liquors, which they robbed others of, at a dear rate to the soldiers. We were obliged to pay for a bottle of the worst brandy, called *aqua riente,* in Spain, from twenty to thirty *francs.* Tobacco, so necessary to the soldier, was worth, during the last days of our retreat, almost its weight in gold, and not always to be procured.

During our stay at Burgos, a revision of the army took place, which did not afford the most agreeable results: our regiment, for instance, which marched out from Madrid, for Valencia, eleven hundred strong, did not now muster more than three hundred. In the company to which I belonged, were only forty men remaining; at the division of the stores, these forty received twenty-five chests of biscuit, each weighing one hundred pounds.

From Burgos, we retreated farther towards the Pyrenees, to Miranda, on the Ebro, and Vittoria, where the main army remained stationary, to await the reinforcements, marching in all haste from Germany. The army was in a miserable condition, quite worn out, and most of the soldiers were without shoes. There was but little to eat, and we lived in holes in the earth, which we dug ourselves; and in which, with scarcely clothes to cover us, we suffered a good deal. A number of our men here deserted to the Spaniards, under pretence of going in search of apples; whenever any one was missing, it was said, "He is gone after apples;" and this saying we long retained.

In this time of need, I found the money, from the treasure-wagon, of great service; one piece after another was changed, and applied to my subsistence; I did not, nevertheless, neglect my comrades, particularly him, whose life I had saved, during the retreat from Valencia. I had long given him and his mule up for lost; but after I had been obliged to quit him, he had followed with the baggage. A good-natured surgeon had dressed his wound, and provided him with bandages; it being only a flesh-wound, he had preserved himself by a regular diet; and, although not yet well, was now much better. Soon after his arrival, he was sent, with the other wounded men, to France, for which journey I equipped him handsomely, considering my circumstances.

After some time, our regiment, owing to being so much reduced, was sent farther into the rear, and posted in the Pyrenees, where the companies were separately detached to Salinos, known for its defiles, to Montdragon, Bergara, and Villa Real. My company was quartered in Bergara, and we were employed in protecting the communication between the army and France. We should have been tolerably satisfied with our situation if the duty had not been so severe: we were scarcely ever off the roads, as the numerous bands of guerillas endeavoured to cut off all communication, and no convoy could pass without an escort, When we obtained any respite from this labour, we were sent round the vicinity, to collect requisitions; sometimes money, sometimes provisions, sometimes beds for the hospitals. At last, we received new clothing, and a reinforcement from the depôt, so that our regiment was six hundred strong. The forces, returning from Prussia, now began to appear; the advanced guard, under Marshal Lefebvre, consisted of Darmstadt, Nassau, and Dutch troops; among which, was a large proportion of light cavalry, particularly Dutch hussars.

How the Spaniards were astonished, when they beheld the advance of these well appointed and excellently disciplined troops! The main army next followed, consisting of French infantry and cavalry, among which, the Spaniards were particularly struck with the appearance of the splendid regiments of Cuirassiers, whom, on account of their size and strength, they named *Colloseros*: last of all, appeared the Emperor Napoleon Buonaparte, usually called by the Spaniards, *Malaparte*. He passed through Bergara, with his staff, in the midst of a tremendous storm of snow and rain; the roads were so muddy; that they were scarcely passable; nevertheless, the Emperor and his whole suite were on horseback, but so completely covered with mud, that the colour of their clothes could scarcely be distinguished.

The army separated itself at Bergara, and marched upon two different roads; one division, by way of Bilboa, which was taken on the 1st of November, 1808, and the other by way of Vittoria; we also received marching orders, and advanced, with the corps of Marshal Lefebvre, to Bilboa. At Durango, we fell in with the enemy; and, after an action, in which we made five hundred prisoners, advanced farther. At Bilboa, the Spaniards were again defeated, the same at Logrono, where we again joined the division of the army, which had marched by way of Vittoria. Between Burgos and Gomala, the Spaniards awaited us, on the 10th November, 1808, with their whole force, and here we came to a serious engagement, The enemy did their duty, and fought like brave soldiers; but they could not long resist the French troops, accustomed to victory; they fled in disorder, through Burgos, part to Madrid, and part to Valladolid. Our division pursued the enemy on the road to Valladolid;

they rallied at Torquemata, and faced us again, but were once more put to flight. Torquemata, as a reward for our exertions, was given up to plunder, and nearly reduced to ashes. After this, we met with no farther obstacles, and entered Valladolid without opposition, on the 12th November, 1808. The army advanced into Gallicia, and the Asturias, but we were left in garrison at Valladolid, along with the Imperial Guards.

After this I had, for some time, no share in the military operations, and can, therefore, give no account of them.

The palace of the Holy Inquisition was appointed for our barracks. The *major-domo* received our colonel, at that time the Prince of Hohenzollern-Sigmaringen, at the gates, and presented him an Imperial order, signifying, that on pain of punishment, nothing throughout the buildings should be damaged. His order was immediately made known to us before our admission, and at first punctually obeyed; but, like all orders of this nature, particularly in an enemy's country, was by degrees forgotten and neglected by the soldiers, and in less than three weeks time, we had pretty well ransacked the whole of the interior.

Here, the horrible secrets of the Inquisition were brought to light, and by this means, I contracted such an unconquerable aversion to the Spanish clergy, as I have never been able to overcome.

The palace of the Inquisition forms a square, having a large handsome court in the centre; the front contains a number of handsome rooms, not at all antique, but fitted up entirely in the modern taste. Upon crossing the court-yard, a flight of steps led to the consistory, where the sittings were held; in this, there was a sort of raised stage, which upon these occasions, was occupied by the Grand Inquisitor and his colleagues. Beyond this, on the farther side, we found the library, the archives, and last of all, the room of torture, about fifty or sixty steps under ground.

The first object which struck us, in this place of horror, was the rack machine, somewhat similar to the lash chamber, with which, to this day, in many countries, soldiers are punished. Two bars, the length of a man, were crossed by two others, of the same size, and formed a sort of bed; there was a board hollowed out, where the head of the unfortunate victim was placed, and buckled tight by a strap. On each side were rings in the wall, through which ropes passed; these were fastened to the body, arms, and legs, and then drawn so tight, that they cut into the flesh. During this operation, the victim had his mouth kept filled with water, so that, in addition to his torment, he had the feeling of suffocation.

The second instrument was for torture, by means of fire; it was a chair, with a footstool, in which two holes were cut; through these the feet were placed, and held over a hot pan of coals, and to increase the pain, were first rubbed with oil. The third torture, for which I have no name, was a rope, which, after the victim's arms had been placed behind his back, was tied to his hands, and by this means, after forty or fifty pounds weight had been fastened to his feet, he was drawn up to the ceiling.

We burned and destroyed all these instruments of torture; the archives we used for lighting our fires, and for a variety of purposes. Had I been at that time more experienced, I might, among these records, have found many things interesting, and worthy of transmission to posterity; but as it was, they were all destroyed, without anyone giving himself the least trouble about them.

In the middle of the court was a well, though it contained no water; but under the colonnade was another, from which, water could be drawn into the uppermost stories. This water, was not very good; having a sweetish decayed taste; but, for want of better, there being no other well near, and the river Pisuerga being at some distance, we made use almost entirely of this, as well for drinking as cooking. No one regiment in the garrison was so unhealthy as ours; and I was told by the surgeons of the regiment, that the prevailing disorder was the putrid fever, of which there was not the slightest symptom in any other of the regiments; at last the reason was found out.

A soldier had let his watch fall into this well; another, a mason by profession, offered to get it out again, if he might be allowed to go down, and the owner would give him half the value.

This was agreed to, and the mason immediately set to work; but he quickly came up again with affright, and said there were skeletons in the well. The matter was investigated, and several were actually taken out; they had probably not lain there a great while, as pieces of flesh were still hanging to them. The well was immediately closed up, and water was brought for us upon asses from the river, and the neighbouring wells; and it was said, that much of the sickness had been occasioned by the water which had been poisoned by the dead carcasses.

The cellars were filled with the choicest wine; these we liked the taste of, and often drank the downfall of the Inquisition in their own wine.

On the first floor were the prisons, which went round the whole building. These were sparingly lighted by strongly barred windows; strong chains, to which the prisoners were fastened, were fixed into the walls; the floor, raised in one part, served for a bed; and the only article of furniture was a necessary utensil, many of which we found filled, a proof that immediately before our entrance, these places had been occupied.

What could the beings, by any possibility, have been guilty of, who in this holy institution were thus tormented in honour of an almighty and benevolent God?

It was sufficient, to become amenable to this horrible institution, to have uttered any expressions in favour of any other and better mode of worship; which, although warranted by conviction, did not accord with the articles of belief of the Catholic church; or to have offended a priest, by word or deed: it was enough, even to have hindered the gratification of the libidinous desires of the holy inquisitors, or the clergy, or to have protected against them the honour of a wife or a daughter. An order for arrest was secretly made out; in the middle of the sight, the officers knocked at the door of the unfortunate person, and demanded entrance in the name of the Holy Inquisition. All trembled at these dreadful words; they sufficed to unclose every door, and no Spaniard dared to refuse admission.

In this manner the victim was carried off; no friend, no relation dared ask after him, or inquire about his fate. He was placed before the dreadful tribunal; a masked accuser and masked witnesses appeared; the one accused him of a crime, of which, perhaps, he scarcely knew the name; the others averred, confidently, that it had been committed. In vain he protested his innocence; to this no attention was paid. In vain he offered to produce proofs in his defence; this was refused. By means of the abovementioned instruments, a confession was wrung from, the unhappy wretch, of a crime which he never had committed. As soon as he had confessed, he was lost without redemption, his property was confiscated, and he was either publicly executed, or privately murdered; if his life was spared, he either never saw daylight again, or only after a long imprisonment.

Near this building in the square of St. Pedro, the *Autos da Fé* or public executions, took place! Within, the walls, we found all the apparatus used upon these occasions, such as caps, ornamented with devils, serpents and all kinds of monsters; dresses painted with flames, and the whole economy of the infernal regions.

But enough of these cruelties, shocking to humanity!

During our stay in Valladolid, several guerilla prisoners were, brought in and executed, These undisciplined bands had. originated in various ways. After the insurrection in Madrid, and our advance upon Valencia, all the scum of the country had turned out against us. These did little service to the nation, as the leaders were usually rogues, who only sought to enrich themselves; they levied contributions everywhere, drove off the cattle, and robbed the poor peasants of everything the French had left them; on which account they were in many places as much dreaded as the French themselves. Afterwards, several bands were formed, under Mina, *El Empecinado*, Jayme, and others, which did us much mischief; they rendered the roads so unsafe, that no convoy could pass without a strong escort. They threw themselves headlong upon the strongest detachment, and not unfrequently gained material advantages and considerable booty.

These guerillas consisted chiefly of French deserters, and but few natives were to be found among them. There were, at least, thirty men belonging to our regiment, in the band of *El Empeci-nado*, who carried on their operations in the neighbourhood of Villa Delpando, Benavente, and Toro. These troops were mostly composed of badly mounted cavalry, who had equipped themselves in a most singular manner, with the clothing taken from the French; many a trooper wore gaiters, had a long cuirassier's sabre, a blanket in the place of a cloak, a *cora*, or cap on the head, and a long musket hung behind, on his lean, worn-out steed. Whenever a French horseman pursued one of these knights of the rueful countenance, he usually looked round, placed his hand upon a part of his body, which shall be nameless, put his horse into a gallop, and disappeared in an instant.

The infantry were just as ridiculously equipped: it often afforded us much amusement to see them stalking about in large boots, a dragoon's helmet upon their heads, and a long sword by their sides. They were once surprised by the 10th and 11th Regiments of Dragoons, and a number of prisoners made, who were all shot, strangled, or hanged by the French as brigands. At an execution of this kind, there were once eighty men strangled; the whole garrison was present, and our battalion kept guard. In the centre of the square, a large scaffold was erected, upon which were several upright posts, to which boards were fixed as seats for the criminals. As soon as they were seated, the executioner placed an iron collar round their necks, which had a screw behind; this being screwed up, broke the neck, and choked the windpipe at the same time. A laughable occurrence happened at this execution, namely, the asses, upon which the delinquents had been brought, all began simultaneously to bray at the moment they were despatched.

At another time, two deserters from our regiment were brought in; one, the drum-major, a Brunswicker by birth, who had also taken with him the regimental staff, which was of some value; the other, quite a young lad, belonging to the band. The latter, not being quite fifteen years old, could not be condemned to death; but he requested this punishment, and both were shot before the gate of Toro.

Prisoners of this kind were seldom kept long, but immediately shot. The prisoners taken, belonging to the Spanish regular troops, were also but roughly dealt with. I once saw, myself, (we were escorting two thousand of them) that a Spanish dragoon, in the vicinity of Valdestillas, who was unable to proceed, was immediately ordered to be bayoneted, by a lieutenant of our regiment.

Here, also, I saw another execution, which was performed by the Spanish authorities, under French inspection. Three Spaniards, who had enticed a French soldier, belonging to the train, into a house, and murdered him, were hanged. The gallows was erected in the centre of the city, in the great square; the criminals rode upon asses, but the priests, who accompanied them, walked on foot, on each side. as soon as they had reached the gallows, the executioner, (*vertugo*) who, in Spain, by way of distinction, wears a silver ladder on his hat, took hold of them, and made them step from the asses to the ladder, without allowing them to touch the ground. When the first one had reached the third step from above, the executioner turned him round, and seated him upon the ladder; he then took the rope, and with much dexterity put it in an instant round his neck. As soon as this was done, he cried out, "*Ave maria purissima*" seated himself upon, the delinquent's shoulders, and riding upon his neck in this way, threw himself from the ladder, and pressed with all the weight of his body upon that of the poor wretch, whose neck was certainly lengthened some inches. Under the gallows stood an assistant, who seized the legs of the criminal, and pulled with all his might; in this manner the execution was performed with the greatest celerity. The bodies were soon after taken down, thrown into a cart, carried out, and nailed upon posts, outside of the city gates. I was surprised that no Spaniards undertook to pull the bodies down, and bury them; I saw them there long after, almost entirely devoured by the birds of prey, which are very numerous there.

The Emperor, Napoleon, came to Valladolid, and reviewed the troops lying here. In passing the front of the regiments, he spoke to several of the soldiers; and struck, perhaps, by my youth, he addressed me also. He asked me: "*Quel age as tu, jeune homme?*"

"Seize ans et demi, Sire."

"Vous etes encore trop jeune. De quel pays etes vous?"

" Je suis Saxon, mon Empereur."

"Ah, les Saxons sont toujours de bons soldats et je crois que vous le serez aussi,—pas vrai, mon garcon?"

With these words he left me, and turned to another. He was accustomed to hold those to whom he was speaking by the button, this he did to me; and during the whole time did not let me go, so that I felt completely confused.

While we were here in garrison, I was made corporal, and I soon after went with a detachment to Madrid, to escort some carriages, carrying household furniture of all sorts, for King Joseph, at Madrid; we passed through Valdestillas, Olmeda, and Segovia; the last-mentioned town has a magnificent cathedral, and an aqueduct, built by the Romans, which is now in ruins, and used by the Spaniards for washing wool. We passed the Sierra Guadarama, and arrived at last at Madrid, where we passed the night in the Royal stables.

The King made us a present of three hundred *francs* for our trouble, but our sergeant deserted with the money, and we received nothing. I saw him afterwards again, as a Brunswick hussar, and reminded him of his shabby behaviour.

I now, as corporal, had the command of the detachment, which accompanied some general officers on the return. In Segovia I was taken suddenly unwell, but I thought I should be able to get over it, and went on; but, between Segovia and Santa Maria, I was attacked with such a violent fever, as not to be able to follow with the detachment, and was obliged to lie down in the road. One of the generals, whom we were escorting, observed my condition, and was humane enough to let me have his mule; upon this I rode to Olmeda, where I procured a carriage, and was brought to Valladolid. I was carried immediately to the hospital of St. Ambrosio, where I remained for two months, in such a dangerous state, that my recovery was despaired of.

Luckily, I fell under the hands of a very skilful French doctor, and of an attendant, who, although a Spaniard, nursed me with the greatest care, and passed nearly the whole day with me. This excellent man spared no pains; he often made my bed five times in a day, and did every thing I wished for, if at all consistent with my condition.

The treasure, which I brought from Madrid, I was yet possessed of, and was still of some value; I was wise enough to keep it hid until I began to get better; I had heard many stories of sick men, who were supposed to be in possession of a little money, being in some way or other sent out of the world by the medical attendants, in order to inherit their property. I had afterwards, when I lay wounded in the hospital, opportunities enough to convince myself, that the attendants made no hesitation of committing such actions. In spite of all my frugality, my property was considerably diminished during my continuance in the hospital; but still applied to my own advantage, as, when I began to get better, I procured for myself more strengthening nourishment; but as this was obliged to be done secretly, (our diet being strictly attended to) it was necessary to pay the attendants well. I also considered it my duty to make a present to the good attendant, who had preserved my life, and thus, when I left the hospital, I was only possessed of fifty dollars.

As a convalescent, I was for some days exempt from service; but I soon became tired of an idle life, and reported myself well before there was any necessity for it.

Our regiment shortly after again joined the main army, which was at Benavente, on the Borejo. We were here, in turns with the 12th Light Infantry Regiment, dispersed about the neighbourhood, to prevent the requisitions of the Spanish troops. Once, when, we were stationed at the bridge of Benavente, and had also a dragoon regiment with us, the 12th Regiment, which was also in Benavente, about half a league from the bridge, was surprised in the night by the Spanish troops. In the utmost confusion, and half naked; the French seized their arms, and retreated; fighting out of the town; many, however, were killed and made prisoners. Among the prisoners was the wife of the commandant of the 19th Regiment; together with several other women. The next morning the Spaniards: sent all these women back to us completely naked.

The Spanish army beginning to show itself in the field, our troops were drawn together and marched against the enemy. In the plain near Benavente, we came to an action, and, after a brave resistance, the Spaniards were repulsed; La Baneza was plundered, and we marched towards Astorga, which city the enemy had already quitted for Galicia and the Asturias, where the Spaniards were posted in conjunction with the English, the former under the command of the Marquis de la Romana, the latter, under General Moore.

The English, at that time, were accustomed only to parade duty, and to a kind of neatness, incompatible with service in the field. This we gave them no time for; we were constantly at their heels, and scarcely allowed them a day's rest. They were also in want of everything, for Gallicia and the Asturias are not the richest provinces of Spain; and the long stay of the army had exhausted all the stores. To this was added diseases of all kinds; and we found whole troops of sick soldiers in the houses, by the road sides, who, for want of means of conveyance, could not be removed. The retreat, altogether, was so rapid, that the enemy left all their baggage, behind; and we captured a great quantity of stores, together with, the military chest.

At Villa Franca and Ponferrata, they were compelled to halt and face us; but the troops were too weak and exhausted to make much opposition. They again retreated, and hastened, by way of Lugo, San Jago, and Ferroll to Corunna; here the English embarked, in all haste, on the 16th of January, 1809, after having destroyed a number of horses, which, in their hurry, they had no time to ship. The Marquis of Romana escaped us, with about six thousand men, retreated by way of Oviedo, and threw himself into the mountains of Asturias.

General Moore was killed at Elvina. At Corunna the French found considerable stores of all kinds, and captured several English vessels, the captains of which, being ignorant of the reverses of their army, and supposing the Spaniards to be still in possession of Gallicia and Asturias, had come into port. Everything which we found of any value was shipped and sent to France. We then set forward in pursuit of the Marquis de la Romana, but we found his positions unattackable. Our division remained in Oviedo and Chigona, as a corps of observation. In Chigona we found considerable English magazines of warlike stores and provisions; among other things, a quantity of coffee, which was applied to our use, and of which we every day consumed a great deal.

After the affair at Villa Franca, as many of the troops as could find accommodation were quartered in the small villages in the neighbourhood of the town; the remainder were bivouacked. Our regiment had the good luck to pass the night in a considerable village, where the privates were quartered in a convent, from which the nuns had all fled; and the officers were lodged in a large house close by, which was empty, and deserted by the proprietor.

The captain of our company, a devout worshipper of Bacchus, ordered his servant, very late in the night, to fetch him more wine; the man, who was a very brave and good soldier, tired and worn out by the numberless orders of his half-drunken master, refused to obey, and, in the heat of the moment, made use of some insubordinate expressions, which put the captain in such a rage, that he drew his sabre to cut him down. This the servant did not wait for, but ran downstairs out of the room, and, hid himself in the cellar, from whence he had not the courage to come; out, although the captain called him several times. Resolving to remain there a little longer, he leaned his back against an empty wine-cask, which, too light to bear his weight, gave way, and he fell down backwards. In falling, he struck his head so forcibly against the stand upon which the cask was placed, that he lost his senses for some minutes.

On his recovery, he found himself sitting in a hole; he looked about him a little, and at last, found, under the sand, some boards, which had been broken by his fall; he raised these up, and very cautiously put his hand into the cavity. At first, he felt something which he thought was a snake, or something of that kind; but, taking courage, he once more put in his arm, and found it was linen, which, owing to the-moisture, felt slippery. He now endeavoured to draw it out, but it was so heavy, that the contents burst the rotten cloth, and fell clattering into the hole. Being now aware that it was money, he ran out of the cellar, and, for want anything better, brought his schako, which he nearly filled with *quadruples*. The next day he begged of the captain, who was now quite sober, the vacant situation of trumpeter; and, as he was somewhat musical, this was granted him. A corporal, a countryman of his, continued, as before, his intimate friend, and the whole company shared in his good fortune, as he treated us every day with something or other.

He remained with us for two years longer, although with his money he could easily have obtained his discharge, At last, at the siege of Rodrigo, his bosom-friend, the corporal, had his leg shot off by the fragment of a bomb: through want of cart, and the heat of the weather, the wound mortified, and he died. He then said, "I have now nothing to detain me here; I will get my discharge and return home; not, however, before the fortress is taken." As soon as Rodrigo had surrendered, he actually bought his discharge for a thousand *francs*. I afterwards heard that he was taken prisoner by the guerillas, who plundered him of all his property, which at his departure, might have amounted to four thousand dollars.

We remained eighteen days in Chigona, and then returned to Castile. The hospital and baggage were sent on some miles in advance, in wagons drawn by oxen. The army followed, and was usually about half a day's march behind. One day, when the column was marching upon one of the worst roads in all the Asturias, with our regiment in front, some hussars came galloping in, and reported, that the escort of the baggage had been attacked by the troops of Romana, and with such an overwhelming force, that they were too weak to resist, and had been obliged to retreat; the hospital the Spaniards had captured, and were making havoc among the sick and wounded. We hastened forward as quick as we could, but we came too late: one half of the escort lay dead upon the field, and the wagons, with the sick and wounded, had been thrown down a precipice, after the oxen had been taken out and driven away.

All those, who, in endeavouring to escape by flight, had been taken, the Spaniards had stripped, and murdered with their knives! It was a shocking sight to behold these poor helpless wretches murdered in this manner; many an eye, which for a length of time had not known a tear, was moistened. and our blood boiled with rage against the brutal assassins of our defence-less comrades. We vowed death and destruction to all Spaniards who should fall into our hands, and this oath we kept inviolate. The village, which had the misfortune to afford us shelter for the night, was burnt to ashes; no living being was spared; all were sacrificed to our revenge; and the Spanish soldiers who were brought in prisoners, were drowned without any mercy! This part of the business was undertaken and performed in a masterly manner by a battalion of Germans, who were with us; the dead bodies were afterwards hung up, and ornamented with their weapons.

CHAPTER 5

The Siege of Rodrigo

We marched into Leon, where we were again, after a length of time, quartered upon the inhabitants. I was lodged in the house of a priest, deprived of office by the French, who used all the means in his power to entice me and my comrades to join the army of Romana; but true to our duty, we withstood all his solicitations. The city of Leon is situated on the borders of Castile; it is not large, but neat and clean. Among the objects worthy of remark, are its fine cathedral, and a monastery, in which the ancient kings of Leon lie buried. Not content with waging war upon the living, the rapacity of the French broke open the long closed tombs[1] of these princes, to search their coffins for treasure; but the result did not answer their expectations—they found but few articles of any value. The old monastery was completely laid waste; the church, which was adorned with fine statuary and valuable paintings, was converted into a stable for the horses of the cavalry and artillery; the basins for the holy water were used as mangers, and the venerable statues of the saints were obliged to look patiently on while the horses were being tied up to their arms.

Not alone here, but every where, the French manifested little or no respect for their religion. I always felt an internal shuddering, when at the command of my superiors, I was under the ne-

---

1. The coffins consisted of a single stone hollowed oat in a square form; the lids were formed of a flat stone, fitting exactly to the coffin, the bodies, among which were some in tolerable preservation, had not the slightest ornament indicative of their former rank.

cessity of assisting in the demolition of a sanctuary of this kind, although to me, as a Protestant, it could not appear so holy as to the French, brought up in the Catholic religion.

After a rest of some time, we broke up, together with a division of the 8th corps, in order to surprise Astorga, in which there was a Spanish garrison. We approached the city without meeting with the least opposition; the *voltigeurs* got into the suburbs, and established themselves behind the houses; the troops of the line halted within musket shot. A tremendous fire was now opened from the walls, which was answered by our horse artillery, (we had no other), with as much effect as possible. By an unlucky accident, a grenade was thrown among a party of eighteen of our own soldiers, of which I was one; it burst, killed some, and wounded several others in a shocking manner. One of my comrades, named Gundlach, from Mühlhausen, was struck by a fragment of the shell, which shattered his musket and bayonet, and carried away the lower part of his face; he fell down senseless, but the wound did not immediately kill him: we laid him upon a sack of straw, and carried him out of the suburbs, under a heavy fire, to a surgeon; but, before we could reach one, a ball struck him again in the foot, and he died very soon after. Another, Roth, from Fulda, had his entrails torn out, and died in unspeakable torments.

The town being very well defended, it was resolved on our side to withdraw; and the inattention of our captain, nearly delivered us into the enemy's hands: he refused to fall back when the retreat was sounded; and only determined so to do, when he perceived the column in full march. In this retreat I ran a great risk of losing both my legs; a cannon ball struck the ground about fifty paces from me, rebounded, and was coming quickly in my direction; I saved myself by a leap; the dangerous ball rolled away under my feet, and shattered the wheel of a cannon.

We marched once more to la Baneza; and this unfortunate place, which had scarcely began to recover itself, was plundered for the second time. The whole of my booty consisted of a few pounds of cinnamon, which I used to mix with my wine.

We were afterwards relieved by fresh troops, and went farther in the rear to Medina del Rio Seco, where we remained for some time, but not undisturbed, as we were every day annoyed by the guerillas.

I often had an opportunity, being obliged to wash my own linen, of observing the method of washing practised by the Spanish women, which is very different from our's. The linen is carried to the river, or any clear stream, and thrown into the cold water, without being, as with us, first soaped. In many places (for instance in Biscay and Navarre,) the women go into the water with their clothes tucked up nearly to their middle, rub the linen over with brown soap, and then beat it forcibly against smooth stones placed for the purpose; as soon as if is clean, it is hung up and dried. In Castile, and in the southern provinces generally, they have boards for this purpose, about two feet long, upon which the clothes are rubbed and beaten until they are clean.

It follows, of course, that by this method the linen receives a good deal of damage; but as linen made of hemp is chiefly used, which is stronger than that of flax, it stands this rough treatment much better. During washing, the women (more than a hundred of whom may often be seen together,) sing incessantly.

We afterwards remained for a length of time in cantonments, in the neighbourhood of Benavente and Leon, sometimes at Valderos, sometimes in Mayorga. While we were lying in Valderos, a serjeant of the 11th Dragoon Regiment, which was in Carion, a German by birth, was sent to us, where the headquarters of the brigade were established, with despatches. About half way, at a place where two villages are situated close to each other, he was attacked by the priest of one of them, with a pistol in his hand; the serjeant, having more presence of mind than the monk, struck the pistol out of his band, leaped from his horse and overpowered him; he then tied him with a cord to his horse, and brought him to the headquarters at Valderos. The priest was instantly brought before a court-martial, and condemned to death. Just before his execution he sent for the serjeant, and made him a present of his gold watch, and four thousand *reals*, which he sent for from home; he then heartily begged his pardon, and prepared himself for death. I with three others, was ordered out to put the sentence in execution; each of our pieces was loaded with two balls, and we shot so well, that he never moved a finger. A piece of his skull struck me on the left side, and stained the belt of my sabre; these spots, in spite of all my endeavours, I was never able to eradicate. In remembrance of this heroic priest, I carried his silver tobacco box, which I took out of his pocket, until I was made prisoner, and it was taken from me by a greedy Scotchman.

From Valderos, parties were often sent out in pursuit of the guerillas, who infested the neighbourhoods. I was once with one of these parties, consisting of a detachment of fifty infantry, and twenty-five horse *chasseurs*, under the command of a captain and a lieutenant. We went to Vincente, and from thence to Villa Leon, which we reached rather late. Here, bread, cheese, and wine, were served out to the men, as was usual upon such occasions. After our meal, we went on towards a village, about three quarters of an hour's distance. Upon reaching the thrashing place, outside of the village, we perceived, in the dusk, a human figure; some of us ran forward and caught the man, who proved to be an inhabitant; we placed our bayonets to his breast, and inquired of him, whether there were any guerillas in the place He answered, "No;" but upon threatening to shoot him, and cocking our guns for that purpose, he acknowledged that there were, and that their leader was in the house of the priest. As the entrances to the village were immediately beset, and under the guidance of the peasant, we proceeded to the priest's house. Here we thundered for admission; but as the door was not immediately opened, we burst it in, and searched the whole house.

The guerilla chief had fled, but he and some of his men were taken by our scouts, in one of the small streets of the villages and placed under a guard. We then began to search the other houses, not only for guerillas, but for provisions, and many of my comrades took whatever else they could lay their hands upon. I went into a decent looking house, where I found several soldiers; upon, asking the woman whether she had anything to eat, she replied, "Yes, Sir, there is the provision-room," pointing to a door which was approached by several steps. I went up, and found a large store of hams, sausages, smoked mutton, and cheeses. To spare my comrades the trouble of coming up, I threw down the cheeses, and they disappeared so fast, that I was glad, at last, to secure a solitary one for myself, which I found behind the door.

As I was going out again, I heard behind me, in the house, a moaning cry; I followed the noise, and found, in one of the interior apartments, a soldier of our regiment endeavouring to force a young girl of very respectable appearance. I earnestly entreated of him to spare her; but as he only laughed at me, I became angry, and told him, if he did not let the girl go immediately, I would run him through the body with my bayonet. As he was unarmed; he could offer no opposition, and went away. I remained a short time with the young woman, until she was a little recovered, and then thought it advisable to be off and join my comrades, who were assembled at the thrashing place, although the girl earnestly begged of me to remain in the house to protect her.

In the corn districts of Spain, there being so little timber, that the farmers are not able to build barns, there is near every village a fixed spot for erecting stacks. As soon as the harvest is over, the thrashing begins, which is performed in a very simple, but very expeditious manner. Every peasant has, in the general thrashing place, a round space appropriated to himself. Around this, the corn which is to be thrashed is placed; to a stake, fixed in the centre, an ox or a mule is fastened by a rope, long enough to allow the animal to perform a tolerable circle. The beast, whose eyes are covered, draws after him a kind of harrow, about four feet long and two wide, under which a number of flint stones are fixed. Without being driven, the animal goes round and round the circle, and the harrow rubs out the corn. In order to make the harrow still more heavy, one or more men or women usually seat themselves upon it; and without troubling themselves at all about the animal, sleep, smoke, or amuse themselves in various ways. When the beast is tired he stops, and another is put in his place. The corn being in this manner rubbed out of the ears, they wait till the wind rises, when, by throwing it up in the air, the wind carries away the chaff, and separates it from the corn, which being heavier, falls immediately to the ground. As long as this work lasts, the whole family is generally, day and night, on the spot. The straw is then put into nets made of *esparto*, and the corn put into baskets, and carried home: in three or four weeks the whole business is usually concluded. One would suppose, that by this means, the corn would be a good deal mingled with sand, but I never found this to be the case.

Throughout the whole country the flour is merely sifted, and the poorest peasant has his meal-chest and fine sieve, with which the mistress of the house sifts, at a time, as much flour as is necessary for making the bread; during this operation she constantly sings, and keeps time with her sieve.

The next morning we again set forward upon our expedition, and had not proceeded far, when we perceived, at a distance, a cavalcade, which several of us took for Spanish troopers; on a closer inspection, it proved to be asses, laden with skins of wine. A few of our horsemen were immediately sent in pursuit, and brought back the convoy. The conductors had forged French passports, and were taking the wine to the Spanish troops. We found it quite good enough for us, and emptied a skin immediately, to "the success of the French, and the downfall of the Spaniards."

Towards evening we came into a town, where we found some French infantry and artillery. These troops being already in possession of the houses, we were obliged to bivouack in an old castle, built by the Moors, outside of the town. Here we were making ourselves merry with the captured wine; when an order for march was suddenly brought in, as there were guerillas in Villa Alba, whose watch-fires were plainly to be discerned. We were immediately in motion, and crept along in the dark, until we arrived before the town, which in former times might have been considered as fortified, as it was surrounded by a high wall, which was, however, now in such a ruinous state, that entrance was to be found every where. Our cavalry now rode forward, and we presently heard a few shots. We hastened quickly onwards, and passed through the town to the other side, where we found our *chasseurs* in the midst of a detachment of the 6th French Dragoon Regiment. The dragoon vidette, who had been posted on our side of the town, had called out to our chasseurs, who gave for answer—"*Chasseurs Hannovriens.*"

The dragoon, not being acquainted with this name, fired his pistol, and galloped off to the main body. The *chasseurs* followed him quickly; and upon his calling out to his comrades—"To horse, the guerillas are coming!" they had not known how to save themselves quick enough, and ran away, leaving their horses behind them. The officer of the detachment was the only one who made any stand. At the arrival of the *chasseurs*, he had snapped his pistols, both missed fire. We passed the night here, and had a good deal of sport with the dragoons, who had shown so much courage. The next morning we set off with our prisoners and our wine, and returned to the regiment. Shortly afterwards, we and the 12th Light Infantry Regiment marched to Mayorga. From hence the whole brigade made a reconnaissance, as far as the frontiers of Asturias and Navarre; considerable bodies of troops having shown themselves in these parts, among others, those under the command of the Marquis de la Romana, which, for a length of time, had been wandering about in the provinces of Asturias, Gallicia, and Navarre.

During this march, which was by way of Mansilla, provisions were so scarce, that on one day we only received twenty pounds of bread for our whole company. The following day we received nothing; but, however, the company killed a calf, which we cooked, with onions, of which there was a great abundance in the place. The whole of the next day our march led over a great heath; we found every where traces of guerillas, but could never fall in with them; we therefore returned, without having effected any thing, to Sahagun, where we passed the night.

On the day before we reached Sahagun, we came late into a village, which was inhabited by a number of shepherds; we quartered ourselves *militairement,* that is, without billets, everyone where he pleased. I, with several others, upon a shepherd, whose flock that night was considerably diminished. My linen was in a very bad condition, for I possessed only the shirt I had upon my back, and that was in such a state, from the frequent Hungarian washing, that I was under the necessity of looking out for another, but hitherto without success. I made a search here, but could find nothing but women's shifts; however, this did not much matter—I made an exchange; but, on the following day, the length annoyed me very much in walking, and my comrades joked me in such a manner about it, that I scarcely knew what to do; but, however, upon halting in the middle of the day, to their great surprise, I began to undress myself, pulled off the shift, and with my sabre, cut off the part which incommoded me so much. Everybody laughed at my scheme, and I put it on again, and wore it until Providence sent me another.

In the middle of the night we received information that a large convoy of wagons, on their way to the Asturias, escorted by guerillas, was not far off. The cavalry was immediately ordered to mount in pursuit, and they soon brought it in, the escort having fled without firing a shot. The wagons were brought into the market-place, and a guard was set over them. I happened, on that day, to be the colonel's orderly, and was at his quarters in the market-place, near the main guard, where I was sent for in the evening to act as interpreter; and the colonel having sent a skin of wine to the guard, I stopped there to drink a few glasses. Returning late in the night, one of the peasants, who were lying with their cattle near the wagons, and anxiously awaiting their fate, took me aside, and said to me—"My good young man, do allow me to return home with my oxen; you can get plenty of others here, and I have got a wife and children sorrowing for me." With these words he put half an ounce (ten dollars) into my hand. As I wished for the money, and the peasant for his liberty, I put it, without hesitation, into my pocket, and told him to take himself off in God's name. The peasant, who was in readiness for starting, took himself very quietly off, and made his escape.

Once, when we were lying in cantonment, in Medina del Rio Seco, our company alone reconnoitred the neighbourhood, owing to some traces of guerillas having been seen; among other places, we visited Villa Alba, a town which I have already mentioned, and where we were tolerably well known. The country is here very fertile, grows a good deal of corn, but not much wine. It is surrounded by a wall, which, in former times, may have served as a defence, but is now quite in ruins, and of no use.

The whole of the troops were lodged in the town-hall, in order to be together in case of any surprise. Sentinels were posted, and it fell to my lot to be detached to one of the gates. My guard consisted of four men, among them some of our most noted wine-drinkers, particularly one, named Thiele, a native of Paderborn, who would risk every thing for the sake of wine. We were sitting very still round the blazing watch-fire, until at last Thiele broke the silence, uttering some rattling oaths before be began his discourse: "What is the use of our sitting here thirsty and cold?" said he, (we had, as yet, received no wine, because the *alcalde* of the place had not sent in any, under the pretence that there was none at hand, and that he was obliged to send for some from a neighbouring village). "Come, let us go and make a few visits, the cellars are not there for nothing; these rascally peasants have, no doubt, wine in abundance." I did not much like it, although I wished for a glass myself; at last thirst overcame duty, and I consented.

Thiele ran in all haste to the cellars, and endeavoured to open one of the doors, but found this would be a matter of difficulty, and occasion some noise, which he did not think advisable; he then tried several others, but found them all alike.

He came back quite discontented, and related what had occurred, and we now consulted what was to be done. "I'll tell you what;" said Thiele, who had always a remedy at hand: "by means of our belts, one of us shall be let down into the cellar, and then what Providence and the cellar affords, shall be drawn up."

No-one, however, would make up his mind to go down the shaft in this manner, until at last Thiele began: "You cowards, you would all willingly drink, but will run no risk for it; if no one else has courage enough, I have. Come along!" Thiele now set off with two others, I and the sentry remained behind; but I did not feel myself very comfortable while they were absent, fearing some accident—either the officer on duty might be going his rounds, and visit our post, or we might be attacked. However, neither of these things happened, and, in about half an hour, the three fellows came back with a *pelecho*, or skin of wine. These are made use of almost all over Spain, and are made of goat-skins, with the hair turned inside: they also brought with them some bread and salted meat.

We were now merry and cheerful, and enjoyed ourselves. As we were sitting comfortably over the fire, and helping ourselves pretty freely to the wine, Thiele began thus: "Only think, my lads, what happened to me! When they were letting me down the hole into the cellar, and I had nearly reached the bottom, one of the buckles broke, and I came quicker to the bottom than I wished. When I had recovered myself a little, I took out my flint and steel and struck a light, to see what the cellar would afford; looked about, first of all, for my schako, which had reached the ground sooner than I did; I soon found this, under an empty cask, but the pompon was wanting; and, in spite of all my endeavours, I was not able to find it. My comrades were anxious to know what booty I had met with, and kept calling impatiently at the hole, until at last I answered their questions with this sack, which they drew up, and you see here."

The circumstance appeared to me rather serious. Supposing, for instance, the owner, on the following day, should find the pompon, he could easily make a complaint to the captain; who, although he was a very worthy man, never suffered mercy to precede his sense of duty, if he caught any one in the fact. We consulted about it, and it was resolved to let some more of our comrades into the secret, upon whom we could rely that they would not betray us, in case the thing should turn out as we feared.

Before daybreak, every thing suspicious was put aside, and the wine was hid in an empty stable, under some straw. At last, the guard was relieved, and we returned to our quarters in the town-hall. We went to work directly; our comrades were willing to assist us; and half-a-dozen pompons were hidden away, without any notice being taken. In the afternoon, (it was the first day of Christmas) the captain came to the company, and asked, in a careless manner: "Have any of you lost a pompon?"

No one gave any answer, "It is very odd" said he; "a peasant brought me one yesterday, which, he said, he found upon the road we passed." We were all still silent.

"Sergeant-Major," said he, "let the men be drawn out, and ascertain which rascal this pompon belongs to: when you have found him, put him immediately under arrest."

The company turned out; but, upon inspection, there was not one, but half-a-dozen wanting. Questions were now asked. One had his broken off; another had lost his; another had his shot off; one had lost his in this, another in that manner. Thiele was also questioned, but replied, very innocently: "Oh, I don't know how long it is since mine has been gone!" The captain did not seem to believe him; however, he was obliged to be silent.

It was Christmas Day, and we had been promised a double allowance of wine; but he now said that we should, as a punishment, have none at all. The whole company murmured at this; and it was unanimously agreed, that the captain had no right to deprive the men of what had been allowed them by the Emperor and the government: upon this the order was rescinded, and we obtained our rations. We remained here a few days longer, and visited the stable every evening, until the sack was emptied, almost without our being aware of it.

On the fourth day we went on again. During the march, the captain, who had no dislike to wine, called to his servant to bring him some. The man brought it, telling him, at the same time, that his whole store consisted in that single glass. The captain regretted this, and blamed his servant for his want of attention. Upon this, Thiele, who was very near, presented himself before the captain, and offered him a glass of his wine.

"Let us see, my lad, is it good?"

"Taste it, and convince yourself, captain."

After he had drank, he asked him where he had got the wine.

"At Villa Alba," was the answer.

"I was not able to get such a good glass of wine there. Did you buy it?"

"Yes," said Thiele, "and I was very near paying a high price for it."

"Well, give me another glass; I will recompense you for it."

"A bargain," said Thiele; "you can do this immediately, if you will."

"How so!" said the captain.

"Oh, give me my pompon back again; that will be a sufficient recompense."

"Rascal!" said the captain, "I thought, at the time, that you, and no one else, was the wine-stealer. Here it is," added he, taking it out of his holster; "but had I known this in Villa Alba, you should have paid for it, by fifteen days' arrest upon bread and water."

"I took good care of that," said Thiele.

The army being now on the march to Salamanca, our company was ordered to join it; but the regiment remained in Medina del Rio Seco. We found the army in Tordesillas; it was on the point of retreating to Simankas, about five miles from Valladolid. Notwithstanding our fatigue, we were immediately, on our arrival, obliged to make this march with it. In order to cover our retreat, the bridge of Tordesillas was strongly defended with cannon, which were not withdrawn until all the troops had reached Toro, a town several miles up the Duero.

During this march I caught a stray ass: I got upon his back, without hesitation, and followed the company very pleasantly. One of my comrades, by way of joke, put a piece of lighted tinder under the animal's tail, who, feeling the smart, began to kick most furiously, and threw me off, without, however doing me any harm. The captain, who saw this gave me a reprimand, telling me, that, as corporal, I ought to set a better example to the soldiers, particularly as I saw that he was walking himself. The ass, notwithstanding, was not set at liberty, but was made use of for the general good: he was. loaded with as many knapsacks as he could carry, and, notwithstanding his heavy burden, he amused us now and then with his loud braying. In the evening it fell to the lot of our company to form a picket, and I, with four men, was detached to the extreme end of a hollow road. It was wretched weather, the rain fell in torrents, accompanied with a high wind, and it was so dark that we could not see our hands before our faces; and yet we could not make any fire, on account of our's being the most advanced post. In this unpleasant situation we remained during the whole night, until at last daylight appeared, and relieved us from our dangerous post.

After we had refreshed ourselves with some wine and meat, we proceeded along the same road, and passed Tordesillas and Medina del Campo, without falling in with any of the enemy's troops: they had withdrawn beyond Salamanca to Alba de Tormes. About this time, I was present at an execution, which, on account of the coolness of the delinquent, made a considerable impression upon me. Near Valladolid, upon a height on the Pisuerga, the French had erected a fort, where a convent had formerly stood. A Spanish officer, belonging to the garrison of Rodrigo, had penetrated into the neighbourhood, and was taken prisoner in the act of making a sketch of the fort.

A court-martial was immediately held, and he was condemned to be shot as a spy. With undaunted courage, and a firm step, he followed his escort; on his arrival at the place of execution, he calmly conversed for a few moments with the officers, then throwing off his large cloak, he advanced a few paces, opened his coat and waistcoat, and cried out: "Now, comrades, fire, and do your duty!" He fell in an instant, without life, there being twelve men upon this occasion, instead of the usual number of three.

As we were in pursuit of the enemy to Alba de Tormes, we were one night lodged (ten infantry and fifteen hussars) in a small cottage; the vicinity of the enemy not allowing the troops to be much separated. No provisions were to be found here, and we came quite unexpectedly upon the inhabitants. Spanish troops had been quartered here the day before, and had given out that the French army had been completely destroyed on the other side of Madrid; and that the troops before them were in full retreat towards France, in order not to be cut off. Our scanty rations were soon devoured, but our hunger was still unappeased; besides, we did not much relish the hard contract-bread, and spring-water.

The hussars had been looking after their horses, and, one by one, came into the kitchen, without knowing any better than ourselves what to do for a supper, until at last one of them, an Alsatian came in, and said: "This rascally peasant has got a quantity of poultry, yonder, in the stable."

We all pricked up our ears; the Germans cried out: "*Wo denn?*" (Where are they?) The French, who understood the German name for poultry very well, "*Où donc?*"

"Close by, where our horses are standing, there is a small shed; there they are."

A council was immediately held, to determine how we should get these fowls into our possession, without the peasant being aware of it. The plan was soon laid, and the hussars undertook the execution; some of whom, going out under pretence of giving their horses water, took a forage sack, and soon bagged the whole of the poor peasant's stock of poultry. As soon as this was done, we all went together into the village, behind the church, and here the fowls were plucked, an operation which, in spite of the darkness of the night, was soon performed. When our fowls were ready (there were eighteen of them) they were put into the bag again, and we returned to our quarters.

We had scarcely entered, when the peasant, of his own accord, asked us if we had received any rations that evening; we told him "No, but that tomorrow the Spaniards should receive theirs;"

One of the hussars then said: "Farmer, have you got a kettle?"

"What for?"

"Oh! only to boil a few fowls, which I have brought with me."

"I have got some too," cried several others; and this was more likely to be the case with the cavalry than with us. The farmer brought a kettle, the fowls were produced, cooked, the peasant was invited to take a share, and we consumed our stolen supper with a great deal of appetite. We marched off very early the next morning, and by the time the peasant had discovered his loss, many a horseman was already in the country where no fowls are eaten; the cavalry having very early in the morning (19th November, 1809), attacked and defeated the enemy at Alba de Tormes, and captured, without the assistance of the infantry, twelve pieces of cannon, four standards, and warlike stores of all kinds. A great number of Spaniards lost their lives in this affair; and most of those whom the sword spared were drowned, for the bridge over the Tormes being very narrow, was completely blocked up with baggage-wagons, and they had no other resource but to throw themselves into the river, where most of them were drowned.

We marched through Salamanca; from thence only one division proceeded in advance; this was entirely defeated near Datames, and came back in confusion. The Spaniards had the barbarity, upon this occasion, to burn the dead and wounded together.

The day after this battle there were a number of prisoners made by detached parties; our company alone brought in upwards of two hundred, and we were appointed to escort the whole convoy to Valladolid. The grenadier company of our regiment was ordered to accompany us, in order to support us in case of any attack from the guerillas; the prisoners we alone had the care of, and the grenadiers marched in advance. The grenadier captain, who was older than our's, had the command; but being angry that his men had no share in the actual escort, which our captain would not allow, contrived, in such a manner, that upon our arrival in Valladolid we should not be quartered in the houses, but in our former barracks, in the palace of the Inquisition. We were all very angry at this, particularly as we had no cooking utensils, for we were here to receive new camp-kettles; and upon our entrance, many were heard to say—"Tonight we will burn down the Holy Inquisition."

At twelve o'clock we were awakened by an alarming voice; the cry of fire was heard on all sides, and the hinder part of the buildings, where we were lodged, was already in flames. Everyone seized his kit, and hastened as quickly as possible through the court into the street. Here we saw that the whole of the back part of the building was in flames; and if we had remained a quarter of an hour longer, we should all have been buried together under the ruins of the building, The inhabitants, awakened by the tumult, rushed in crowds to see what was the matter, but made no attempt to extinguish the fire; many were even rejoiced at the fate of this den of iniquity; others stole the iron, or any thing they thought might be useful, without any step being taken to hinder them. We endeavoured to extinguish the flames; but only for the sake of appearance, for we were all inwardly rejoiced that there was one barrack less, and that we should the sooner be quartered upon the inhabitants. The whole back part of the building, therefore, together with the archives and the library, where the fire had broke out, was entirely consumed; the front remained in tolerable preservation.

Early in the morning our two captains had a serious quarrel. The captain of grenadiers insisted upon it that we had purposely set the building on fire, while our captain denied it most positively. We had piled our arms, and were quietly awaiting what was to take place, when suddenly a battalion of the 122nd Regiment marched up in line, loaded their muskets before our eyes, and then shouldered arms. We were ordered to retreat thirty paces from our arms. An adjutant of Marshal Kellerman shook up a number of tickets in his hat, and ordered the grenadier company to draw lots, after which our turn came. We now learned that, owing to a complaint which had been lodged, two of our men were to be shot, on account of this cursed Inquisition. We were thus obliged to draw lots for our lives, and the fatal lots were drawn by a grenadier corporal, named Tischner, and a serjeant of our company, named Emmel. Our colonel, who, on account of ill-health, was staying in Valladolid, no sooner heard of this than he came and protested violently against it; he declared that if two brave soldiers, of whom the Emperor could not have too many, were to be shot for the sake of an old barrack, he would immediately throw up his command, and complain personally to the Emperor. All this was of no use, and the two men who had drawn the lots were carried off by the *gendarmes* to the military prison. However, the punishment was afterwards remitted, and the men came back again. When the danger had passed over, we learned the origin of the fire; it had been kindled by one of our voltigeurs, who had got secretly into the library and thrown a torch among the papers.

In this manner a German soldier caused the destruction of a building, in the interior of which so many cruelties had been committed; a building, of which no Spaniard would have dared, for the riches of the whole world, to have injured a stone; he would have been considered as an offender against his religion, and punished in such a manner, that no-one would have henceforward dared to undertake the like.

From Valladolid we did not immediately return to our regiment; we were employed for some weeks in collecting requisitions, which afforded me an opportunity of earning a few dollars in a very harmless way. I was one day quartered upon a farmer, who requested me to write out for him a quantity of receipts, for articles delivered; such as bread, wine, meat, wood, salt, &c. amounting altogether, to more than ten thousand *reals*. Being fully convinced that he would never receive a penny for them, I refused for some time, but he pressed me so much that I did it at last to oblige him, and he gave me for my trouble an ounce (twenty dollars) in gold.

Another time, passing through Villa Leon, we came in the evening, to a handsome village, called Fuentes de Navas, which had to pay a contribution of twenty-seven thousand *reals* (one thousand three hundred and fifty dollars) in hard money. On our arrival, we found all the doors closed; a dragoon regiment

having, shortly before passed through in pursuit of the guerillas, which did not behave very handsomely, and the inhabitants
were therefore, in a state of consternation. The *alcalde*, however,
was soon found, and obliged to furnish us with billets. I stood
at the farther end of the company, and received a billet for six
men, although there were only three of us remaining. We, therefore, on this account, promised ourselves good quarters. We set
off in the dark, and knocked at the first house we came to, in
the military manner, that is, with the butt-ends, of our muskets.
For a length of time no one answered; but as we only, knocked
the louder, and the door began to shake with our blows, a voice
called out at last—"Who is there?"

"Peaceable people" the usual answer given after knocking.

"What people?"

"*Militaires Françaises.*"

"*Ave Maria purissima!*" cried the peasant, as he came and
opened the door. We showed him our billet; he read it, and said,
joyfully: "This is not for me, but down below, yonder." With
these words he would have closed the door again, but we being
weary of seeking about; seized him by the collar, so that he could
not escape, and obliged him to show us the way with a light. As
we explained our wish pretty clearly to him, he went along with
us without opposition, and took us to a house in which a dead
corpse, was lying, which was to be buried that night. We did
not trouble ourselves about the dead, but our visit proved very
disagreeable to the living. He begged of us, in the most pressing manner, to allow him to procure us another billet from the
alcalde, and engaged to procure us as good, if not better, quarters.
As the man was really to be pitied, and had behaved very well
to us, we agreed; he went away, and very soon returned with
the billet. He accompanied us to the door of our new lodging,
and then went away, while we were knocking. After the usual
questions and answers, an old man opened the door, and desired
us to walk in. We had to pass through a large court before we
reached the house, where the mistress came out to meet us, with
her two daughters, both handsome brunettes.

Soon after we had entered the apartment, supper was brought in; we had soup, ham, and sausages, in abundance: there was likewise no want of wine, and I was entertained so well by the family, that I could not have wished for better quarters. My comrades paid their respects so frequently to the bottle, that their conversation soon gave evidence that they had drank more than was necessary to quench their thirst. After supper, a young Spaniard came in, who, the mother having just left the room, gave himself out as a son, drank with us, and mixed in the conversation. During this time the old servant prepared some beds for us, mattresses and horse cloths, near the oven, round which the whole family usually lie. It did not escape my observation, that the young man, whose name was Christoval, entertained more than a brother's love for the eldest daughter; they were very loving together, and I also never heard her call him *hermanno*, (brother) but always *amico* (friend).

At last the mother came in again, and said: "It is now time to go to bed, and for you, Christoval, to go home." Christoval went, but I remarked something about an assignation; for as they thought I was drunk, they were not very cautious about what they said. I did not wish to interrupt their amusement, and pretended to stagger to my bed, where both my comrades were snoring like rats. The young lady accompanied Christoval across the court, and I distinctly heard her wish him a good night, and close the door. It was now quiet through the whole house; and I lay perfectly still upon my bed, although I could not sleep; when presently the door of the room was opened very softly; this I heard very plain, and could see it, as I had ordered that the light should not be extinguished. Peppa, this was the girl's name, put her head in, listened a little while, and as she thought we were all fast asleep came in, and crept softly past our beds to the oven. I now became attentive, and being heated by wine, all sorts of ideas of being attacked, &c. came into my head.

Presently the door opened again, and my friend Christoval crept in in the same manner. I could now bear it no longer, as even if there was no intention to murder us, yet I did not like that the room we were in should be made use of for their nocturnal meetings, and began to make a noise: my two comrades sprang up, but the effect of the wine was too powerful to allow them to get upon their feet. The Spaniard immediately called out: "Be quiet, I shall do you no harm?" Peppa came up, and went with him into a side-room, The intention of this nightly visit being now evident to me, I troubled myself no farther about it, but laid down and went to sleep. The next morning we got up early, it being Sunday; and having dressed ourselves in our new clothing, we looked very well. As we all pretended to be Catholics in Spain, we were going off to mass, when Peppa called me on one side, and said: "Where are you going, Pedro?"

I replied, "To church, with my comrades, to hear mass."

She then said, "Stay at home. I have something to say to you; but do not let your comrades remark it."

Not being able to refuse so pretty a girl her request, I went out with my comrades, but turned back after I had reached half way, under pretence of having no particular desire to hear mass on that day. When I came back again, I found Peppa quite alone: she said to me, "Pedro, you were very uncivil last night."

"Uncivil," replied I, "how could I tell what you two were going to do; you might have been going to murder us, for you Spaniards are not to be trusted?"

She replied, "Pray be quiet, and tell no one of this; be silent in particular towards my mother; if it was to be known that Christoval came to me at night, I should be pointed at and despised by the whole village."

With these words she put a quarter of a gold ounce (five dollars) into my hand, and laid her fingers across her mouth, which is in Spain a token of secrecy. Christoval just then came in, and addressed himself to me in the following manner:—"You rascal! you frightened us properly last night: it was fortunate for you that you remained quiet! I trust you will be silent for the future, else you will feel my knife in your body; there is a dollar for you, but hold your tongue."

He told me afterwards that Peppa was his intended bride; but being first cousins, the priest made a difficulty about marrying them, and they were obliged to petition for a dispensation from the bishop. As neither their relationship nor their meetings were any thing to me, and feeling no inclination to disturb their pleasure for the future, which would have been the case if I had said anything to the mother, I kept their secret very faithfully, and was glad to find myself six dollars richer without any trouble.

We were again very near Valladolid, but were not able to reach it that evening, on account of our mules being very tired, We were afraid to march the few remaining leagues, as we feared they might lie down on the road, or become restive, which is often the case with these animals. It was resolved, therefore, to pass the night in a considerable village, and to set forward very early in the morning, in order to arrive in good time.

The name of the village I have forgotten; but it was remarkable on account of two white towers belonging to the church, which may be seen a great distance off, on which account, it went by the name, among us, of the place with the two white towers.

Though we had received our rations, we were not satisfied, particularly with respect to wine; for the Spanish *vino tinto* is a delicious beverage, as every one must allow who has tasted it.

After we had rested a short time, a reconnaissance was made, to find out where the wine-cellars were. This was soon done; for they are very easy to be seen by any one who looks, about in earnest for them. They are never far from the village, and somewhat resemble another small place, the air-holes having the appearance of our chimneys, and are usually so large, that a man may easily get in. We soon returned from our survey, in order to procure some information from our landlord, as to which cellar held the best wine. "Gentlemen," said he, "close to the one belonging to me is the cellar of a *grandee*, residing in Valladolid, and whose estates are managed by a steward: he is immensely rich, and you can do him no harm by paying him a visit; you will find wines of all sorts, and of several years' growth; but," added he, "my cellar is close by; spare that, for I am but a poor devil, and have altogether but two casks in it."

We promised, as men of honour, to spare him and his wine too; but requested, that he would come with us to point out the cellar, and this he readily did. About eleven o'clock at night we went out; nine of us, loaded with pots and pitchers, and proceeded to the cellars; as soon as the peasant had pointed out to us the right one, and also his, we went to work. The doors, which could not withstand the attack of nine powerful men, were soon opened. We went in, struck a light, and such a battery of wine-casks presented itself to our eyes, as we had scarcely ever seen, though we had ransacked many a cellar. Hogsheads of the largest size we found here, all filled; not a single one empty, We now tasted and rejected; tasted again, and again rejected; until, at last, we came to a small cask of a white sort; this was unanimously pronounced to be the best. All our vessels were now filled; and, after passing a jug or two round, we departed; meeting, as we came back, a number of our comrades upon the same errand.

Upon our return home, our host and his wife were invited to join us: they played their parts well at the Spaniard's expense. Our hostess was soon satisfied, and withdrew; but our host must have been one of the best drinkers in the place, and was a good match for us. However, in time, he became sensible that he was but a man, and was as little able to empty his glass as the rest of us. Upon this, the president of the company endeavoured to compel us to obedience, by ordering, that every man who did not empty his glass, should have a stroke on the hand with a cane. However, this was of no avail; we were obliged to give it up, and to go and lie down; and in a very short time we were all fast asleep.

In the morning, about six o'clock, we were awakened with the cry of, "Get up, you lazy rascals; the company is already under arms." We did not take long to rub our eyes, but jumped up immediately, took our knapsacks and muskets, and staggered, rather than walked down the steps, to the place of rendezvous; where we found the company assembled, and the captain, who saluted us with an oath or two, walking up and down.

Shortly afterwards a man came up, with a long face, the captain said to him: "Do you know, any one of the men who have stolen your wine?"

"Yes, Sir," was the answer; "There was one with red hair."

"I advise you," said the captain, "to be sure that you can point him out; if so, he shall be punished as he deserves: but if you do not you shall be punished in his place I do not suffer thieves in my company, neither do I allow any one to call my soldiers thieves."

The peasant now had his choice which he would do; however, he was foolhardy enough to run the risk, and began to search. After going through all the ranks without finding his man, he returned with a woeful countenance to the captain; he, in a rage, kept his word, ordered out a couple of corporals, and had the peasant well flogged, who, between every stroke, called upon all the saints in the calendar to help him; but not one of them appeared, to receive a single stroke for him,

After the peasant had been well flogged, they let him go; and the captain began a not very complimentary speech to us, calling us "rogues, &c". He concluded, nevertheless, by saying we were "brave fellows."

"However," he continued, "I will convince myself whether you have any store in your quarters."

This; put many of us in fear; but our host was a cunning fellow, and had hidden away what remained of the wine, with the exception of a small pitcher, which he had not thought it worth while to put out of sight. The captain, with a sergeant, then went round to all our quarters, but all our hosts had some excuse; in one house, the soldiers had bought the wine; in another, they had had nothing beside their rations, &c, &c. In our's, where the pitcher was standing upon the table, our landlord, in reply to the captain's question, "What there was in the jug?" gave for answer: "Water."

"Oh," said the captain, "if you say it is water, I do not mean to say it is any thing else."

On the captain's return, he said to the company: "I find your hosts are greater rogues than you are. Get along home, and drink your wine, if you have any; we shall begin our march directly." In this manner the storm passed over our heads without bursting.

We were now incorporated in the third division, under the command of Loison, in the brigade of General Simon: and thus, in the sixth corps *d'armée*, under Marshal Ney, and went into cantonments in a large village, called Almeide San Jago, in the neighbourhood of Ledesma and Zamora. We remained here for some time, and, with the exception of being continually exercised, were pretty well off. I, in particular, was well situated; for owing to my long stay in the country, I was become so well acquainted with the language, as to be able to make myself understood upon all ordinary subjects. This qualification procured me to be employed as interpreter, and I was every day orderly to the general or the chief officer on the staff, by which, means I not only procured the best quarters, but had likewise a very easy service.

We had here just provisions enough to support us, but not so much as to have our fill everyday, and we often went hungry to bed; it was natural, therefore, for us to take every opportunity of quieting our hunger at the expense of the inhabitants, and in this we were assisted by our landlord, as great a rogue as any of us. Our operations were sometimes attended with danger, but this we despised, if we could only get our fill. We went out, one day, to get a calf from a pasture ground, which was surrounded by a wall; one of us, a tall stout grenadier, leaped over, seized the calf, and put it on his shoulders; the mother was, luckily, not aware of it at the instant, or he would have been lost; and he had got close to the wall when the cow came after him at full gallop. With the utmost celerity he climbed the wall, and was saved. The calf was brought into our quarters, and *Señor* Manuel Rodriguez, this was our host's name, helped us diligently to consume it. This prize was soon devoured, and we were obliged to look out afresh.

There were several horse *chasseurs* with us, in order I to keep up the correspondence with the head-quarters in Ledesma, and we were conversing one evening, at our quarters, about our straitened supplies. "The devil fetch all the Spaniards," said we, "we must see tonight whether we cannot steal a head of cattle, somewhere! If we only knew where the sheep were!" These the peasants had very wisely driven off into the mountains, where they were more secure from our attempts than in the stalls in the village. We determined that night to make a search, and, about eleven o'clock eight of us set off. We passed by one of the posts of our regiment, where we were stopped; but, upon our telling the sergeant on duty what errand we were upon, he gave us some men along with us to take a share in the booty.

After we had walked about half an hour, we came to a small wood of green oaks, of which the acorns were eatable; upon them we afterwards, in Portugal, made many a meal, for want of any thing better. Here we found a number of oxen, but, as usual in Spain, they were so wild, that we had the greatest difficulty in the world to catch one. Our chase lasted a long time; at last we succeeded in getting a very fine ox into our power. One of the horse *chasseurs* cut the sinews of one of his hind legs with his sabre, we then all rushed upon him, and threw him down. A soldier, who had been a butcher, took out his knife and cut his throat, and almost before the beast was dead we had his skin off. This business had nearly cost us dear; for the other cattle, of which there was a quantity here, assembled by degrees, and, made wild by the lowing of their companion, approached every moment nearer. We finished our operation as quickly as possible, hung the meat upon branches of trees, and carried it off; those who carried nothing, were occupied in keeping off the other oxen with stones.

We reached the village in safety, where I, and the two comrades who were quartered with me, received upon the division a piece large enough to last us for sometime.

The ignorance of the French language among the Spaniards often gave rise to very comical expressions. *Dites donc,* which occurs so frequently in a Frenchman's discourse, the Spaniards took for a name common to all French people. When they spoke to any one of that nation, therefore, they always said *Señor Liton;* (not being able to articulate the words correctly) the ladies they always called *Señora Litona.*

In this same village, I had an opportunity of admiring the skill and dexterity of a French grenadier. The Spaniards usually amuse themselves, before they slaughter an ox, with baiting it, somewhat in the manner of a bull-fight: they lead it about by ropes; fastened to the horns, and endeavour to excite its fury in every possible way: some hold their great cloaks before it, and when the animal rushes upon them in a rage, they slip on one side with much skill. This seems to afford them a great deal of pleasure: the meat is by this means much deteriorated; it is of a deep red colour, and full of small bladders.

One day, when I was on guard in the place where the cattle is slaughtered, there were several oxen, which were going to be killed, made wild in this way. One of these enraged animals broke loose, and ran at a voltigeur, who was carrying his comrade's dinner to the guard-house. The man was knocked down; but owing to the violence with which the animal ran, and the slight opposition he met with, he was unable to stop, and passed over the man's body without doing him any harm. Before the ox had time to renew his attack, the voltigeur got up quickly, and escaped by leaping a wall. While this was going on, a grenadier happened to come the same way, and the furious animal made a rush at him. He, being a tall strong Hungarian, seized the ox by the horns, twisted his head on one side, and, with the utmost dexterity, threw him on the ground. The animal rose again, and rushed once more upon the grenadier, who sprang aside, seized him by the tail, and threw him down a second time; meanwhile a number of men hastened to the spot, and one, with a blow of a large axe, deprived the animal of life.

Upon the whole, the Spaniards are a lazy, idle race, but easily excited to anger: their greatest pleasure seems to consist in doing nothing; and they lie for whole days together in the sun, wrapped in their large brown cloaks, amusing themselves by picking the vermin from each other, without being concerned in the least at the presence of strangers. They have a proverb, which says, a country without lice is a miserable country! They never kill these insects, but merely throw them away; for what reason I know not. Their food is very simple, and, altogether, they are very temperate; but they use a great quantity of red pepper, garlic, onions, &c. in the seasoning of their dishes. They never drink much wine, excepting on festivals, and at the time of the carnival, at which times they are in a state of the greatest excitement.

They are very reserved towards strangers, are excessively proud, and pretend that every one should talk their language; a common expression among them is, "speak like a Christian;" which is as much as to say—talk Spanish.

The dress of the middling and lower orders is brown or black; many wear sandals of *esparto* or untanned leather, instead of shoes; the shoes which are worn are made of brown, and very seldom of black leather.

The upper ranks dress quite in the modern fashion; among the men I never could perceive any difference from the French or German; but among the women, the *mantilla* (a large wrapper of a white or black colour) is an indispensable appendage to their dress, and this is worn so as to prevent the face being seen, unless the wearer chooses to show it.

The natives of Galicia are the only race which are at all distinguished for their activity. They are to be found all over Spain, particularly in Madrid, where they exercise the trade of water-carriers, (*aguadores*) and, procure a very good livelihood. Many are employed as servants, and are noted for their fidelity and obedience. During the time I was in Spain, I travelled in all parts, but never found the natives busily employed as with us; just so much land is cultivated as to prevent them from starving. Immense plains, over which the eye can scarcely reach, lie waste, and only serve for pasturage for the sheep. In short, the Spaniards are, in every respect, far behind the Germans.

The clergy, at that time, were almost adored, by the populace, and the weal or woe of many depended upon them. If a French prisoner was about to be murdered, and the priest took him under his protection, not a hair of his head was injured; but if he only called out "crucify him!" the man was lost beyond redemption. I have often heard that the priests have said: "As many Frenchmen as you kill, so many steps you advance in your ascent to Heaven!"

As our regiment consisted chiefly of Germans, and the Spaniards had an idea that all Germans were Catholics, we took care not to undeceive them, but crossed and blessed ourselves in the same manner that they did, which procured us this advantage—that they liked us better than the French: they also believed that we were compelled to fight against them, and were in hopes that, sooner or later, we should come over in a body to their side. This belief, however, was only prevalent among the lower orders.

Every Spaniard, though ever so poor, possesses an ass, which forms one of the most indispensable articles of his household. This animal, miserably fed, principally upon straw and thistles, getting corn but very seldom, and still worse treated, is used for carrying every thing necessary for domestic use; neither man nor wife ever think of going a quarter of a mile on foot; both mount the ass, and, if going into town, the beast is loaded besides with baskets of provisions or other articles. These animals, in spite of their bad treatment, are strong and lively, and apparently want for nothing. It is particularly droll to see a whole caravan of them coming along the road, consisting of the women belonging perhaps to three or four villages, who often, in addition, have baskets on their heads, and perhaps children in their arms.

The inhabitants of Biscay and Navarre are particularly distinguished by their industry. These two provinces, consisting almost entirely of mountains, and having but very little level ground, the inhabitants make use of even the smallest spots for the cultivation of maize, beans, &c. One looks for nothing of the sort among the barren rocks, and is, therefore, often agreeably surprised by meeting with small plots of ground covered with maize, and beans growing between. The want of other necessaries of life is, however, abundantly replaced by the numerous forests of chestnut trees, the fruit of which is particularly large and fine.

The inhabitants here are much cleaner and more civil; the Spanish national character, however, may still be traced. Their wagons are of a very peculiar construction, and often, during my three months' residence in these parts, made me almost mad: they are small, have two wheels, and are drawn by a pair of oxen. The wheels do not, as with us, turn upon the axle, but are fastened to it, and thus the wheels and the axle-tree turn round together. This motion, added to their never making use of any grease, occasions an incessant and almost unbearable noise. We often had the misfortune to escort wagons of this kind, and the noise, until we became accustomed to it, always occasioned us violent head-aches. In addition to this, the progress of these machines was remarkably slow, it usually taking an hour and a half to get over two and a half miles of ground. However, at last we became pretty well used to it. I often enquired why they did not build their wagons upon a better and more convenient construction; but always received for answer, that owing to the badness of the roads, no better could be made; that they were very safe, and ran no risk of being overturned. No-one felt the inconvenience of these carts more than the sick and wounded, who were conveyed in them from Vittoria to Bayonne, and in addition to their bodily sufferings, had to endure this abominable noise for five or six days together.

Wolves are also found here, but not so large as in the north of Europe; however, I never had an opportunity to see one.

The muleteers and ass drivers, by way of precaution, hang large bells upon their beasts in order to drive away the wolves by the noise. The mules and asses in Spain have all grand and high-sounding names: one is called captain, another colonel, another beauty, *(hermosa)* another San Miguel, and so on. These animals are very safe and easy goers, and if even six or eight are harnessed to a carriage, a bridle is never made use of—the driver merely calling each by his name, and telling him what to do. It is to be remarked, however, that they are all harnessed singly, and never in pairs. They are also used to carry a sort of sedan chair. A mule is harnessed in before and behind; these are handsomely ornamented, and hung with bells; the driver is also richly dressed, and either walks by the side of the beasts, or sits on the hinder one, which usually carries a saddle. This method of travelling is by no means disagreeable in a country like Spain, where very little has been expended on the roads; and as the beasts are very sure footed, the most dangerous places may be passed without fear.

In the spring of 1810, the siege of Rodrigo was undertaken; this I was a good deal interested about, never having been present at a siege. The troops appointed for this expedition were drawn together, and marched by way of Salamanca to Rodrigo, which place we reached just, at the worst season of the year, in the beginning of March, during the whole of which month it rains incessantly, and we remained encamped till the middle of June. The heavy artillery was brought from Salamanca; but owing to the badness of the roads, the transport was excessively tedious. I recollect, one day, thirty-six horses being harnessed to a twenty-four pounder; and although more than one hundred men were employed in mending the road with faggots, and making it passable, yet it could not be got forward more than five miles during the day.

The woods round Rodrigo abounded with oxen, sheep and hogs, which immediately on our arrival were taken possession of, and every regiment had fresh meat served out. It being the general opinion that the siege would not last long, proper care was not taken of this supply, and a scarcity was soon felt, the roads being so bad that few convoys of provisions could be received. Our rations became every day more scanty: fortunately, there was no scarcity of bread; for the supply of this article, ovens had been erected in several places.

The most dangerous part of the service fell to the lot of our regiment, namely, being posted in support of the artillery: for this service we received thirty sous, in addition to our daily pay; this was regularly paid to us every day! Besides this, we were allowed a pint of wine and a glass of brandy to our breakfast. Nevertheless, the other troops were, in some respects, better off; their lives were not in danger for the whole of the day. However, this troubled us but little, and we made the best use of the advantages accruing to us from our increased pay and allowances.

The trenches were opened, and the works at the batteries diligently carried on, in spite of the heavy fire from the Spaniards, who often made sallies, without, however, doing us much harm; once only they drove us from our work, but they were soon repulsed in such a way that they did not venture to repeat the experiment. Our work at last was so far advanced, that the guns were placed in the batteries, and in the beginning of June the place was cannonaded with seventy mortars and guns.

At first we did not succeed very well; the Spaniards silenced the breaching-battery, and also another, and succeeded in blowing up a powder magazine belonging to the former. This misfortune happened very near our battery, and occasioned a great deal of mischief; the shock was so great, that we all took it for an earthquake. Fascines were torn in pieces; casks, pick-axes, shovels, stones, and men's limbs were blown into the air, and several men were buried alive.

The 25th light regiment, which was just then doing duty in the trenches, lost the whole of its voltigeur company, which happened to be posted dose behind this unfortunate battery. No one troubled himself at first about the dead bodies, which remained scattered on the ground; all were occupied in making good the damage. The next day a soldier of the 27th Regiment of the line, in stripping the coat from one of the dead bodies, in order to mend his own, found it very heavy, and upon searching farther, found eighty quadruples sewn into the lining.

The works in the trenches were usually carried on in the evening, when it was dark. The Spaniards, however, found a remedy for this; they threw up lights, in order to find out the places where the works were carrying on, and then fired grenades at the workmen. When these lights were thrown up, we always laid down and covered ourselves with earth, as we knew that a volley of grenades usually followed. I and an old artillery-man with whom I was working, had, with no little trouble, half buried ourselves in the earth, when an artillery officer came by, and wished to drive us from our asylum. Accustomed to military subordination, I was making ready to creep out and repair to the place directed by the officer, when the old soldier took me by the arm, and said, "Stay here, you fool! if he says any more, I will split his skull with my pick-axe! We are not the first whom he has ordered out in this way, and the others would have paid him just the same compliment! We are here at our posts, and as useful here as any where else; I understand that quite as well as his reverence." I followed this good advice, and the officer took himself off.

It was wonderful, the number of balls, shells, and bombs we threw into the town; every piece of artillery, of which there were seventy, fired everyday from ninety to one hundred shots. One day, after a very heavy fire, I felt a strong inclination for a hard ship-biscuit, which I happened to have in my knapsack, for we had no want of appetite after our work; I then took the drinking vessel belonging to the battery, and went to the well to fill it, in order to refresh myself with a drink of cold water. The well was at the end of the battery, not far from the river, which flows close under the walls of Rodrigo, in a garden where the Spaniards often threw their shells, as they knew the soldiers often came here to fetch water. I met several comrades on the same errand as myself, filled my pitcher very comfortably, and soaked my biscuit in it. After it had lain a little while, and was become soft, I ate it, and as it was too little to satisfy my appetite, I drank a tolerable quantity of water, and then, contrary to my inclination, fell fast asleep.

I can say with confidence that Providence watched over me; for upon awaking, after some hours' sound sleep, and returning to the battery, I found that the gun, an iron one, which I had to serve, was burst, and had knocked down thirteen men, eight of whom were dead, and the others severely wounded. I was very glad to have escaped this accident, and thought myself very lucky to have been asleep at the time of explosion.

I will in this place give an account of the death of one of my comrades, owing to the remarkable circumstance attending it. He was a native of Brunswick, named Langkopf, and had acquired a considerable booty in Galicia, about one thousand six hundred dollars. He had with this money been leading a true soldier's life, until the siege of Rodrigo: here he was obliged to part with his gold watch, the last article of value he possessed. He had often treated me, without my being able to make him any return, owing to fortune not having been so favourable to me. Just, however, on the evening of his death, as we were being dismissed, he asked me for some tobacco, which I willingly gave him, as I had at that time a store of some pounds. We were just then at the entrance of the battery, and he said to me: "Comrade, my money is all gone; I must now either earn the cross of honour, procure more money, or die." He had scarcely uttered the last word, when a four-pounder came, shattered his head into a thousand pieces, and laid me senseless on the ground. It was a long while before I recovered, when I found myself in the hands of my comrades, who were sprinkling me with water. Langkopf, in the mean time, had been thrown over the breast-work; and thus his wish was fulfilled at the very moment he expressed it.

During this siege, I was almost daily very near losing my life. One evening, being in front of the battery, a shell struck the ground not four feet distance from me, and threw the earth up in all directions. I cast myself into the trench, and the shell burst without hurting me in the least. In this manner I once more escaped from danger, not, however, without loss; for in the mortal leap I was compelled to take, I lost my last half *franc* out of my pocket, which constituted the whole of my property.

The adjutant-major of our regiment was a man of no courage whatever, and took every opportunity of withdrawing himself from danger; and as he had little or nothing to do in the trenches, his life was pretty safe. One day, however, the colonel happening to visit the trenches, he could not very well remain behind. Just at that time, to our infinite amusement, the Spaniards happened to be firing away merrily at our battery: this caused our adjutant a slight attack of cannon fever, and the balls beginning to strike the earth around him in all directions, he did not well know what to do. The colonel, too, took him purposely into the most dangerous places, so that at last he pretended to be taken suddenly ill, and made his escape as quick as he could.

One morning, just at sunrise, as the Spaniards were beginning their fire from the walls, a bitch, big with young, belonging to the artillery captain, was lying on the top of the battery. The night had been very cold, and several of us, myself among the number, were lying in a sunny corner, having as yet received no orders to fire. All at once came a four-pounder, which tore the dog in pieces, so that entrails, young pups, and blood, flew into our faces. We were all completely stupefied; when suddenly a shell fell among us, which brought us instantly to our senses. We threw ourselves on the ground, and each made up his mind, on its bursting, to be damaged, more or less. We waited a short time; at last it exploded, and crushed the arm of a soldier, named Hahn. He had, on that very morning, refused to assist one of his comrades who was wounded; on which occasion, the head-surgeon,[2] had said to him: "I could, if I pleased, compel you to assist this wounded man; if, however, you have not yourself regard enough for your comrade, you may go, in God's name."

Now, being wounded himself, he could cry out "Comrades, help me!" On the instant after, a second shell came, burst immediately, and shattered his skull. So quickly was his want of feeling towards his comrade punished.

As long as the Spaniards kept possession of the suburb, upon which the left flank of our battery rested, they did us a great deal of mischief, as they well understood the use of the rifle. A few marksmen, posted in a small steeple, particularly distinguished themselves by their dexterity; one above all the others, named Manuel, was an unerring shot, and the greatest caution was necessary when he was at his post. The garrison were incessantly calling out to him: "*Manuel tira!*" (fire, Manuel.) We, by way of joke, used often to call out to him ourselves. After-

---

2. Dr. Homann, a Brunswicker.

wards, some batteries being erected close to the suburb, the Spaniards withdrew into the fortress, and we were no longer annoyed from this quarter.

The fearlessness and audacity of the *Tirailleurs du depôt,* I shall always recollect. This was a corps formed of volunteers from all the regiments, and they occasioned the enemy considerable loss. These men sat two and two, in holes of the ground just in front of the batteries, about fifty paces from the glacis of the fortress, and firing incessantly at the walls, frequently shot the artillery-men at their guns; the bombs and grenades that were constantly falling and bursting around, did not in the least deter them. By habit, we were certainly become so much accustomed to danger, that every thing was done with the utmost coolness. At the beginning of the siege, when the first cannon-ball whistled over my head, and killed and wounded several men and horses in a cavalry patrol, I did not feel quite, at my ease, but afterwards I often slept as sound at the before-mentioned well, which was exposed to the enemy's fire, as if I had been lying at home in my bed, and have eaten my hard biscuit, soaked in water, with as much appetite as if my life had not been in the slightest danger.

At last, however, it fell to my lot to be wounded, a musket-ball having grazed my knee. The wound indeed was slight, but my knee swelled immediately very much, and I was obliged to be taken to the field-hospital. Here, along with two Frenchmen whose legs had been shot off, I was placed upon a tumbril, and conveyed to Salamanca. The field-hospital being behind an eminence, was tolerably secure from the enemy's shot; but the road to Salamanca was completely exposed to the fire; and when we reached the most dangerous place, the men belonging to the train galloped their horses as fast as they could go. The bullets whistled round us on all sides, but no one was struck.

We were four days on the road, without our .wounds being dressed. On our arrival at Salamanca, we found, owing to this want of care, that maggots had generated in the wounds, and occasioned a stench which was almost intolerable. We were taken to the hospital of Real, which was already so full of sick and wounded, that we could scarcely find any accommodation.

While I was lying here, sick and wounded were constantly being brought in from the army, and I had many opportunities of observing how many lives were lost through the barbarity of the attendants. A soldier of the 39th Regiment of the line, who was brought in very ill, had a bed directly opposite to me, and we often conversed together. He told me that he had got some money about him, and that he would willingly pay the attendants if they would nurse him properly. I dissuaded him from this, and warned him by the relation of several occurrences I had witnessed during my stay; but, in spite of my advice, he trusted to the medical attendants, and allowed his purse of money to be seen. He got everyday worse; and one night, the medical attendant and his worthy colleagues, who were become impatient that he did not depart in peace, and leave them in possession of his property, filled his mouth with water, and held it close until he was suffocated.

The next morning he was found dead, and was carried out to be buried, along with several others, who had either died a natural death, or had been murdered in the same way. Although I had witnessed the perpetration of this cruel deed, I remained silent for some days, until I received my certificate of health, and was thus safe from the revenge of these inhuman murderers of the sick.

Upon the surgeon-major coming to visit me, I related to him the whole occurrence in the presence of the murderers. They denied it steadily at first; but my word was taken in preference to theirs, and they were brought before a court-martial. They then confessed their crime, and were shot without mercy. In this manner numbers of soldiers lost their lives. In the breasts of these wretches every feeling of humanity was extinct; they were actuated only by a thirst of gain; and without reflecting that they deprived their country of a protector, aged parents of a support, or infant children of a father, they murdered everyone whom they knew was possessed of money, and was too weak to oppose them. In four-and-twenty days I was entirely recovered, and returned with several other convalescents to the regiment, which was now before Almeida. During my stay in the hospital, Rodrigo had surrendered, (on the 10th July, 1810) and the besieging force had marched to the former place.

CHAPTER 6

Besieged in Almeida

At the siege of Almeida there was harder work to do than at Rodrigo: the ground was here so rocky, that several of the batteries could not be thrown up with earth, but were constructed with sand-bags. However, we got through with this, and bombarded the town. The Portuguese did their duty; and many a brave soldier would have lost his life before the fortress, if, by an extraordinary misfortune, the commandant had not been compelled to surrender. On the 26th of August, 1810, a French artillery-man, either by chance or skill, succeeded in throwing a shell into the principal powder-magazine. It happened just at the moment of relieving guard in the trenches, and we all had the opportunity of observing it. First issued a tremendous smoke, which at once darkened the whole atmosphere; then came the explosion, and after that—a death-like silence! All the camp were struck motionless. Presently was heard a whistling in the air, occasioned by the materials thrown up by the explosion. Stones, some hundred of pounds' weight, were hurled into the trenches; cannons were burst, and there was not a single house in the town which did not receive some damage.

On the following day the fortress surrendered, and we marched in. The soldiers of the garrison, who were prisoners of war, were reviewed by Marshal Massena, and asked if they would not serve France, in order to drive the common enemy (the English) out of the country. The Portuguese agreed immediately, and took the oath of fidelity to France. This they did not keep long. Very shortly, with the exception of a few, they deserted, and formed bands which very much impeded the communication between Portugal and Spain. Upon this, Massena disarmed the remainder, and sent them to France: the chief part, however, had escaped.

During the siege of Almeida, the English had constantly annoyed us, but without any particular result. After the surrender, they retreated into the interior of Portugal. We were also now unoccupied, and nothing hindered us from marching against the enemy, whose advanced guard was in the neighbourhood of Pinhel. The two fortresses of Almeida and Rodrigo were first put into as good a state of defence as possible, to serve as magazines for provisions and ammunition. We received fourteen days' allowance of bread and biscuit: but who could carry such a load on his back Everyone made what use he pleased of his portion. After this we advanced, and in September passed the Alva.

Every place we came to we found empty. The English retreated as we advanced, and we began to think we should reach Lisbon without opposition. We passed through several towns, all deserted by the inhabitants, until, at Busaco, a village in the neighbourhood of Coimbra, in the province of Beira, the English army halted; and, on the 27th of September, 1810, for the first time faced us. On the same day there were several skirmishes at the advanced posts—fore-tastes of the battle which was fought the next day.

The position of the English was a most advantageous one; and it was easy to be seen, that it would require both courage and skill to dislodge the enemy; and at all events would cost the lives of many men. Our troops attacked with their usual impetuosity, but were so warmly received by the riflemen of the German legion, and of the 60th and 95th Regiments, that they fell in all directions; every shot told, and our regiment alone had seven officers killed, besides the wounded: in my company there were forty-eight killed and wounded; the captain was shot through the body, and was carried to the hospital at Coimbra. General Simon, who commanded our brigade, was also wounded and made prisoner. We attacked the heights at the point of the bayonet; but before we had reached half-way, we were driven back with great loss. The battle lasted two days; and the scarcity of provisions was so great amongst us, that we were compelled to subsist upon maize and oranges from the neighbouring fields. Here we often met with the Portuguese; and, notwithstanding our natural animosity, agreed upon these occasions tolerably well.

At last a corps received orders to turn the heights, and take the English in the rear; this the English commander perceived, and retreated in the best order, without awaiting the result of the operation. From hence the enemy's army retreated towards Lisbon; and with the exception of a few skirmishes of cavalry, nothing of any consequence occurred during the march.

When we reached the Tagus, there were two ways of getting possession of Lisbon; either we must have crossed the wide river, or have stormed the formidable batteries, erected by the English and Portuguese; these we were told were built of large wine-casks, and reached a distance of three hours' journey from the city. Massena, who commanded us, considered it most, advisable to try the passage of the Tagus; with this view the army was quartered in Santarem, Thomar, and the adjacent villages; and the pontoneers and marine artillery-men began to construct bridges of boats. The Portuguese guerillas swarmed on all sides, and did us a great deal of mischief; captured transports of all kinds, and many soldiers, on foraging or plundering excursions, fell by their hands.

Although at first, owing to the abundance in the neighbour-hood, we were well off for provisions, yet, through the improvident use of them, a scarcity soon began to be felt, and detachments were obliged to fetch corn in their haversacks, from a distance of several miles. This was afterwards ground, made into bread, and served out to us. We chiefly lived upon Indian corn and beans; but by degrees these became scarcer, and we suffered severely from want of all kinds.

For five month we remained here, and during this time the

army was so much reduced by the sword, but still more, by sickness, that Massena could not venture to prosecute his operation; but giving up the idea of the capture of Lisbon, on the 3rd of March, 1811, resolved upon a retreat into Spain. The work of three months was destroyed; the small remaining stock of provisions was divided, each man receiving thirteen biscuits; the baggage, and the sick and wounded, owing to the want of horses, were left behind, and everything got in readiness for the march. The army was in a miserable condition; without clothes, without shoes, without provisions, and reduced one-half in numbers, was on the point of commencing a retreat through a devastated country, with roads in the worst possible condition, and pressed on all sides by an enemy eager for battle, and provided with every requisite.

Many a soldier, in the first two days, had consumed his scanty allowance, and found himself obliged, if he did not choose to die of hunger, to procure himself provisions by whatever means lay in his power. No-one could assist his comrade, because no one possessed anything. The soldiers were compelled to plunder, and this occasioned the greatest disorder on the march: whole companies left the main body, and did not rejoin it until their arrival on the Spanish frontier, when they were received without punishment. Many returned with booty, in addition to their provisions; but many, owing to their thirst for plunder, as the gratification of their unbridled appetites, fell victims to the revenge of the Portuguese peasantry: woe to him who fell into their hands; if innocent, he was sure to suffer for the deeds of others.

At the commencement of the retreat, I had fortunately a small store of beans; this, notwithstanding my being tolerably loaded, I did not leave behind me; and these beans, when my biscuit was consumed, saved me from starvation. Towards the end of the retreat, the scarcity was so extreme, that many soldiers collected the undigested corns of maize from the dung of horses, washed and ate them. During the retreat we lost a great number of men. As the Portuguese were well acquainted with the country, and as swift as deer, awaited us at all the most dangerous passes, and fired upon us, without our being able to prevent it. The English light cavalry also allowed us no rest, and were literally always at our heels; so that we often had scarcely time to take even scanty meals.

In this manner we left Portugal quicker than we entered it. Halting was out of the question; for in addition to the enemy's troops, we were daily attacked by the peasants, who followed the army in bands, and our only safety consisted in flight. At last we reached the long-wished-for frontier. On the 17th of March, 1811, the army crossed the Alva, passed Almeida, and entered the Spanish territory: I, however, was not so fortunate, as I belonged to the detachment which was left in Almeida.

At San Felice the army halted, under the idea that the English would discontinue the pursuit, but the enemy's columns passed the Alva, and before we could look about us, we were blockaded in Almeida.

As the town was at first not very strictly blockaded by the English, the corn for the garrison was ground at a mill in the neighbourhood; and in order to protect it from a surprise, a strong detachment from the garrison was every day sent there. There being a depot for all the regiments in the army here, it happened there was among the detachment a soldier of the 39th Regiment. Before we went to our posts, our. muskets were always fresh loaded, and in so doing, this man placed the ball under the powder, and thus prevented his piece from discharging. On being reproached for his unskilfulness and want of attention, he gave the following laconic answer: "*Je n'ai pas envie de faire mal à personne, Messieurs.*" (I do not wish to hurt anyone, gentlemen.)

The French now began to perceive that matters were serious, and used all their endeavours to relieve us with the assistance of the fresh troops which were arrived from France, but it was too late; the English had now learned to fight, and looked their hereditary enemies, the French, steadfastly in the face1

One day an hussar of the King's German Legion rode close under the walls, and challenged the French to come out. The sentinels shot at him, but missed. He saluted with his sabre, and rode slowly away, although they fired grenades at him.

During this blockade we made several sorties, one of which was interesting to me, from having been present. A captain of the 15th Light Infantry regiment, a brave and skilful officer, commanded us. I was sent with four men to reconnoitre an old house, in order to see if any of the enemy's sentries were there. We approached very cautiously, and had reached within five paces, when the cry of "who comes there?" resounded. We rushed forward, the sentinel fired his piece, but in the next moment was transfixed by our bayonets. Scarcely forty paces' distant, a party of English soldiers were posted, who, alarmed by the shot, advanced and fired upon us; but as the night was very dark, and we did not return the fire, they could not see us, although we could plainly distinguish them. As we did not wish to make the sortie known, we withdrew silently to the main body, and made a report of what we had discovered. At a ruined windmill, close to the side of the wood, there was a strong English outpost, which it was our intention to surprise; but warned by the noise, they were on their guard, and received us with a heavy fire. We advanced quickly, and when close in, fired, and rushed forward with our bayonets. Too weak to withstand our force, they retreated: we, however, having no inclination to advance beyond the reach of the cannon of the fortress, withdrew, carrying with us only a few wounded, whom in their hurry they could not take with them. These prisoners we brought into Almeida, where they were strictly interrogated respecting the strength and condition of the enemy's force; however, they would confess nothing.

The fortifications, which were much damaged by the before-mentioned explosion, had been put into a tolerable state of defence, but still not sufficiently so as to be able to stand a regular siege, much less a bombardment. The houses were in a still worse condition; for what the blowing up of the magazine had spared, had, owing to the scarcity of wood, been consumed by the besieged for fuel. Provisions also began to fail, for the Ninth Corps d'Armée, and the detachments passing to and from the main army through the town, had always received at least six days' provision, and the present garrison, consisting of two thousand men, was much too large for the small stock remaining. Few inhabitants were left behind, and they were possessed of nothing; the chief part were buried under the ruins of their houses by the explosion, and many had left the town in the night.

At this time the English sent in a flag of truce, to require the surrender of the place; but this, although we were in such a bad condition, our general would not hear of, and the flag of truce returned with refusal. We were constantly in expectation of being relieved, until at last a messenger from Marshal Massena arrived, (how he got into the fortress I know not) with an order to blow up the fortifications, to destroy the town, and all the guns and stores; and we were afterwards to cut our way through the blockading force. This was a hard undertaking for our weakened and worn-out force. However, we went cheerfully to the task, and in less than a fortnight had undermined the walls in fourteen places, which were in communication with each other. All who were in a condition to work were employed upon this, and those who were not able were posted on the ramparts, so that we had scarcely any rest.

During the blockade I became better acquainted with the effects of the explosion, which had been occasioned by a shot from one of our batteries. A shell had fallen in the vicinity of the magazine, just at the time that the wagons were standing there, in order to convey ammunition to the ramparts, and had set fire to one of them; this communicated like lightning to the magazine itself. A number of the workmen were at the time employed in filling bombs and shells; these were all destroyed. Among the numerous victims of this unfortunate accident, were upwards of six hundred persons, who had fled for safety into the fortress, with the chief part of their effects: they had been lodged in a casemate, which was close to the powder magazine, and were there, with all their property, in an instant overwhelmed. They could not escape their fate, and would have done wiser to have remained in their dwellings; as although they might have lost everything else, they would probably have saved their lives.

The place where they and their treasures were buried, was well known to us and the inhabitants, and the search would have well repaid us for our trouble; but this was strictly forbidden, and a sentry was constantly posted on the spot to prevent it, from the fear that the disinterment of so many dead bodies would produce some pestilential disorder in the town.

The stock of provisions decreased every day; the small remaining quantity of corn was ground by hand-mills, the finer part of the flour was made into bread for the officers, and the remainder served out to us. This bad fare, added to our hard work, made us very discontented, and we earnestly wished that the English would undertake something in order to decide our fate; but they remained perfectly quiet, they well knew that we could not escape them. The scarcity, at last, became so great, that we began to slaughter the horses, mules, and asses. The governor himself gave one of his best horses, and every day several of these animals were divided among the troops. Water was also scarce, for in Almeida there was no good drinkable water, and we were obliged to procure it from a place about fifty yards distant from the gate. This the English discovered, and erected a battery which commanded it, and we could procure no water but at the peril of our lives. We were thus restricted to what was in the town, and was called sweet water; this we only used at our utmost need, as it had such a disagreeable taste.

On the morning of the 6th of April, 1811, General Brenier assembled the whole garrison in the principal square of the town, and, appearing on horseback in the centre of the circle, made a powerful speech to us. He praised our exertions, and the steadiness with which we had undergone so much without murmuring; he then stated that we must make up our minds to still greater exertions—that we had yet a hard battle to fight, as there remained no means of safety for us but in cutting our way through the blockading force of the English, in order to reach the French army, which was distant about six miles. He hinted how shameful it was for a soldier to display meanness and cowardice, or to desert his colours in the hour of need: he hoped none of us were capable of such an action. Last of all he told us, that those who wished it were at liberty to go over to the English. As no one answered to this, he cried out: "Well, then, swear all of you that you will do your duty like brave men:" all swore to conquer or die. After this all the remaining provisions were served out to us, and we spent one more pleasant day.

At eleven o'clock at night we silently broke up, passed out at a small side gate through the trenches, which were filled with spiked cannon, ammunition-wagons, &c., all of which were afterwards destroyed by the blowing up of the walls. When the whole garrison was assembled on the glacis, a detachment of artillery received orders in ten minutes time to spring the mines, and presently every thing blew up with a tremendous crash. At the same moment, the advanced guard fell in with a Portuguese picquet, who were bayoneted in an instant. We perceived movements in the English camp; but, as we afterwards learned, they concluded our powder magazine had blown up, and troubled themselves no farther about the matter.

General Brenier had very wisely escaped before into the French camp: he had capitulated with the army of Marshal Junot, in Lisbon, and had taken the oath not to serve against the English during the war; had he been, taken prisoner, his breach of parole might have cost him his life. We marched, under the command of the colonel of the 82nd Regiment, during the night, without molestation, by an unfrequented route; but, as soon as the day dawned, the English perceived our retreat; and we were immediately attacked by a Scotch infantry and an English hussar regiment, which happened to be near us.

The neighbourhood of Almeida, towards the Spanish frontier, is level for miles, with here and there isolated rocky eminences and ruined watch-towers, On approaching San Felice, however, the ground became hilly and uneven. We had nearly crossed the plains, and began to approach the hills, where the cavalry could no longer have done us so much mischief: we were, however, hard pressed, and the enemy's artillery beginning to bear upon us, we fell into disorder. Our ranks were every moment thinner, and at last entirely broken up. Everyone sought his own safety, or endeavoured to sell his life as dearly as possible, so that the cavalry which pursued us lost several men. A small, number of our men were fortunate enough to reach the French line, a greater part were killed, and the remainder made prisoners, which fate I also experienced.

A sturdy Scotchman seized me by the collar, and an hussar flourished his sabre over my head; but when they perceived that I made no opposition, they desisted from hostilities. These two gentlemen, without further ceremony, took possession of my small stock of money and my knapsack, out of which they selected what they pleased. I was obliged to look patiently on, as, had I made the least opposition, I should only have experienced worse treatment.

I was now a prisoner, and, with many others, was driven off like a drove of cattle by the English: a good pair of shoes which I had on I lost by the way; an English soldier exchanged them for his, which, unluckily, I could not wear. We were brought to Villa Formosa, where the English head-quarters were established under Lord Wellington. He came with a number of other generals to see us, and all reproached us, particularly those who were Germans by birth, for having so long served the usurper (for so they denominated the Emperor Napoleon). One general above all others, he was probably a German, abused us most unmercifully: this cruel treatment, as we were already unhappy enough, made a very unfavourable impression upon us.

We were again led away, placed in some old stables, and strictly guarded; we were about four hundred in number, and so crowded together, that we were very much incommoded; but, to the honour of the English, I must allow that we were excellently well fed; our rations, which we received direct from the commissary, and according to the regular allowance, were as good, and often larger than those of their own soldiers, which, on the contrary, passed through the hands of the regimental quartermasters, who seldom forgot to exact their tithes, and thus they came, somewhat diminished, into the soldiers' hands.

The French also treated their English prisoners much better than their Spanish. The latter received, if they were in want of clothing, shoes, shirts, trousers, and great coats. The Spaniards, on the contrary, treated their prisoners most shamefully: in proof of which, I will only relate what occurred to those unhappy beings who were carried to the island of Cabreara, one of the Baleares. This island is quite uninhabited, and only visited during the fine season by the goat-herds of Majorca. On the arrival of the captives they found no shelter, and were afforded so few tents, that the chief part remained at the mercy of the elements, and were finally obliged to dig holes in the earth, in order to shelter themselves. The subsistence which was furnished them consisted of bread, horse-beans, and oil; but the rations were so scanty that they were frequently nearly starved.

Once, owing to the unfavourable weather, they were several days without provisions, and their misery was so extreme, that several threw themselves into the sea to avoid starvation: and a Pole was discovered, who had murdered a cuirassier, his comrade, and was in the act of eating his heart As I learned these particulars from a creditable eyewitness, named Schwein, who was afterwards my comrade, and had passed five years on the island, I can answer for the truth of them, as well as if I had seen them myself. To provide, at least, for the welfare of their souls, as that of their bodies was so much neglected, a priest was sent to them; but this personage, instead of endeavouring, by pious exhortations, to alleviate their misery, on his arrival, struck his staff into the earth, and exclaimed: "When this staff puts forth leaves, then, and not before, will you be released from this island."

By degrees these unhappy beings endeavoured to make their condition more tolerable, by building huts and cultivating the soil. They procured all sorts of seeds from Majorca, such as tobacco, cucumbers, pease, beans, &c, and by selling the produce, procured themselves some few of the necessaries of life. When a prisoner died, he left his small plot of ground to his favourite comrade; when another enlisted, either in the English or Spanish service, for which there was always a recruiting depôt in Majorca, he sold his little possession. After the treaty of peace concluded at Paris, and not sooner, were these prisoners released; and on their disembarkation in France, they were not known to the Frenchmen, so much were they changed by sorrow and misery.[1]

On the second day of our captivity we were marched farther into the interior of Portugal, escorted by but few military; but before our departure, we were warned by the general not to separate from our escort, as enraged Portuguese peasants were every where to be met with, eager for any opportunity to murder us. When we-had marched some little distance, I began to feel great inconvenience from the want of shoes; the stony roads wounded my feet in such a manner, that it was with the utmost difficulty I was enabled to reach our quarters for the night, which were in an old church. I should scarcely have been able to have proceeded the following day, had I not remarked among the Portuguese, who were looking at us, one like myself, without shoes; but this want he had skilfully remedied by a pair of sandals. I resolved immediately upon following his example, and took my empty, and now useless, knapsack, and out of it made myself a very masterly pair of sandals: these I bound to my feet with the cords of my cap, and in less than half an hour I was so handsomely shod, that I reckoned upon being able to walk at least a hundred miles.

On the third day we reached Pinhal, where we were joined by more companions in misfortune, particularly of the 5th Regiment of Hussars, who had been made prisoners the day before. Here I also saw, for the first time, the black Brunswick Oel troops. These had been described to us as warlike, fierce, and blood-thirsty; they did not, however, at all correspond to the description: they were discontented, and not at all pleased with the mode of living in Portugal. I even heard that in a short time a great number of the corps had deserted, on which account they had been disbanded, and a company placed with each division

---

1. The relator of these circumstances, Philip Schwein, is now living in Rheinzabern; he is happily married, and keeps the inn known by the sign of the lamb. His story is told in *A Conscript for Empire* available from Leonaur.

of the English army. The soldiers of the German Legion called them, in derision, "The Brotherhood of Revenge."

From Pinhal we proceeded farther, under an escort of heavy cavalry of the German Legion; and a circumstance occurred here which may serve to characterize the brutality and blood-thirstiness of the Portuguese. There was a prisoner among us, named Stern, who, on account of sickness not being able to walk, was carried in a cart.[2] A peasant, happening to perceive this sick man, asked a dragoon to sell him, and actually offered for him forty *crusados*. Upon the dragoon asking what he wanted with him, the peasant coolly replied, "to torture him." The dragoon, enraged at such inhumanity, drew his sabre, and gave the Portuguese a good-drubbing, The same feeling existed throughout Portugal; men and women, children, and aged persons, took up whatever lay near them to throw at us, and to kill us; and I once saw an old woman, in passing through a village, endeavouring, with all her might, to take up a large stone to throw at us; not being able to compass this, she took up, in order to satiate her revenge, a lump of mud, and threw it in my face, as I happened to be near her. Such indignities we were obliged to buffer in a country which we had so lately passed through as lords and conquerors; and, under these circumstances, we had truly very little wish to escape.

Upon reaching the Mondego, we were embarked in boats, which had brought up provisions from Coimbra. Had I made this journey under happier circumstances, the magnificent scenery of the country would have afforded me abundant gratification; but situated as I was, a prisoner, and kicked about by the rough boatmen, the beautiful views on each side, drew too little of my attention for me to be able now to describe them. I can, however, recollect, that the river winds through high rocks, and that the banks particularly on the right side, are adorned with pleasant country houses and fine gardens.

At Coimbra we were landed at the bridge, where a crowd

---

2. This man is living now as an invalid. He is an Alsatian by birth, from the neighbourhood of Strasburg.

of the inhabitants received us with curses, blows, and showers of stones. Our guards were too weak to protect us from this ill-treatment, and were obliged to look on quietly, if they did not wish to render themselves liable to the same treatment from the enraged populace. With God's help we at last reached our prison, which protected us from the rage of the Portuguese, who assembled round the building, and with violent outcries demanded our death. The officer in command here procured immediately a reinforcement from the garrison, and ordered his men to load. This operation intimidated the Portuguese, and the chief part of them left us. The most violent, however, did not stir from the place, and continued uttering curses and threats against the walls of the building: we, nevertheless, looked at them through our iron bars, and laughed at their impotent rage, which only rendered them more furious. Among the mob was a Portuguese officer, who passionately drew his sword, and brandished it at us poor unarmed prisoners. As soon as our guard perceived that the number of our enemies was diminished, they came out and drove the crowd away with their bayonets. When we received our daily rations, we were taken under a strong guard to the magazine: this was absolutely necessary for our protection.

One day it was my turn to go to the wine-store: our cans had been filled, and the commissary was in the act of presenting each of us with an extra glass, when a Portuguese, who was at work in the magazine, came up, seized me by the collar, and drew a long knife from under his jacket—"You French son of a w—," said he, "shall I rip you up?" I did not understand this alarming threat, but an Englishman explained it to me. "If you were not here, under English protection, your blood should soon flow." He then turned round to the English, and added—"You English are likewise rascals, and not better Christians than the French; you may all of you go to the devil together." This, uttered in a threatening tone of voice, and the sight of the long knife, alarmed me so much, that I should have suffered myself to be ripped open without making any resistance; the man, however, contented himself with the threat, and I escaped with a blow in the ribs, which for a few seconds deprived me of sense.

During the fortnight we remained at Coimbra, many of these scenes occurred; we, however, escaped without injury, the presence of the English preventing them from putting their dangerous threats in execution.

Between seven and eight hundred prisoners were by this time collected, and we were once more embarked on the Mondego, to be sent down to the coast. On our embarkation, we experienced the same ill-treatment as on our arrival—we were pelted with stones until we reached the boats. We reached Figueiras late in the evening, where some English seamen were ready to convey us on board the transports. It was already dark, and at the mouth of the Mondego the waves rocked our boats about so much, that we, unacquainted with the sea, expected every instant to go to the bottom. The sailors laughed at our fears, tumbled us into their boats, and we soon reached in safety the transport ships, which were appointed to receive us, eight hundred in number. The manoeuvres of the sailors on board the ship very much surprised us, particularly as every movement was accompanied by a sound very much resembling the cry of a man in pain, and we thought at first, deceived by this cry and the noise occasioned by their movements, that some punishment was being inflicted. We would willingly have asked the reason of all this, but nobody understood us, and we were obliged to wait patiently until we could see matters with our own eyes.

Immediately on coming on board, we were confined between decks, with only a few holes left open to prevent our being suffocated. Everyone took possession of the best place he could find; those who came first, of course had the best. I was one of the last, and was obliged to content myself with what remained, and took up my abode for the night quite in the forepart of the ship, between two beams. I soon found out, that if my quarters were not the most comfortable, yet that they protected me from many inconveniences experienced by my comrades, who, from various causes, were quarrelling the whole night; in short, every thing disagreeable, which the crowding together of so many persons in so small a space can occasion, fell to our lot. By degrees the air became so foul that we could scarcely breathe; for, in addition to our natural perspiration, we had been wetted through by the rain the day before. Our clothes began to dry, and occasion such a steam, that it was absolutely insupportable. Under these circumstances, how earnestly we wished for day-break, any one may easily imagine. At last, daylight appeared, and we were allowed to go upon deck. Here I, for the first time, duly appreciated the luxury of fresh air; I drew in my breath with ecstasy, and glad enough I was to have escaped from my nocturnal abode between the two beams.

A marine officer, probably the commandant of the port, now made his appearance, and ordered one-half of us, of which number I was one, to be conveyed on board another transport, which had been fitted up for cavalry. Here a number of prisoners had already been confined, and had left us a very disagreeable legacy: the ship swarmed in such a manner with lice, fleas, and bugs, that it was almost insupportable; whenever we went below deck we were covered in an instant. Oh, how often, when I shook these vermin from my body, have I thought of my beloved Weimar! When in trouble, and without occupation, thoughts of happier days always press heaviest upon the recollection.

The want of good water was our greatest evil; we had nothing wherewith to quench our thirst but foul and stinking water, the smell of which alone deprived us of all desire to drink, and we suffered the greatest thirst before we could resolve to use it.[3]

Soon after, the vessel was anchored farther in the bay, and we were then, fortunately for us, enabled, at ebb-tide, to procure water fit to drink. At flood, however, the water was again salt, from the coming in of the sea. We often stood for hours

---

3. I since that time, have often heard sailors say, that the more foul and stinking the water was, the better it was to drink on shipboard; I, however, could never accustom myself to it I afterwards used to mix it with either vinegar or sugar, which made it at least drinkable.

on the deck, anxiously waiting till our wish could be fulfilled. Eagerly we quaffed the precious liquid: many injured
themselves by drinking excessively, even of this simple fluid.
In about a fortnight, came an order to send us to Lisbon; and
two frigates, which were cruising before the harbour, were
appointed to convey us. The harbour being so shallow, that
only small vessels can run in, all the boats belonging to the
ships which were lying here, were put in requisition to convey
us on board. More than a hundred boats were assembled, and
we were then embarked.

A Portuguese merchant-vessel, which was going out, took
our boat in tow; to our's others were fastened, and formed
altogether a chain of more than fifty. In the next boat to us
were only Frenchmen, who suddenly set up a loud cry: they
had, some how or other, pulled out a plug, (which there is in
every boat, in order, when hung up, to let out whatever water
may be in it) and it naturally began to fill. The sailors soon
remedied this, quieted the noise of the Frenchmen with blows,
and compelled them to bale out the water with their caps. The
weather had been stormy the day before, and the sea still rolled
very much, which made the boat pitch about in such a manner, that we thought ourselves every instant in danger of our
lives. No-one gave utterance to his fear; but it was clearly to
be read in every countenance. We got, at last, safely on board
the frigates, which were lying still before the wind, that is to
say, without being anchored, having their sails crossed. By way
of precaution, a rope was made fast on each side of the ladder,
and two sailors stood on the deck ready to receive us. I did
not understand, at first, what this ceremony meant; but when
it came to my turn to ascend, I soon found out. Owing to the
heavy rolling of the vessel, every one, on stepping upon deck,
(unless he took the precaution to hold fast, or was held) was
sure to fall backwards, and would either have been pitched into
the sea, or the boat underneath. To hinder this, the two sailors
stood ready, and on my running up, seized me by the collar
and threw me down on the deck, where I found my comrades

crawling about on their hands and knees: standing was out of the question, as we were afraid of being thrown down, and breaking our heads against something or other.[4]

After remaining in this manner for some time, and experiencing some of the sensations of sea-sickness, all our names were taken down, and we were put below. I crept immediately to one of the port-holes, where there was a current of air, and soon found myself a good deal recovered. In a few hours I found myself so well, that I felt a wish to go again upon deck. Unfortunately, but few of us were allowed to go up at a time; and I was thus obliged to wait with patience, until it came to my turn to breathe fresh air above. When I came up, we were approaching the entrance of the Tagus; and I could discern, at a distance, the forts of St. Julian and Margareta, which protect the entrance to the port of Lisbon.

What a magnificent prospect offered itself to my view! Level plains extending along the coast; beyond these, hills varying in height, bounded in the distance by the lofty Portuguese mountains, the tops of which were lost in the clouds, and formed the back-ground to a most lively landscape. The Tagus was covered with boats; farther on was seen the port, with hundreds of vessels, the city, with its magnificent palace, and the castle rising above all. We passed, first, the forts of St. Julian and Margareta;. then the Castle of Belem; and anchored close to the marine arsenal. All, who were not prevented by sickness, were now allowed to come upon deck. As soon as the Portuguese perceived us, they began, as usual, to curse and to pelt; but we were too distant for them to do us any harm. On the same day, we were landed and conducted to the prison, which was in the arsenal. Fortunately for us, there was a palisadoed way from the port to the arsenal, otherwise many of us might have fallen victims to the hatred of the inhabitants.

---

4. I wondered much, at first, how the sailors could walk about without staggering; but by degrees, after several times measuring my length upon the deck, I learned to walk about as well as the best of them: but it is singular, that, after having been for some time at sea, one walks on shore as if one was stepping over something.

Here we were kept three whole days without receiving any provisions. Several had been fortunate enough to bring something from the ship; but these were few in number, and what they had was soon consumed; and we then had nothing but what our neighbours, the galley-slaves, spared us, out of compassion, from their own allowance!! These; however, were but sparingly fed, and could afford us but little. Those among us who had any article of clothing to spare, parted with it to procure bread. He who was in possession of both a shirt and a coat, sold either the one or the other, in order to satisfy that most pressing of all wants—hunger. Those unfortunates who possessed nothing, were seen on their knees before those who, by the sale of their clothing, had been able to procure some food; begging in the most moving terms for the smallest morsel to still their gnawing hunger. This was of no avail; for each individual was too much occupied with his own misery, to pay any regard to the distresses of others. These distressing scenes our guards regarded with indifference; and it seemed as though we were fast approaching to a country where plenty for ever reigns. At last, on the third day, at noon, each soldier received thirty *reals*, which were instantly exchanged for bread. With what appetite this was devoured, after so long an abstinence, those only can conceive who have ever been in a similar situation.

Early in the morning of the fourth day, some English recruiting officers paid us a visit, to recruit for the foreign regiments in English pay: our necessities compelled four hundred of us, Germans, Netherlanders, and Poles, to volunteer; we were accepted, and immediately separated from the remaining prisoners.

CHAPTER 7

The King's German Legion

It is a certain truth, that not man alone, but every living being, feels a lively sense of joy at being released from a state of confinement, particularly from so irksome a one as we had been subjected to. With us this was considerably increased, by the hope of being once more enabled to eat our fill. Heartily pleased, therefore, we followed the steps of our conductors.

The arsenal is situated nearly in the centre of the city; to reach our new quarters, therefore, which were in Belem, we had a considerable space to traverse. Among other places which we passed was the fish-market, which happened at the time to be filled with people. Along the whole of our road, we had to put up with numberless insults from the populace, which yet seldom proceeded beyond words. Here, however, it was scarcely to be borne; we were assailed on all sides by a furious cannon-ade of stinking fish, rotten oranges, and filth of all descriptions; the wandering dogs were even set upon us.[1] Our conductors begged of us, in the most urgent manner, to avoid showing any signs of resentment, for that if we made the slightest opposition, we should be torn in pieces by the enraged populace. We were, therefore, obliged to submit with patience to this ill-treatment.

Completely disfigured, and scarcely to be known, we reached Belem, which is almost entirely inhabited by shop-keepers, who gained their livelihood by supplying the large depôt there. These

---

1. In this city dogs without owners wander about in countless multitudes, par-ticularly in the neighbourhood of the fish-market, and the butchers' stalls.

people, more accustomed to the sight of French prisoners, allowed us to pass along in peace. A cavalry stable was appointed for temporary quarters; but provisions, which we so anxiously looked for, were not forthcoming; we saw no symptoms of any being about to be served out. We waited a couple of hours, and our patience being quite exhausted, became furious; and a corporal of our regiment, named Lattner, and myself, made use of not the most polite expressions, which, I think, no one can blame us for, upon considering we were nearly in a state of starvation.

Information was sent to the officer of the depôt, that the recruits, (for so we were called, although many of us had smelt and fired away ten times as much powder as the Englishmen,) were in a state of mutiny. He came immediately, and addressed us in a threatening manner:

"You rascals, if you are not quiet immediately, I will have you all well flogged, and sent back to the arsenal!"

We muttered out in answer: "If this is done, the King of England will be spared the shame of suffering his newly-acquired soldiers to die of hunger." These remarks drew the officer's attention; he ordered us to be quiet, and requested one of us to step forward and relate our complaints; and promised, if they were just, that they should immediately be remedied. Upon this, I stepped forward, and began in the following manner:—

"If you, Sir, captain, or lieutenant, whichever you may be, were in our situation, I am convinced that you would not be more peaceable than we are; and, when you come to know, that many of us, for the last three or four days, have scarcely had any thing to eat; and that, according to all appearances, we are not likely to get any thing this evening, I am sure that you will excuse this disturbance, which despair and hunger alone has caused."

"My God!" exclaimed the officer, whom I afterwards found to be a most excellent man—"I knew not a word of all this; it was reported to me, that the newly-enlisted men had been brought here, and had received their provisions for the day."

Upon this he sent a corporal, with orders to the quartermaster-sergeant, who had made the report to him, to come directly;

he made his appearance, and the officer addressed him very seriously, in the following words: "Sir, have these men received their full rations, after the usual manner of English soldiers?"

"Captain"—was the only word the sergeant could utter: he stood confused before the brave officer, who thus proceeded:

"I command you, within half an hour's time, to have every thing provided; after that, you go under arrest. Fie! are you not ashamed of yourself; a German, and to act in this manner? For a trifling gain you would endanger the lives of many men, and thus deprive the King of soldiers he wants so much: you may thank my good nature, and your length of service, that your punishment for this time is so slight, but let it be a warning to you for the future."

The man went away quite cast down, but the captain remained with us until he had seen the provisions delivered into our hands, he then said: "Now, my lads, I hope you will relish it, tomorrow you shall receive more!" After this, he wished us a good night, and went away.

We received bread, rice, salted meat, and each one a pint of good Portuguese wine. We eagerly devoured the excellent bread, and drank our wine with it; the latter proved too strong for our weakened stomachs, and soon got into our heads, so that in less than half an hour all who had drank their allowance were intoxicated. I made up my bed in a corner of one of the stalls, and slept soundly; my stomach was filled, all my troubles were forgotten, I felt nothing of the vermin with which I was covered, and it was broad daylight when the noise made by my comrades, already up, awakened me. All were busily employed! the meat was on the fire, the rice was boiling, some were already eating, and the gloomy silence caused by our distressed situation, had entirely disappeared, and given way to an expression of comfort visible in every face.

The captain came to visit us very early, and asked us how we found ourselves today? "Very well," was the general answer.

"Are you now satisfied at becoming English soldiers?" This was a question which we would rather not have answered; however, to oblige him, we unanimously assented, and this pleased him. We were now taken to the surgeon and examined; and, with a few exceptions, were passed. I must observe, to the credit of the English, that those prisoners unfit for service were not sent back again, but were taken with us to England, and from thence were sent home to Germany, with an allowance of £2 for travelling expenses. How happy these men were when they took leave of England; how much they rejoiced at the prospect of a return to their native country, which they proposed taking the first opportunity to effect.

At the conclusion of the surgical examination, we were all taken down to the sea-side; here we were ordered to undress; every one received a piece of soap, and leaped joyfully into the waves, to which our whole French wardrobe, with its contents, was consigned. How readily we assisted each other in getting rid of our dirt and filth, and how pleased we were when, on coming out of the water as if newly born, we found ready for each of us a shirt, a pair of linen trousers, a cap, and a flannel jacket.

A lively barter now took place among us; one called, "who will exchange trousers, or cap?" another, "who will exchange shoes?" and so on, until at last we were all tolerably well fit-ted. While this was going on, we were highly amused by seeing the Portuguese engaged in collecting our cast-off clothes: these they sought after with the greatest avidity, and deposited them in their boats; the competition became at last so great, that they actually fought for the possession of these rags.

After being so completely transformed, we were not taken back to our former quarters, but embarked immediately on board the *Doris*, a large transport, which accommodated us all, with the exception of about a hundred, who were put on board a smaller vessel. Here every one of us received another shirt, and 15s. 6d., being a month's pay, (about five dollars of our money) and likewise a new blanket.

We had been but a few days on board, when a tragi-comical occurrence took place. Owing to the extreme heat and fine-ness of the weather, a number of us who were able to swim were bathing in the Tagus, among others a Dutchman, who was an excellent swimmer. The captain of the vessel had a beautiful Newfoundland dog, who was trained to save persons who might have the misfortune to fall overboard, and to fetch any thing which might drop into the water. This Dutchman, in order to show his skill, played all sorts of antics in the water; among other things, pretended to be in danger of drowning. The dog, who was usually lying on the ship's side, no sooner perceived this than he darted like an arrow into the sea, swam towards the man, and endeavoured to get hold of him. The Dutchman, taken unawares, would now actually have been in danger of drowning, if assistance had not been immediately afforded him; the dog following his natural instinct would not quit him, while he was using his utmost endeavours to keep him off. A rope with a large loop was thrown out to the dog, into this he laid his fore paws, and in this manner was drawn up into the ship.

The chief part of us slept in beds, but several in hammocks, one of which I had, and I can only wish that every one may always sleep as comfortably as I did in my hammock; this sort of bed, however, is only calculated for those who can bear the motion. Our daily fare consisted of bacon, beef, cheese, butter, and ship biscuit; in the place of vegetables, we received pudding, pease, oatmeal, grits and rice; besides which, every day, the third of a pint of rum, tea and cocoa. This good nourishment, and the pure healthy air, soon freed us all from the effects of our former troubles. Our rations were so abundant that we were none of us able to consume what we every day received; and we got fat and healthy beyond measure. Tobacco, which during our troubles we had been entirely deprived of, was now again procured, and it was really a pleasure to see the men, either stretched out on the deck, or leaning on the ship's side, looking out towards the city, smoking their pipes as happy as kings. To pass away the time, a number of amusements were found out, in which the captain and the sailors frequently shared.

This pleasant life lasted for six weeks, until from eight hundred to one thousand recruits had been collected; and towards the end of August, 1811, we received orders to go to England. The transport, on board of which we had until now been living, remained here, and we were put on board of a man of war of seventy-four guns, named the *Leyden*. On board this ship of war, we missed many of the conveniences we had been accustomed to on board the *Doris*. Our blankets, in particular, were kept back, which would have been very useful to us during the voyage. No smoking was allowed, excepting in the fore part of the ship; no one was allowed to wash himself upon deck, and not on any account with fresh water; every day, from ten to four o'clock, we were obliged to be upon deck, if the weather permitted. However, we had an excellent opportunity of becoming acquainted with the exterior and interior of such an interesting object as an English ship of war. The sailors, a good-natured though rough class of men, very readily showed and explained to us everything worthy of remark on board. The following is a short description of the ship:

It had been captured from the Dutch, and taken into the English service; the guns had been taken out of the lower deck, which was fitted up for the transport service; it held nearly six hundred men very conveniently, who slept, in beds, each of which was arranged to hold six persons. There were four anchors, of an enormous size and weight; the cables were almost as thick as the leg of a middling-sized man, and we were told that they cost a guinea per foot. The cables, when the ship is under way, are placed below deck, and the anchors are hung on each side of the fore-part of the vessel, fastened by chains and cables. On approaching the place of destination, the cable is brought out from the hold, and in transport ships placed upon deck; but in ships of war under the upper deck, where it is run out, through holes made for that purpose, and fastened to the anchor; the whole weight of which is afterwards sustained by a small rope. Immediately on arriving at the place of anchorage, on a signal being given by the captain, this rope is cut, and the anchor falls as quick as lightning to the bottom. The cable is afterwards drawn in as far as may be considered necessary. The ship immediately turns round towards the wind, and in places where the tides are very strong, the ships turn regularly four times in the four-and-twenty hours. When the anchor is to be weighed, it is wound up by means of a sort of capstan, and this business is performed on board ships of war to the sound of drums and fifes, but in transports to the sound of the sailors' voices. The whole ship is divided into three parts; the after, middle, and fore-deck.

The after or quarter-deck is reserved for the officers alone, and any persons of distinction who may happen to be on board as passengers; the middle and fore-deck is for the soldiers and the ship's company. On the quarter-deck are the cabins, consisting of several apartments, often very handsomely decorated and furnished. Directly in front of the cabins is the wheel belonging to the helm, at which two sailors are constantly posted, in order to work it; this is not performed, as has been often falsely reported, by the steersman alone. Every sailor must know how to steer, otherwise he is not a sailor, but only a cabin-boy, even if he is a hundred years old. Immediately in front of the wheel stands the compass, at which, during the night, a lamp burns, and close by is the ship's bell, which rings the hour. Near the mainmast are the pumps, by which, every morning, and if necessary oftener, the water is pumped out of the hold. Farther back the long boat is placed, which is the largest on board,—the smaller ones hang overboard, on each side. The kitchen is below, as well as the magazines for stores of all kinds. The ship's company is usually divided into three watches, which are relieved every four hours; but in case of need, "all hands on deck" is called; everyone hastens up immediately to be in readiness, whenever his assistance is required. The hammocks are every morning rolled up tight, brought upon deck, and placed in rows on each side, and covered with tarpaulins, to secure them from being wetted.

At night, upon a given signal, when the guns are drawn in and the ports closed, they are carried down again. Over every gun there is a table fixed, where the sailors take their meals; these can be removed, so as not to be in the way of any manoeuvres.

The crew of a vessel like this often consists of seven or eight hundred men, many of whom have their wives and children on board; for the latter there is a schoolmaster appointed, who also acts as a sort of police officer, and punishes old as well as young for every trifling fault, with a few strokes of a cane, which he always carries with him. Once, at the closing of the port-holes, I came in for a few strokes, which operated as a useful lesson to me; for, upon giving a signal at sunset, every thing being done with the utmost punctuality, the ports are all closed at once, and had not my attention been drawn by this means, I should have been miserably crushed. The children of the sailors are all under the control of this teacher; they are kept in strict subordination, and their faults severely punished.

In the daytime, the sailors are occupied in various ways—mending sails, making ropes, &c. &c. The utmost care is taken of the fresh water, and all unnecessary consumption of it is strictly forbidden. The sailor sitting on the top-mast has to look after everything which may show itself in the horizon, and to report immediately. He is relieved every four hours; but in bad weather, every two hours. In transports and merchant-ships, many of these regulations are not in use; but a good captain always endeavours to keep up as much order as possible on board, without which a ship can never be well managed.

In fleets, the following customs are in use. The signals are always given by the commander of the fleet or squadron, and must be answered by every vessel under his orders. If this be not done, the commander is allowed to fire at the vessel disobeying, and the captain of her is obliged to pay for the shot. In the night, signals are made by lighted lanterns hung up to the masts, and must be answered in the same way. No captain of a ship, if sailing under the orders of a commodore, knows at his departure the place of his destination. He has sealed orders on board, which he is not allowed to open before the time appointed. All the sailors on board ships of war are obliged to go up aloft as well as to work the guns, which is not exclusively the province of the marines, although there are a number of these men on board every man of war. They are dressed in scarlet, exactly like the troops of the line, with the exception of wearing hats instead of caps. They assist in the work below deck, but are not obliged to go aloft. Besides this, they guard the cabins and the powder-magazine. On board of our ship there were only twelve of these men. Every sailor is armed with a sabre, two pistols, and a boarding pike. The marines are armed in a similar manner to troops of the line.

In ships of war the captain gives directions what is to be done; these orders are repeated by the boatswains and under officers to the crew, by means of a small silver whistle. Upon a signal of this kind being given, every sailor is instantly at his appointed place, to perform immediately what may be required.

During this voyage, it happened that a sailor, who had been for some time ill, died. If possible, the dead are always kept in the hold until the arrival of the vessel in port, so that they be buried ashore; but if circumstances do not allow of this they are thrown, into the sea, which was the case in this instance; as on account of the intense heat, the body could not be preserved until our arrival in England. The corpse is wrapped up in a piece of sail-cloth, and then fastened to a board of the same length as the body; at the feet is fastened a sack, filled with ballast or some cannon-balls, in order to sink it the quicker. When these preparations are completed, the body is taken up by two sailors, and placed on the ship's side; the captain, or one of the officers, in case there is no chaplain on board, then comes and reads a short but appropriate prayer, and on a given sign, the two sailors cast the body overboard. The whole ship's company are obliged to be present upon these occasions; and with their heads uncov-ered, offer up a prayer for the dead, after the body has been cast into the sea. After this the man is no more thought of, and every thing goes on as before. On shore, however, the sailors bury their comrades in a very appropriate and solemn manner.

As soon as the convoy which was to accompany our ship was collected, towards the end of July, 1811, we set sail; and as all the vessels which were to sail under the command of our's were in readiness, we went down the Tagus like an arrow, a cannon-shot giving the signal for our proceeding on the voyage. In a very short time the coast of Portugal resembled only a cloud, and then disappeared entirely. Our vessel sailed majestically among the small transport and merchant-vessels upon the dark blue surface of the sea; but, although large in proportion to the others, it was yet, in comparison to the boundless ocean, but as a grain of sand. We proceeded rapidly on our voyage with a favourable wind; and in less than a week we came in sight of the coast of Brittany, and soon after perceived the western point of England, Cape Lizard. Several small French vessels were cruising along the coast, but none ventured to approach us.

In the channel or narrow sea between France and England, the colour of the water began to change from a deep blue to a dull green; this may be caused by the want of depth, and the chalky nature of the English coast. We soon afterwards saw Falmouth, the first port on the western coast of England, then Plymouth, and at last, ran in between the Isle of Wight and the main land, and about the middle of August, 1811, came to anchor at Portsmouth.

The weather on the day of our arrival was cold and foggy, but the ship's company was in the highest spirits. We were also rejoiced at having reached the place of our destination in good health, and without any misfortune, and were in anxious expectation of what was next to happen. The sailors had certainly more reason to be pleased than we had, most of them not having seen their native land for three years. All received their three years' pay and prize-money, amounting together to a considerable sum. Shortly after our arrival the paymaster made his appearance, and everyone received his due to the last farthing.

Such a scene then took place on board as I never before witnessed. Many of the sailors dressed themselves, went on shore, taking all their money with them, and soon returned without a farthing; others, who could not get leave to go ashore, amused themselves in a different way; dealers in all kinds of wares established themselves on the deck, and eating and drinking went on in all directions. Ladies of pleasure came on board, and carried on their trade in the most shameless manner. The English amusement of boxing was not forgotten, and in a short time few sailors were to be found without black eyes. This they called liberty!

The sailors, who at that time were mostly pressed, that is, compelled to serve by force, being taken wherever they could be met with, were, when ashore, as well as when on board, (particularly those belonging to ships of war) a merry, but rough class of men, most of them lived only for the present moment, and forgetting the past, thought only of the future, in what way they should best get rid of their money, if they had any due to them. When sailors receive any money, their only wish is to go on shore; should their desire be fulfilled, they are happy beyond measure.

No sooner do they quit the boat, than they rush, with all their money about them, usually tied up in their neck-handkerchief, into the nearest public-house, where their first call is for a glass of rum, which generally means a pint; they then drink and amuse themselves with all sorts of jokes, until at last, quite intoxicated, they fell down, and sleep on the spot. If they happen to fall into good hands they are well off; but this is seldom the case, as upon these occasions they are usually accompanied by women, and their whole stock disappears, these harpies taking good care not to leave the poor devil a single penny; and on awaking after their debauch, and perhaps complaining of their loss, they are usually kicked out of doors. Notwithstanding the loss of their money, they do not return immediately to the ship, but begin to sell whatever articles of clothing they can possibly spare, and this only to procure liquor. At last, barefooted, and with scarcely enough to cover their nakedness, they return to their ship, the captain being frequently obliged to pay the expense of bringing them on board.

In this manner many a one dissipates the fruits of several months hard and dangerous labour in two or three days; others, in scarcely one, or even less. However, it is all the same to them; they never give themselves the least uneasiness about it, and only think how they shall manage matters the next time.

We quitted our jovial companions, in the midst of the enjoyment of their liberty, and went on shore in the Isle of Wight, near the village of Yarmouth: Here we were quartered in the neighbouring military barracks—at Coldwell, Freshwater, and other places, forty or fifty men being lodged in each.

The Isle of Wight is of very small extent, and may easily be rambled through. This we often did after we became a little domesticated. We visited Yarmouth, Newport, and all the adjacent places. For these rambles we had plenty of time, our only occupation being in the morning and evening to answer to our names, to show that we were not absent.

During this state of inactivity we amused ourselves in various ways, in order to shorten the time. We caught oysters and crabs, went out fishing, collected shells, &c.; we also visited each other in our barracks, lying at a short distance apart. In this manner the time passed quickly and agreeably, and much more pleasantly than in Spain and Portugal. When the autumn approached, we assisted the inhabitants to get in their harvest. For this we were very well paid; but we saved nothing, as we liked the taste of the English beer so much. This is much dearer than with us, the quart costing sixpence. During this time I once crossed over to Lymington, where, among the prisoners detained there, I found my former captain, who had been taken prisoner by the Portuguese, in the hospital at Coimbra.

One night we were roused by a smart and continued cannonade; we actually thought that the French were not far off, but we soon learned that the shots were signals of distress from a frigate, which had been wrecked, owing to the want of attention on the part of the captain, in not taking a pilot.

The next morning we went down to the beach to see the ship; the crew and chief part of the cargo was saved, but the vessel was fast between two rocks, and wwent to pieces by degrees.

Planks and pieces of timber were afterwards continually washing ashore, and of which we collected the large copper nails, and sold them; by which trade I myself gained upwards of seven dollars. All property of this kind, strictly speaking, belongs

to the persons who farm the beach, for which they pay a considerable sum to the government; but we, notwithstanding, took
advantage of the opportunity.

At last, in October, the government considered that we were
sufficiently restored, and fit for service. We took the oaths, made
an agreement to serve for seven years, or until six months after the signing of a treaty of peace, and received four guin-
eas bounty. Shortly afterwards, we received a complete English
equipment, and orders to join the regiment. We were taken over
to Portsmouth in small pilot-boats, and marched the same day
to Chichester, a neat and not very small town; from thence to
Lewes; then to Brighton; then to Helson barracks; and at last
reached Bexhill, the place of our destination. We were very well
pleased with this march: the roads were good, the distances not
too long, and the best of all was, that on our arrival we everywhere found our meals prepared; these were likewise abundant,
the inn-keepers being obliged to furnish a good meal to soldiers
on their march, for which the King pays two shillings and sixpence. In addition to this good fare the soldier receives daily
two shillings, marching money; out of which he is only obliged
to pay the inn-keeper eight-pence. Thus a march is much more
agreeable in England than in France, where the inn-keeper is
bound to give so little; and even that he often gives very unwill-
ingly. On arrival at Bexhill, we were immediately incorporated
in a battalion of the King's German Legion. I was entered as a
private in the sixth company, with a promise, however, of being
soon appointed to the same rank I held in the French service.
We were exercised every day; and in less than four weeks, I
mounted guard for the first time as a regular English soldier.

In December, 1811, the battalion received orders to hold itself in readiness for marching; and soon after the orders came.
On the 26th of December we returned by the same road to
the coast; and at Portsmouth we were immediately embarked
on board a transport, named the *Harriot*. Our destination was at
this time not finally decided: we were either to go to Spain and
Portugal, where the English had gained several victories over

the French, or to the Mediterranean. We sailed several times, but were always driven back by contrary winds into the harbour of Lymington, where we were detained full two months.

At last, on the 1st of March, 1812, we proceeded to sea; but had scarcely lost sight of the English coast, when a tremendous storm arose, which separated us and seven other vessels from the fleet. At the beginning of the storm we were enveloped in such a thick fog, that we were unable to see ten paces before us; we could not see from one end of the ship to the other. The band which was on board was obliged constantly to play the loudest music, in order to give warning of our situation to the other vessels, that they might not run foul of us. This contrivance soon became useless; for the storm increased so much, that the vessel was no longer manageable, and was suffered to drive as much as possible, certainly under the captain's direction. All the ports and gang-ways were closed, and tarpaulins nailed over. Those who were below deck were obliged to remain there, owing to the waves breaking so furiously over the ship that we expected every instant to founder.

We should, without doubt, have been lost, had our vessel been less sea-worthy, and our captain less skilful and active: but, during the whole time of the danger, he never quitted the deck for a single instant; and whenever there was need, was always the first on the spot. We remained in this manner for several days, at the mercy of the waves; until the weather became more calm, and the sails would be again made use of. We had been driven to the farthest point of the Irish coast, and were obliged to steer again towards England, and run into Falmouth harbour, where the damages which the ship had sustained were repaired.

As soon as every thing was once more in order, we weighed anchor, and quitted the coast of England a second time. At first, although our ship was an excellent sailer, we did not proceed very rapidly on our voyage; being obliged, on account of the privateers, to tow a small vessel along the French coast. But on reaching Cape Finisterre, we were freed from this encumbrance; and, together with the other vessels, sailed rapidly along the coast of Portugal, reached Cape St. Vincent, passed Cadiz, and, in about eight days, in the middle of March, arrived at Gibraltar, where we cast anchor opposite to Algesiras. Here we again fell in with our fleet: they had been a long while expecting us, and had began to give us up for lost.

The harbour and bay of Gibraltar is very roomy; but being a good deal exposed to the wind, is unsafe; the bottom is likewise so rocky, that large vessels are obliged to make use of two or more anchors. Notwithstanding this, they are frequently driven out, and the utmost precaution is necessary at the turn of the tides, and at the time of a change in the wind.

The town of Gibraltar lies close to the sea, in a kind of bay, and reaches from the plain on which San Roche is situated, nearly to the end of the rock, which is surrounded entirely by the fortifications. In the back-ground, at no great distance, is San Roche; on a hill opposite is the town of Algesiras. The rock on which Gibraltar is situated is fortified, not only all round, but also up to the very top. On the highest point stands the telegraph and the alarm gun. Monkeys likewise inhabit this rock, which are preserved and fed by the government; they not unfrequently come down into the town, and steal whatever they can find.

We also experienced the effects of the gusts of wind in this place; the vessel in running out, some days afterwards, was several times laid completely on her side, and all sails were obliged to be taken in. However, we got safely out of the bay, found ourselves in the Mediterranean, got sight of Ceuta, opposite to Gibraltar, and, farther in the distance, of the mountains of Barbary. We had plenty of time for these observations, as there was but little wind, and our ship sailed very slowly, though all sails were set. We proceeded in this manner, until at last the Spanish coast disappeared; a gentle breeze then sprung up, which carried us forward quicker.

We saw in the distance the Balearic islands, then Corsica, passed the channel of St. Bonifacio, between Corsica and Sardinia, and at last got sight of the continent of Italy. The coast of Sicily soon rose before our eyes, and we all believed this to be the place of our destination, and that we were to be landed here, when suddenly we tacked about and steered to the eastward. It was about noon when we took this direction; and the next morning, when we came upon deck at daybreak, a rock appeared before us rising out of the sea, upon which was situated a beautiful city, whose harbour was filled with numberless vessels.

It was Malta which we saw. How pleased I was to have come here, as I had read so much about the knights of Malta, and their expeditions against the unbelievers. I was anxious to behold such men, whom my fancy had portrayed as a strong and powerful race. Nevertheless, during my stay I saw but few of them, and these by no means answered my expectations.

The whole fleet lay to before the wind; as owing to the narrow entrance to the harbour, the ships were obliged to run in singly, and just then a French man of war of seventy-four guns, taken near Toulon, was being towed in. The English ship which had gained the victory, and was leading the captured one in tow, was a sixty-four, accompanied by a brig; she passed close to us, and we were enabled to perceive that the enemy had done his duty. Masts, sails, and rigging, were cut to pieces, the hull was full of shot-holes, the French flag, which was flying underneath the English, was almost burnt; in short, every thing showed that the French had made a brave resistance, and that the English had not obtained the victory at a cheap rate. We had a farther proof of this afterwards, upon seeing the wounded brought on shore. Our ships were next towed in one by one, by a rope made fast to a small boat; for large vessels, two, three, or more boats were requisite. In a short time we were all lying together inside of the harbour, close under Fort Ricasoli.

There being a scarcity of troops here, we were much wanted, and on the third day after our arrival, the 4th April, 1812, were disembarked without performing the usual quarantine. The distance from the shore to our new quarters, the casemates of the Fort Ricasoli, was scarcely fifty paces, but these I trod very reluctantly; for, alarmed at the name of casemate, I fancied our destined dwelling to be a damp hole, in which in winter time the water ran down the walls, and rendered the floor always damp, as I had seen in the casemates of the Spanish and Portuguese fortresses; but upon entering our quarters, how agreeably was I surprised to find large stone buildings, vaulted and provided with numerous air-holes, roomy, and particularly clean, as was every thing provided for our use, such as beds, cooking utensils, &c.

At first we had nothing else to do but to get ourselves in order, and to clean up our arms and accoutrements, which had been damaged by the sea-air and water. In point of cleanliness and neatness the English soldier may compete with the military of any nation. To this part of his duty he is obliged to attend most strictly, but every thing necessary is furnished him, and he is suffered to want for nothing; it becomes therefore his own fault if he makes his appearance dirty, and is punished for it.

We had the good luck to be in Malta during the finest season; the air was pure and refreshing, the heat, though great, was not oppressive, and was constantly cooled by the breezes from the sea, and our casemates were cool and airy. I enjoyed myself here very much, and often reflected with a thankful heart upon the happy turn in my destiny: a year before I had, in the most miserable condition and constant danger, been marching through the devastated provinces of Spain and Portugal, little dreaming of so pleasant a futurity. My being taken prisoner, therefore, which at that time I considered a misfortune, had proved my greatest benefit; had I remained with the French army, a hostile ball or an assassin's knife would probably ere this have deprived me of life; or if even my life had been spared, I should still have had to contend with hunger and thirst, and been exposed to dangers of every description. Now, on the contrary, I was well fed, well clothed, had no hard duty to perform, and was living in a beautiful country without any cares.

The island of Malta, although only a barren rock, not capable of affording subsistence to the inhabitants, is never in want of provisions, every thing being brought here in abundance, and at very low prices. Every day we saw large and small vessels coming in loaded with produce from all parts of the Mediterranean, and large ships often came in bringing the productions of the most distant parts of the world. The entrance of the harbour is protected by two forts opposite to each other: one is called St. Elmo, and the other Ricasoli, where we were quartered, and from whence we could every day enjoy the, to us, novel spectacle of vessels of all kinds running in and out. The city is properly called La Valetta, and is joined by several suburbs, named Floriana, Victoriosa, and Burmola, which are all surrounded by strong fortifications. The harbour runs through the midst of these places, and is so deep that the largest ships may lay themselves close to the shore in any part. The climate is particularly healthy, and we were all in good health, until an epidemic disorder in the eyes broke out in the regiment, which deprived many soldiers of sight, and alarmed me excessively. However, luckily I kept free from this evil. Our lives passed very peaceably, undisturbed by any warlike occurrences; and owing to our distance from the seat of war, we heard but little of what was going on, so that at last we began to get tired of this pleasant life, and to wish once more to be placed in a state of activity.

I cannot refrain from taking this opportunity of recalling to mind my old commanding officer, Major Thalman, and of relating a few traits of his original character, of his benevolence, and also of his strict attention to discipline. He was a worthy old man, about seventy years of age, had been a soldier from his youth, and had risen from the ranks. He began his career as a drummer, and frequently proved to us that he had not forgotten his first occupation, by beating some old marches of the time of his youth. His constitution was weakened by his various services; and owing to attacks of the gout, he frequently appeared on horseback in front of the battalion with one leg in a gaiter and the other in a boot. He was partial to every soldier who did his duty, but did not easily pardon those who were guilty of neglect; he looked after the soldiers' wants, willingly listened to anyone who had a just reason for complaint, and redressed every grievance without the slightest respect of persons. Old as he was, he still preferred service in the field to the veteran-service, although he frequently had been offered an appointment in a veteran-regiment.

Cleanliness, order, and decency, he prized above every thing. I will relate a few anecdotes which I myself witnessed.

He was very particular that every soldier should keep his hair cut close, and not unfrequently took off the schakos to see whether his orders were obeyed. Once, during an inspection of this kind, he came to a soldier who had very long hair in front; without farther ceremony, he laid down his stick, called for a knife, and cut off the whole of the hair. At this time he inspected no farther, but on the following day there was no long hair to be met with. His regulations were the same respecting whiskers; no one throughout the regiment was allowed to wear them lower than the tips of the ears. He reprimanded the officers publicly for their ignorance, and called them by their names, and told them before us all that he would not suffer the soldiers to be put to any inconvenience on their account. Owing to this, he was disliked by most of the officers; but the soldiers held him in high estimation. Upon falling from his horse, one day, during exercise, without however doing himself any harm, he expressed himself in the following words: "There are many of you who would, no doubt, have been glad if the old man had broken his neck; but take care, that if he leaves the regiment you will not be sorry for it."

He was a soldier in every respect, did every thing for himself; and as I was often his orderly, I have many times seen him sewing on buttons, mending stockings, &c.

Liars he could not bear. If any one once deceived him, he could never reckon upon his favour afterwards. He had a very strong memory, and knew every man in the battalion by name. He never excused a single iota of a soldier's punishment: if any one made use of entreaties, he always told him he had brought it on himself, and he must bear it. If he was told it was the first offence, "Well, then," said he, "the punishment must be severe, that you may be deterred from coming again."

Once, when we were in Messina, going out early in the morning to exercise, we came about five minutes too late to the Terra Nuova, our place of exercise; General D———, who expressed himself rather angrily about it, received from him the following answer:—"I beg your Excellency's pardon, but at Talavera de la Reyna I was not a moment too late, and on such occasions I was never the last."

The general was silent, and rode on. He, however, with the utmost indifference, ordered the battalion to shoulder arms, and fall into the line.

About this time an English expedition, under General Maitland, had been despatched to the east coast of Spain, and the troops cantoned in Sicily had been employed upon this service; in consequence of this, we were ordered to supply their place, but before our departure we celebrated, on the 4th day of June, the birthday of the King of England; a few weeks afterwards we were embarked on board some Dalmatian vessels. Our ships were lying close to a squadron of seven or eight Turkish vessels, and I thus had the pleasure of seeing some Turkish ships, after having seen in Malta those of almost every other nation. I had always imagined that every thing belonging to the Turks was quite different from any other nation; but I saw here that this was not the case, at least with their vessels, for they were built in a manner very similar to the English. The crews certainly were dressed in a very different manner; their turbans, caftans, and large wide trousers, presented a very singular contrast to the neat dress of the English sailors and marines. In going out, we by chance got entangled in the tackling of one of these ships; the Turks were not idle, for in an instant they cut the ropes of our Dalmatian in pieces, and the poor fellows were employed for half a day in putting every thing in order again.

At our departure the weather was. beautiful, a gentle breeze filled our sails, and we glided softly over the smooth surface of the water. Sicily lay before us, enveloped in mist, occasioned by the smoke of Etna. While one of my comrades and myself were eating our breakfast, which consisted of tea and biscuit, the sailors behind us called out suddenly, in bad Italian: "Get out of the way of the holy Michael;" but before I could look round, I received a blow on the back, which stretched me almost senseless on the deck; it was one of the sails, probably a god-child of this worthy saint, that had given me this blow, which I felt for some time afterwards.

The island of Malta began by degrees to recede; the coasts of Sicily began to draw near, and Mount Etna was already to be seen, with its snow-covered top reaching to the clouds. Malta always remained in sight like a small cloud upon the horizon; for in dear weather, such as we had, it is always to be seen from Sicily. Upon sailing a little farther, the continent of Italy began to rise out of the sea, and the high mountains of Calabria were plainly distinguishable. At last we directed our course straight upon the Sicilian coast, passed by Syracuse and Catania, in the channel of Messina; and on the evening of the second day of our voyage, on the 1st of July, 1812, ran into the harbour of that place. During our voyage along the coast we never lost sight of Mount Etna; for although it lies on one side of the island, it is, owing to its great height, to be seen all round. We could also plainly perceive that it was planted up to the region of snow with vines, olives, and chestnuts.

The next morning we were landed, and lodged in the English barracks, on the Terra Nuova, near Castelmare. We remained in these quarters only a few days, and the companies were then placed separately in different convents; these we found by no means unpleasant dwellings. The city of Messina is regularly built, and is completely intersected by two streets of considerable length, the Via Nuova and St. Ferdinand. The citizens are a good sort of people, compared with the other inhabitants of the island; but a well-meaning German must never trust an Italian: this lesson we were taught by a tragical occurrence, which took place a few days after our arrival. Some of our men had gone into a tavern, and were enjoying, in the fullness of their hearts, the excellent wine the country produces. Several Sicilian soldiers who were present were invited to join them at their table, and were treated with the best the landlord could produce.

Both parties relished the wine; they drank more and more, and became at last somewhat heated. It so happened, that some incautious words were made use of, and the anger of the Italians was excited against our countrymen; however, they combated the fury of the Italians so far, that nothing passed beyond words; unluckily some other Sicilians, who happened to come in, could not brook the expressions made use of, and in going out they fell upon two of the most intoxicated of our men, and stabbed them to the heart. They then made their escape so quickly, that they never could be discovered, although the strictest search was made after them. After this event we were more upon our guard, and a strict order was issued, prohibiting all intercourse with the Sicilian garrison.

Shortly after we left Malta, the plague made its appearance, and all connexion with the island was forbidden. Gibbets were erected at all the landing places in Sicily with ropes attached to them, to punish those who should attempt to evade the quarantine laws; but I never observed that recourse was had to this severe measure. We were in this respect the worst off, for the pay-master-general residing at Malta, we were unable to procure our pay, as was likewise the case with the troops in Spain, and in other quarters. Letters and other things, which at that time came from Malta, were pierced through, and fumigated with vinegar, before they were delivered to the owners. When the plague had ceased raging, we received our arrears of pay; nevertheless all the money was washed and fumigated before it was distributed to us.

In each company of the battalion there were at that time six riflemen, but an order arrived from England, that in future each battalion should have a rifle and a grenadier company. Upon putting this order into execution, the company to which I belonged was dissolved, and the rifle company formed out of it. As soon as this was done we were posted at the Faro Tower, where there were some strong batteries which we had to guard, and were lodged here in some large barracks, which take the name of Curcuraci, from a village so called, situated close by.

The time which I passed here I look upon as the happiest and most pleasant of my whole military career. We lived without care or trouble, and had ample opportunities of enjoying the beauties which were constantly before our eyes. In front of us we had a most delightful view of the channel of Messina, of Reggio and Scylla; the whole of Calabria lay before us; farther to the left we beheld Italy and the Island of Lipari; to the right was the valley of Messina, the harbour, and the stupendous Mount Etna, with its top covered with eternal snow. The channel was enlivened with vessels of all kinds, both for the purpose of trade and for the protection of the coasts; almost daily actions took place between the Scampavias[2] which came over from the Neapolitan coast, and endeavoured to land at different places, and the English vessels appointed to protect the coast of Sicily; in short, the prospect was so rich and varied that we were never weary of gazing on it. The surrounding vineyards were frequently visited by us, and figs and other delicious fruits were here in abundance. The sea afforded us as much fish as we could wish for, and the neighbouring villages most delightful wines. Every morning we went out walking, and enjoyed the splendid scenery; and one of our chief pleasures was at daybreak to behold the sun rising magnificently out of the sea. One morning, during one of these walks, I had an opportunity of seeing a water-spout; a vessel of war, cruising in the channel, fired several cannon-shots towards it, and ran into the harbour without sustaining any damage.

Sicily altogether pleased us uncommonly well, and I found everything I had read respecting the natural riches and fertility of this country fully confirmed. I also saw evident marks of the dreadful ravages caused by the earthquakes and eruptions of Mount Etna; whole streets in Messina were still in ruins; the finest palaces were destroyed, and the inhabitants, with whom we conversed upon these subjects, could never find words strong enough to describe the horrors of this earthquake. Near the sea, in particular, were heaps of ruins to be seen, which no one had

2. A Scampavia is a flat sort of boat with one mast, usually manned with from twelve to twenty men, and carries a single gun, from twelve to twenty-four pounders.

ever been at the pains to remove, and here everything remained just as it had fallen. I was often present when researches were made among the largest houses, and, half-decayed carcases were found, which were then taken away and buried.

After we had become sufficiently practised in our rifle exercise, we were reviewed, and then embarked at Messina to proceed to Palermo, where the second expedition, destined for Spain, was being collected. In passing the channel near the Faro, we were saluted by the French from the opposite forts of Scylla and Reggio with a few cannon-shots, which, however, did us no farther mischief than damaging our rigging and main-mast, which was speedily repaired. We had scarcely cleared the channel when the wind dropped, and we remained becalmed the whole of the night. During the night a grenadier belonging to a regiment which was embarked with us fell overboard, and in spite of our utmost endeavours we were unable to save him. Towards morning a cool breeze sprung up, which carried us gently past the promontory of Milazzo to Palermo. Immediately upon our arrival, we were incorporated in a battalion, consisting of five companies of riflemen, taken from various regiments.

The inhabitants of Palermo differ considerably from the rest of the Sicilians, but by no means to their advantage. It seems, rather, as if the scum of all Sicily was collected here; not a week passed without the occurrence of assassinations, not to mention the robberies committed in the streets and houses; and it very seldom happened that the criminals were discovered and brought to justice. During the fifteen days we remained here, several persons were murdered, but in no one instance was the perpetrator discovered. Beggars may be seen in every corner, either half or wholly naked, suffering under the most disgusting complaints, or covered with loathsome sores, often occasioned by art. These they exhibit to every passenger, and roar out, for I can give their horrid cries no other name, for alms, in the name of God and the Virgin Mary.

A Swiss, who had been twenty-five years in the Sicilian service, told me once that many of these beggars were far from poor, but, on the contrary, possessed of property; that once one of these wretches had been found dead in the street, and upon examination it was found that he had upwards of two hundred *ounces* (the *ounce* is more than three dollars) concealed about him. This story appears to me incredible, or that time the natives of Palermo must have been much more charitable and generous than. they were during the time I was there, for I have often enough taken notice of the beggars and their benefactors, but always remarked that they received but a trifle; a *grano*, or at most a *bajocco*, was the usual coin, and the greater part of the passersby gave nothing but the pious wish—"God help you." Besides these beggars, there is an idle and lazy race of men in Palermo, whose numbers it is difficult to estimate, as they have no home or settled place of abode; sleeping one night with a stone for a pillow, and an old rag for a covering, in a church; the next night perhaps under a shed, and the following, in a boat on the beach; and in this manner they wander about every day.

The police give themselves no trouble about them. Should any one be taken up for a crime, he endeavours to save himself directly by running to the sanctuary of a church,[3] when the populace immediately interfere to save him from justice. These men are called *Lazzaroni*. Their manner of living is very simple: they sleep the greatest part of the day, and never think of earning any thing until driven by the utmost necessity. They then go down to the harbour, and work for half an hour, unless a lucky opportunity should present itself for gaining a trifle by a *coup d'industrie*. At the harbour, they earn a few *taris*, upon which they can very comfortably subsist for a day; if they are frugal this will even suffice for two days. Three *grani's* worth of bread, some offal broiled upon coals, and a glass of wine, at three *grani* the pint, is a sumptuous meal for them. When they have filled their stomach with this, they lie down in the first sunny place they come to, and sleep away the time until again awakened by hunger.

The Sicilians, generally speaking, live very temperately, in the

---

3. The rights of these churches formerly extended so far, that if the criminal could only reach the shadow, no civil power could arrest him.

midst of the abundance furnished by the fertility of their country; and I have very seldom seen drunken persons among them. This is a most fortunate thing; for, as in their sober senses, they are passionate and revengeful enough, what would they be if they were given to drinking, and their hot blood was still more inflamed by their fiery wine. However, I will now proceed with my narrative, as I shall have an opportunity, in giving an account of my second stay in Palermo, to allude again to these people.

After fifteen days' stay, we were embarked, six thousand in number, and shortly set sail. We saw Sicily for a long while behind us, having but a very light breeze, which impelled us towards Spain. However, at last we lost sight of Sicily, the Lipari Islands, and the Continent, passed the channel of St. Bonifacio, ran into the harbour of Minorca, where we remained a short time; and then, after a voyage of fifteen days, cast anchor in the roads of Alicant, the place of our destination. I was now once more upon the coast of Spain, but in better circumstances than when I left it. At that time I was starving and in rags; now I was well clothed and fed. At that time, I was among the oppressors of the people; now I belonged to an army appointed to deliver Spain from a foreign yoke.

Alicant, which is not a large, but a populous city, lies close to the sea, and has no harbour, but only open roads, where vessels cannot lie in perfect safety, and in stormy weather are in danger of being wrecked on the coast; small vessels, which can run up to the town, lie tolerably secure at the mole; but ships of war, owing to the shallow water, cannot come in so far.

At the time we were there, the place was remarkably lively, owing to the presence of the English troops. It is very well fortified, and the works were in excellent order. To the north of the town, upon a rock, is the fort of Santa Barbara, existing since the time of the Moors, and built quite in the ancient style. The casemates for the garrison resemble prisons much more than places of residence for free men. The water which they have is cistern-water, which at the time I was here was filled with worms. Spring-water is altogether very scared in the neighbourhood of Alicant, and that which is procured from the aqueduct is scarcely fit for use, hardly good enough for washing. The fortifications of the city are closely connected with the fort of Santa Barbara, and there is a communication between them. On the east side, the fort is close to the sea, and its guns command nearly the whole of the roads. Towards the south, it commands the city; and to the westward, in conjunction with a newly-built fort, it covers the main road leading to the city.

Another fort was at that time being built, and the French prisoners were employed upon the works; they received six *reals* daily pay, and were not very badly off. The houses outside of the town had nearly all been pulled down, in case of a siege, which was anticipated.

The valley of Alicant, where the so well-known Alicant wine is produced, is several miles in extent, and is almost entirely planted with vines. The numerous detached houses scattered about, give them almost the appearance of gardens. The village of St. Vincent, about three miles off, was, before our arrival, sometimes occupied by the English, and sometimes by the French, and not unfrequently the scene of bloody reconnoitres.

CHAPTER 8

The Campaign Against Suchet

We were quickly disembarked, and the same evening detached to the outposts, the French being only about ten miles from Meant, and their cavalry made frequent visits to the neighbourhood. We were first of all quartered about two miles and a half from the city, in detached houses. I, with eighteen men, was lodged with *Señor* Pasqual. The poor man, who wore a pair of breeches which had served already eight-and-forty years, and had yet more service to perform, did not manifest the slightest joy at the honour his house experienced; he clasped his hands together above his head, when he saw us coming in. However; he soon formed a better opinion of us, upon seeing our bags filled with provisions, which we had saved from the abundant rations furnished us on board the ship. We invited him to partake of our fare, and gave him some English rum to taste; he soon began to get lively, and called out "*Vivan los Ingleses*," and said we were *buena gente*.

He also endeavoured to show his gratitude towards us, and during our stay, furnished us with the best *tabago negro* at a very moderate price: we paid for the pound four *reals*, although in Alicant the same quantity cost two *duros*.[1] He was a smuggler,

---

1. In the largest cities in Spain, there are never more than two or three shops for the sale of tobacco to be met with. These are usually distinguished by a sign, and the inscription, "*Real Estango*;" those only being allowed to sell tobacco who are in possession of Royal Monopoly. A soldier in a Spanish Swiss regiment, a Prussian by birth, who was taken prisoner at the battle

and paid to his friends the smugglers, who landed secretly on the coast, two *duros* for the *aroba* (twenty-five pounds) no doubt, had his occupation been known, he would have been compelled to visit the galleys with us, he said, he was perfectly safe, for that we were soldiers, and consequently persons who willingly bought cheap, and sometimes even forgot to pay.

During the day we were in our quarters, but at night we were assembled at the captain's, where the whole company slept in a stable, in order to be together in case of being surprised by the French. One morning they did make an attack upon our advanced posts, which immediately retreated to the main body: the Frenchmen advanced, but we received them so warmly with our rifles that we made them halt, they having expected to surprise us. A venturesome trumpeter, who approached too near, was dismounted by a well-aimed shot; many others were killed, and a few prisoners were made, without our having even a single man wounded: this was not much to be wondered at, as the French troops consisted of cavalry, and we riflemen were hid in the vineyards, or protected by the olive-trees, and shot at them without their being able to approach us. Upon perceiving that their undertaking was useless, they withdrew, and did not again repeat their visit.

Shortly after, a part of the army was moved forward; some in the direction of Xixona, others towards Monte Forte, and we on the road to Tibi, In Tibi we entrenched ourselves very strongly, and remained full six weeks in the face of the enemy's army, without any thing taking place. Once only an alarm was given, owing to a certain Lieutenant Freitag, who being at one of the picquets, took a drove of oxen, escorted by two English dragoons, for the enemy's cavalry. We were quickly assembled at the point of rendezvous, but soon found out what sort of an enemy it was; the officer received a reprimand, and was for a long time an object of ridicule.

---

of Jena, and sent to France, had entered the Spanish service, owing to the flattering representation of the persons employed to recruit; among other things, he had been told that for a single *quarto*, tobacco and pipes were to be had in Spain, because for that sum one may obtain three paper cigars, weighing altogether not the sixtieth part of an ounce.

I was quartered, with five others, upon a barber, or rather letter of blood, as he was called Sangrero; soon after I was appointed permanent orderly to the adjutant, and was lodged at his quarters, also with a barber, who was at the same time church beadle; and notwithstanding both him and his wife had nearly lost their sight, he regularly performed the duties of both employments. On Sunday morning early all the congregation assembled at his house, seated themselves upon a bench, where he lathered, and his assistant shaved them. I often took up a razor and assisted, and thus proved to him that I was not inexperienced in his art. He expressed himself very thankful for this: at breakfast I got a glass of *aqua-riente,* and he every day treated me with wine. His wife was very stingy, and did not at all approve, of her husband's generosity; she blamed him so often for this, that he at last hit upon a scheme which answered very well—he gave me money secretly; with this I bought wine, and treated him in my name, and this satisfied his wife perfectly.

I will here relate a trick I played this old man, which, though not strictly justifiable, does not, I think, deserve much blame. It became, perhaps, rather annoying to him, not to be able to drink his wine, alone, for as I bought it for him with his own money, I, as a matter of right, helped him to drink it; and he once endeavoured to cheat me. One evening, as I was sitting quietly in the kitchen, by the fire side, I heard the old fellow coming up the steps; he muttered at first a few words to himself, and then called out aloud, "Pedro:" (this was the, name I gave myself in Spain, as it was much liked; I also observed all the ceremonies of the Catholic religion, in order not to be taken for a heretic.) I saw that he had got something under his cloak, and suspecting what it was, I remained silent and kept myself quite still, in order to see what would take place. He called out again, but I was still silent: upon this, he came into the kitchen, and began to feel about every where to find out if any one was there. I crept about from one place to another, without his being at all aware of my presence. At last he came to the seat I usually occupied, felt it, and said: "Hum! it is still warm, somebody must have been sitting here."

Upon this, he began to call "Pedro," till the kitchen echoed again. I still made no answer, and by this time had discovered that he had got a large flask of wine. He then went grumbling up stairs; I listened where he went, and while he was coming slowly down again, I slipped out of the kitchen, down the steps, and then came singing up again. As soon as he heard me, he called out, "Hallo, Pedro!"

"What's the matter?"

"Where have you been, you rascal?"

"Among my comrades; what news have you got, that you call out so lustily, are the French coming?"

"Oh! Heaven defend us from that, my lad!"

After he had convinced himself, by a number of questions, that I had not been in the house, he became quiet, and went into his room. Soon after he went out to the church, where the *Ave Maria* was being said. During his absence I crept upstairs, and soon found out the flask hidden up in a corner; I tasted the contents, and found it excellent. I took my prize with me, went downstairs, and filled my canteen, (this, which holds about two quarts, together with a haversack, every English soldier is furnished with) and then hid the bottle with the remainder. I then went very quietly into the kitchen with my canteen, and seated myself by the fire; soon after, the old man came back from church, and I called out to him: "*Bona noche, Cavallero!*"

"*Gratias, Señor Millitar.*"

"Will you drink a little?"

"What have you got?"

"An excellent glass of Don Francisco's best." This was a wine-merchant who lived at the farther end of the town.

The old fellow tasted, and found the wine excellent. We emptied the canteen together, and were very merry. The next day, having been out with the adjutant to visit the advanced posts, he saluted me, on my return, with a volley of Spanish curses of all kinds; such as "curse your soul, your body, your eyes; you are all rascals alike," and so on. Upon this, I became apprehensive that I was discovered, but waited patiently to see how the thing would end, and was soon convinced that he was aware of nothing but the theft. There was quartered in his house, besides me, the adjutant, a sergeant-major, and a Spanish dragoon of the regiment of Olivenza. This last was a native of the province of La Mancha; the old man generally called him "Mancheco," and could not bear him, because he always sold half the corn and straw he received as forage for his horse; on this account he suspected him of the theft.

To me, however, he said very candidly: "Only think, Pedro, they have stolen a flask of wine from me, which I brought home yesterday; and yet there was nobody in the house, for I hunted and felt about everywhere. I almost bit my tongue in half to prevent myself from laughing. In the evening I filled my canteen again, and came into the kitchen, and invited him to partake of it, so that he did not lose all his wine. He praised the wine very much, and said over and over again that it was the sort which he had had in his bottle, for that he had got his from Don Francisco. Upon our departure from Tibi I could conceal it no longer, but told the old man that I had been the thief. He said: "Go along, I forgive you, for you have always been a good lad, and conducted yourself well in my house; but if I had known it at the time, you should have had a taste of my knife."

Upon his wife too, I passed many jokes: among other things, she asked me one day why some of the soldiers wives in our battalion wore white, and others black stockings. I told her very seriously that this had a meaning; the wives who were really married, wore the white stockings, and those who only passed for such, wore black.

During our stay here, the battalion was frequently exercised in shooting at a mark, in order to make us more skilful as riflemen. As we were one day occupied in this manner, the adjutant came riding by, who had orders to take to the different companies, and stopped to look on. Our captain, who was a brave officer, but fond of a joke, and a most excellent marksman, invited the adjutant, who gave himself out for an excellent shot, to shoot with him for a wager. He refused for a long time; but the captain pressed him so much that he at last consented, and the trial took place. The captain fired first, and shot very well. The adjutant next presented, and fired; but the ball flew wide of the mark and scarcely five paces distant from the soldier, who, during the first firing, was placed behind an almond-tree, to mark the shots on the target. The soldier, alarmed at the ball, put his head out from behind the tree; and, to prevent any more such skilful marksmen from taking aim at him, called out, thinking it was one of the riflemen who had fired: "You ox! there is no target here." All burst out into a loud fit of laughter; and the adjutant leaped upon his horse and galloped away from the place where he had so well proved his skill as a marksman.

In addition to our battalion, there was also here the second battalion of the 27th Regiment of the line; a detachment of the 20th Light Dragoons: a battery of mountain guns;[2] and a corps of Calabrians. These last the Spaniards liked better than us, as they were good Catholics, although the greatest scoundrels in the universe: but they went twice a week to mass, and we were heretics; and, of course, according to our landlord's opinion, must be inferior to good Christians, even if, as these Calabrians did, they cheated and robbed them everyday.

The inhabitants here had never had an opportunity of witnessing an English military punishment; and the flogging of an artillery-man made a considerable impression upon them: they cut down the fig-tree to which he had been tied, and even grubbed up the roots; and abused the King and the officers for allowing such barbarous punishments. The criminal received all sorts of presents from them, was much pitied, and, as long as he was suffering under the effects of his punishment, was allowed to want for nothing. The flogging certainly is a tremendous

---

2. These guns, in general, are not half the size of the usual field-pieces; so that to each piece, and the necessary ammunition, only three mules are required. One (usually the strongest) carries the gun; the other the carriage; and the third, the ammunition. They fire balls of three or four pounds weight; and as they are formed something like a howitzer, they carry quite as far as the field-pieces, although much shorter. Two strong men can place one of these guns, without much trouble, upon a mule's back.

punishment; the delinquent is stripped to the waist, tied up, and flogged with a whip having nine lashes, with three knots in each; so that each cut makes twenty-seven wounds; and if the capital sentence is awarded upon him, he receives nine hundred and ninety-nine of these stripes: and at every twenty-five strokes, the drummer who performs the sentence is changed. This punishment occurs very frequently in the English army; drunkenness and other acts of insubordination being often punished with from one to two hundred lashes.

The Spaniards did not at all dislike furnishing quarters to the English, as they circulated a good deal of money. The French, on the contrary, who had been here before, took every thing, and paid for nothing. With us it was quite the contrary: we paid for every thing, and took away nothing; and they were very sorry when we left them.

We were once called up in the middle of the night, and ordered to assemble ourselves without noise, as it was proposed to surprise the French, who were in the village of Ibi, about a league from Tibi. We marched out, and about four in the morning reached Ibi;—but we found the nest empty, and the birds flown. The French had collected contributions of all kinds, and about an hour before our arrival, had retreated to Alcoy. We went in pursuit, but could not get a sight of them, until arriving very near Alcoy, we penetrated through some underwood, and found them posted in a valley, ending in a narrow pass. Their position was so good, that we had no inclination to force it: we rather waited patiently tor an attack from them. Our cavalry made several movements, as if about to advance; but these were only feints, in order, if possible, to draw the enemy out; but they .never moved from their position. After waiting a good while, until we were quite impatient at the delay, our artillery fired a few shots, and we then returned to Ibi. It was high time also for our hungry stomachs; for we had been obliged to break up in the night, without being able to take the least thing with us: during the whole day we had been manoeuvring, and had no time to think about eating and drinking.

The quarter-master and two men from each company (I among the number,) were sent forward to Ibi to provide quarters.

Along the whole of the road we were accosted by peasants, who annoyed us with a thousand questions about how many Frenchmen we had killed; and we answered them all according to their wishes, in order to satisfy them, without any particular regard to truth. On approaching Ibi, we were received with shouts and huzzas; old and young came out to meet us; and here we were absolutely overwhelmed with questions. We were requested by everyone to give them a minute account of our meeting with the enemy; until at last tired out, we hastened to the *alcalde*, where the quarter-master explained his business, and proceeded immediately to arrange the quarters. This gave us very little trouble: we wrote merely on the doors of the houses how many men each occupier should receive, and the thing was done. I now went in search of my lodging, which I considered to be the best in the place. I had not chosen amiss, but had fixed upon a house where I was very hospitably received. But here the questions began again: they would insist upon knowing how many Frenchmen we had killed. In order to get a little rest we quieted them, as we had done the others, mixing up truth and lies together. The wine which they placed before us was excellent; but we did not dare to take much of it, as we had eaten nothing, and were therefore fearful of becoming intoxicated.

Just as we were sitting down to a comfortable meal, the bugle blew; an alarm, and we found that counter-orders had arrived; that the troops should merely take some refreshment, and then return to their old quarters. The necessary arrangements were immediately made; bread was procured from all the houses, and packed upon mules; and, together with the wine, which the people willingly presented us with, was carried to the place where the troops were halted. Here also the Spaniards brought wine in abundance, and gave it to whoever would drink it; so that many were almost drunk, and the whole corps in such a joyous state, that, if the French had advanced upon us just then, they would have found a merry enemy: however, they kept away, and after two hours rest we returned to our quarters. On arrival at Tibi we were pestered with the same questions we had already been obliged to listen to so often, and our hosts were considerably displeased, that we had brought neither prisoners nor booty back with us. At this time deserters came in daily, who described the situation of. the French very differently; but never estimated the amount of their force too low; and added to this, that every day fresh troops were coming in from France.

At last we left this place, and occupied Ibi, Alcoy, and Baneros; the two latter places the French had just left, and retreated to San Felipe. We, together with a grenadier brigade, were posted at Unil, and our advanced posts reached to Biar and Baneros. I was quartered upon a wine-merchant, who supplied us plentifully with this liquor, and was altogether a good sort of man. His son was a spy; he showed me at least twenty passports, made out by different officers in the English and French armies. The old man had a considerable store of gunpowder, consisting of more than two thousand cartridges; these, during the stay of the French here, he had concealed underneath the roof of his house. He also possessed a *trabuko*, or *Musquetoon*,[3] which is much used in Spain, and in riding is fastened to the saddle. He was also provided with knives, daggers, and weapons of all sorts, which he had managed to conceal from the researches of the French. This man was of a peculiarly active and restless disposition, although considerably advanced in years; he was a bitter enemy to the French; even the word Frenchman was sufficient to put him in a rage, which he accompanied with a sort of pantomimic action, as if he had his deadly enemy under his knife.

Here the French once again endeavoured to surprise us, and at first succeeded. During the night they drove in our out-posts, and fell upon us all at once, before we were in the least aware of any attack. At first we were in such disorder, that they succeeded in gaining a slight advantage, but we soon collected, and under

---

3. This weapon is very generally used by the smugglers, and may be loaded with several balls.

the skilful direction of Sir William Bentinck, made a determined opposition. The second battalion of the 27th Regiment of the line, in particular, performed wonders; they charged three times with fixed bayonets into the enemy's ranks, and at last succeeded in driving them back.

Upon the failure of this attempt, the French retreated still farther, probably induced to this by the bad success of their army in the west, and gave up to us all the towns and villages as far as Valencia; they even quitted San Felipe, a fortified place, and Valencia. I searched in the neighbourhood of Valencia for the traces of my first campaign, which I had made in the French service, but in vain; all had passed away: high grass had long been growing over the graves of the fallen warriors, and over some the ploughshare of the farmer had drawn its furrows; even the bones of the horses and asses, shot at that time, some thousands in number, were no where to be seen; so quickly does time blot out all traces of the mightiest armies. When I considered what countries I had passed through, and what I had suffered since that time, I could not repress an anxious feeling for the future, and a wish for repose; this, however, was not to be thought of, for the flames of war had burst out anew, and the track of the French army, which we were following, was marked out by plundered towns and smoking villages—the usual accompaniments of a retreating force.

Tarragona and Tortosa, two important fortresses, were both still in possession of the French, and the garrisons had been reinforced before the retreat of the army. Suchet, the commander of the French forces, still retreated, and was followed by our general, Murray. Tarragona was besieged: the ships of war provided heavy artillery, and the place was bombarded by land and sea. The advanced guard of our corps, in which I was, was stationed about ten miles in advance; it was a small but brave band, of about four thousand men, consisting of a battalion of riflemen; the Calabrian corps, the 27th Regiment of the line, four squadrons of Brunswick hussars, as many of English dragoons, and some artillery. In the middle of the night we were attacked in a defile by General Suchet, with thirteen thousand men, a force treble the amount of our's.

We defended ourselves for a long time with the utmost bravery, and not without effect; but our brave commander losing his arm by a shot, the command devolved upon the colonel of the Calabrians. The fortune of war then took a different turn, and we fell into disorder. The French pressed forward and outflanked us, and we had no resource left but in flight, if we did not wish to be cut down or made prisoners. We fell back in the utmost haste. Luckily the night favoured our retreat, for the few cavalry we had with us was not sufficient to cover it. We reached the besieging force of Tarragona; and as a strong column of the French army followed the troops we had been fighting with, we were compelled to raise the siege: the troops were embarked with the utmost celerity, without the loss of either artillery or baggage. Upon landing a second time at Alicant, we learned that the army under Wellington had been acting against the French with much greater effect. This compelled the French army again to withdraw, and we once more advanced in the same direction as before. We now received orders to return again to our regiments, and we embarked near Tarragona (which was not yet in our possession) for Sicily, on board a cavalry transport, which had brought Brunswick hussars from Ireland to Spain.

Our voyage on board this cavalry transport was not the most agreeable; we were so closely quartered, that we laid over one another like herrings; in the hold were some artillery horses, which made it very disagreeable to those who could not bear the smell. These poor animals are certainly in a worse condition than men on board a ship. In shipping and unshipping they suffer a good deal; horses also which are embarked for the first time, frequently become wild, and occasionally fall into the water.

In shipping and unshipping them, the following method is practised:—a strong girth is fastened round the body; they are then raised up by means of a crane, in such a manner that they always preserve their balance, and are gently lowered into the vessel. During this operation the horse kicks without intermission until he is lowered, into the hold; here they are during rough weather suspended in the same way. Those who have made several voyages become accustomed to this operation, and bear it all patiently, with the exception of some few, who never take it quietly. During the whole voyage they are not suffered to lie down, because, owing to standing so long, they become so stiff that they would not be able to get up again. Every night they are suspended in their girths, by which means they can rest and sleep a little. During bad weather these animals suffer like men, from a sort of sea-sickness; they eat nothing, hang down their heads, and evince their uneasiness by continual snorting. They well know when they are about to be released from their torment, and never move when they perceive that they are to be disembarked.

Besides us, there were on board some soldiers of the train, to whom the horses belonged, and some artillery-men of the Italian Legion. Almost all these men had either a lawful or a temporary wife: quarrels and tumults were incessant among these people, for the women, being allowed only half rations, claimed from their husbands or lovers, at least a quarter of theirs. This occasioned reproaches on both sides, which were not seldom followed by blows. Nothing was to be had on board for money, excepting what any man could spare from his rations, and we were embarked so suddenly, that no-one had time to provide himself with a stock of provisions. Our vessel was in a very bad condition, old and out of repair, had several leaks, and in addition to this, the captain was a drunkard of the first class. He drank every day two or three bottles of rum, and troubled himself neither about his crew or his ship. He put his head out of his cabin at most twice a-day, asked what sort of weather it was? at what rate we were going? and so on, and then crept in again. Through this inattention, the sailors were so disorderly that they did just what they pleased, and often paid no attention whatever to the orders of the mate, who, luckily for us, was a clever active fellow. However, he taught them a little manners with his rope's end, and he was the more encouraged in this from knowing that he could rely upon our assistance, else the sailors, from their superiority in numbers, might have gained the upper hand.

Contrary winds detained us nearly a week upon the coasts of the Balearic Islands; the weather was bad, and we sailed so slowly, that the *Leyden*[4] would have taken us in tow; but in spite of the utmost endeavours, the long-boat was unable to get a rope to us, and after four hours' labour, was obliged to return to the ship. We were in much anxiety, for if our ship had struck against any thing, we should all have been lost, for she was as badly manned as commanded. But Providence watched over us, and saved us from this danger, and in ten days we arrived safely in the port of Mahon, in the island of Minorca. Upon our arrival, a naval officer came immediately on board and inspected the condition of our ship, reported the captain as unfit to command, took the most mutinous of the sailors into custody, and sent us a naval officer to take the command of the vessel until her arrival at the place of destination, and also some sailors. While the vessel was being repaired, I was fortunate enough to get on shore for an hour. I was surprised to see the difference in the appearance of these islanders from the Spaniards. Comfort was visible everywhere, and everything more resembled an English than a Spanish colony: the houses were all neat both inside and out, the inhabitants clean and well dressed, the taverns in the best order, so that I half thought myself once more in my native country. All this, however, may perhaps be ascribed to the English ships of war stationed here, the crews of which spent a great deal of money.

For the neatness and cleanliness in the taverns, the landlords, to be sure, charged rather high. I, and one of my comrades, had a bottle of wine and something to eat in one of them, and for this we were charged a Spanish dollar, although the wine here does not cost more than a *real* the bottle. However, I did not regret my dollar, for I was rejoiced once again to be able to make a meal in a comfortable manner, after having been so long deprived of

---

4. The same which took us as recruits from Portugal to England.

this pleasure. When we went away, I took the loaf which had been placed before us, weighing about four pounds, with me. Upon coming out, I met a Spanish soldier accompanied by a woman; he spoke to me in German, and it turned out that he was a native of the same town as myself, and the woman from a place about ten miles distant. In my joy at this meeting, having nothing else at the moment to offer, I made him a present of the loaf I had brought out.

The harbour of Mahon more resembles a large river than a harbour, as it reaches nearly three miles into the interior of the island. In the background, close to the harbour, is the city of Mahon. The entrance to the harbour is very narrow, and well defended by batteries. In the centre of the harbour are several small islands, upon which are buildings of various descriptions—such as the naval hospital, magazines for stores, the arsenal, and in some of them French prisoners were kept. The inhabitants much resemble the natives of the provinces of Valencia and Catalonia, but their complexions are of a deeper brown.

Upon going again to sea, we did not find that our ship sailed any better; but we were no longer under any apprehensions of being wrecked by a drunken captain, and in a few days reached the coast of Sicily. The captain of the man of war which conveyed us, thought that we had now no farther need of the officer who had taken the command of the ship from Mahon, as we had scarcely fifty miles to sail. He, therefore, recalled him, and we proceeded.

Our present captain was unacquainted with the coast, and perhaps knew very little about navigation; for as soon as we had lost sight of the vessel before us, he was more at a loss than we were, for each of us, from our former voyages, were pretty well acquainted with the coast from Trapani to Palermo. In spite of all our representations, he would have his own way. and steered right upon the coast, under the impression that Palermo was situated in that direction. At last we compelled him by force to lay the ship before the wind, and a boat was sent off with one of our officers to obtain some information from the fishermen who were cruising about. The officer soon came back, and brought a fisherman with him, who offered for two *scudi* to conduct the ship to Palermo. The captain, an avaricious fellow, refused to give so much; but our officers interfered, and gave the man a *scudi* more than he had demanded, in order to get released from this unlucky vessel. The wind began to sink, and it took us the whole day and following night to get off the harbour of Palermo.

At last we reached the entrance, close under Monte Pelegrino, upon which there stands a chapel with a miraculous image of St. Rosalia, the tutelar saint of the city of Palermo. Here the wind all at once died away, and we advanced no farther than we were impelled by the waves. This calm lasted several hours; the wind then rose again, and the captain, who did not choose to trust to the fisherman, gave orders to put out to sea. It being very dark, we were all upon our guard, and no one left the deck, for the careless captain might easily have run us upon one of the numerous rocks, which make the navigation here very unsafe. About midnight we tacked, and steered right in for the harbour, which we entered about ten o'clock in the morning, and cast anchor in front of the mole.

During this voyage, I witnessed another example of coolness in a soldier, which is worthy of being recorded. This soldier, named Consilla, was sitting on the ship's side, cleaning his accoutrements, when by an accidental movement, he lost his balance and fell overboard. The ship's sails were put back immediately, but the vessel was, notwithstanding, impelled forward by the wind, and had reached a considerable distance before the boat could proceed to his assistance. We saw him contending with the waves, and as he was a very good swimmer, he soon reached the boat, which brought him on board again. When he got upon deck, the captain asked him how he felt when floating in the sea? "Oh," replied he, "I could have kept it up for half an hour longer."

A small flask of rum was given him to recover himself, he drank it off, and throwing himself down, said, "after this exercise, I must take a little sleep."

By means of the man of war which arrived before us, the

battalion had received intelligence of our return, and upon our making our appearance in the harbour, our comrades came off in boats to welcome us. Many sought in vain for an old comrade, for several had fallen in Spain, and were gone to the land from whence there is no return. The lost were lamented, and the living heartily welcomed; and for the moment, we had nothing to do but to relate our mutual adventures. We had suffered much in Spain, and they, during our absence, had lost several men by assassination, without the perpetrators ever being discovered. On the same day we were disembarked, and joined our battalion in their quarters at Noviziata. We were allowed three days' liberty to get everything in order, and to refresh ourselves. We made use of this time to celebrate our return from Spain, in the wine-houses of Palermo, where we had many a carouse.

Shortly after our return, news was brought that the French were completely defeated, and soon after, the treaty of peace concluded at Paris was made known. This news re-animated our hopes of a return to our native land, as we were only engaged to serve during the war; but under different pretences our discharge was refused, and we were obliged to remain. The black Brunswick Hussars now came to Sicily, where they were known, by the name of "*Reggimenio del morte*," owing to their wearing deaths' heads on their accoutrements and horse furniture. They were not distinguished by orderly behaviour; on the contrary, by committing excesses of all kinds, they so much enraged the people against them, that they were one day besieged in their barracks by the populace: the Sicilian military hastened to the spot, and had some difficulty in dispersing the enraged mob. It was very easy to cause an assemblage among this mass of idle people. As soon as only a few were collected together, the thieves hastened from all quarters to see what was going on, and to make the best use they could of the disturbance. I advise every stranger in this country to keep clear of quarrels; for owing to the general feeling against foreigners, he is sure to get the worst, and if he even escapes public revenge, he has constantly assassination to fear.

Among the troops lying here, I found out by degrees a number of my countrymen, several even from my native town; one of them is now living with me in Weimar, and can testify the truth of my assertions at any time.

The life we now led was the most unvaried of my whole military career, and its sameness almost wearied us to death. With the exception of exercising, mounting guard, and escorting the priests in their processions, we had nothing to do; and every soldier, accustomed to war, will dislike this manner of living, if it lasts long, quite as much as we did.

The priests, as we were not Catholics, thought that we were honoured by being suffered to attend upon their saints. We, however, troubled ourselves about nothing but the compensation we received for attending these processions, for what do soldiers care about saints?

The English were particularly anxious to retain the good opinion of the clergy and the nation, for they not only readily granted whatever number of men were required to attend these processions, but. every sentry was also obliged to present arms when. these saints were carried past: this annoyed us a good deal, as it frequently occurred several times in the course of the day.

Saint Francisco de Paolo, who was the patron of the convent in which we were quartered, and especially worshipped by sailors and fishermen, and who had performed I know not what miracles, if the pictures are to be believed which hang up in the church, was annually brought out from his residence in the convent known by his name, and carried in procession to the cathedral, where he remained a short time, and was then carried back with much pomp, amidst the "*Vivas*" of the assembled multitude. During the advance and return of the procession, a quantity of fine fireworks were let off, and festivities of all kinds took place.

We were also told that the eyes consisted of two valuable diamonds, worth thirty thousand *scudi*. This *si non e vero, e ben trovato*. The ringing of bells during the whole day was incessant, and we were sometimes nearly stunned by the noise. In the passion-week alone every thing was quiet, and the usual expression was: "The bells are gone to Rome." At that time the inhabitants were reminded of the hours of mass, by rattles similar to those of our watchmen. On the first day of Easter the old trade began again, and continued without any farther intermission.

That the vows of chastity, made by those devoted to religious services, are not very strictly observed, the following occurrence, related to me by a person deserving of credit, may evince:

A soldier belonging to a Swiss regiment, having strolled into the garden of a nunnery, remained there too late; and upon wishing to come out again, found the gates closed. The walls being high, there were no means of getting out, and he began to bawl aloud, but no one appeared to set him at liberty. Tired out at last, he laid down upon a bench, and fell asleep, and did not awake until aroused by some one shaking him. He opened his eyes with astonishment, upon seeing a veiled female before him, who beckoned him to follow. He got up, and followed her without suspicion into the convent, where, at first, he found himself very comfortable; but at last, tired of the business, he begged for his discharge, which was absolutely refused. In this manner he was imprisoned for several days, without hopes of escape, being confined on the side of the convent looking into the garden, and not into the street.

At last he found an opportunity of making himself remarked by a sentinel, posted on the other side of the convent. The soldier at first was astonished, and quite surprised to behold such a wolf among the lambs, but went and told it to the commandant, who inquired into the circumstance, it was discovered that a soldier was missing from the regiment, whom, from his character for steadiness, it was considered impossible should have deserted; it was, therefore, immediately conjectured that this might be the man. On the following day an inquiry was secretly made at the convent, and the bird was found in the cage, sighing for liberty, and joyful he was to find himself released.

A great number of the inhabitants of Palermo occupy themselves with gardening, and I often took the opportunity of observing their methods, which I found much more simple, and less laborious, than our own.

All sorts of garden-plants thrive here, and grow with such celerity, that three and sometimes four crops are raised from the same ground. The manure they chiefly collect from the streets, carrying it away in baskets, loaded upon asses. They draw the ground very much, by the constant watering they give to the plants; this, owing to the great heat in the summer months, they can very well bear, and it causes them to grow incredibly fast.

Their method of watering, too, is very simple. It may be remarked, that water is very plentiful in the valley in which Palermo is situated; and the city is not only so abundantly supplied, that almost every house has one or more wells, but also all the gardens around are provided with them. The water is usually drawn up by means of an ass, and conducted to a sort of basin, placed in a part of the garden most exposed to the sun. This is always done either in the evening, or at midday, in order that the water, if drawn at noon, may remain till evening; or, if drawn in the evening, remain till the following noon, in order to become warm; for if conducted at once to the plants, it would, owing to its coldness, do. more harm than good. When it has become sufficiently heated, it is let out of the basin, and conducted by means of small furrows, in whatever direction it may be required.

The cactus, or prickly pear, and the black fig, are here in abundance; the former is used for hedges, and its fruit is excellent. The bread-fruit-tree, and all southern fruits are found here; but the northern fruits do not thrive so well as with us; and potatoes were wanting, certainly not altogether, but they were too dear for us often to taste them. This want was supplied by macaroni; but having once witnessed the manufacture, which, at least where I saw it, was not of the cleanest description, I took such a dislike to this preparation, that it was with the utmost difficulty I could ever be persuaded to taste it.

Among the idlers and unnecessary consumers of provisions may be reckoned the innumerable quantities of dogs, wandering about without owners, and which readily make themselves at home wherever they can find any thing to eat. We being now abundantly supplied with every thing, and meat in particular, (each man being allowed a pound per day) a number of these dogs collected about us, many perhaps having masters, but only a scanty allowance of food, in order to assist in the consumption of our superfluity. I can assert, with truth, that by degrees a band of forty or fifty collected at the quarters of our regiment, who kept excellent order among themselves, but treated all newcomers very roughly, until they became accustomed to them. It was also just the same with the other regiments.

Among the number, two dogs of the wolf breed were particularly distinguished. They would take nothing but what was given them by the soldiers of the regiment, and were most deadly enemies to the cats of the convent, whom they persecuted in every possible way. One day these two dogs were in pursuit of a cat, who seeing no other place of refuge near, made her escape into a long earthen water pipe, which was lying on the ground. These two inseparable companions, who always supported each other, pursued the cat to the pipe, where they halted, and consulted what was to be done to deceive and get possession of their enemy. After they had stood a short time, they divided, took post at each end of the pipe, and began to bark alternately, to give the cat reason to suppose they were both at one end, and to induce her to come out. Their really astonishing cunning soon had a successful result, and the cheated cat left her hiding place. Scarcely had she ventured out, when she was seized by one of the dogs; the other hastened to his assistance, and in a few moments deprived her of life.

The monks, exasperated, at this, poisoned many of these dogs; but this availed them nothing; for fresh ones constantly came, who, however, fared no better than their predecessors. The two before-mentioned dogs still remained, in spite of all the endeavours of the monks to destroy them, for they would eat of nothing which they placed in their way, nor indeed of any thing out of our quarters. A soldier of our regiment afterwards took them both with him to Germany.

After some time we were removed from Noviziata, and placed in the convent of Saint Francisco de Paolo, where we were quartered with a battalion of the 10th Regiment of the line. A number of soldiers in the battalion had just concluded their seven years' engagement; but as they could not well be spared, all possible means was resorted to, in order to induce them to conclude a second engagement. Instead of the usual strict state of discipline in which the English soldier is kept, an extraordinary relaxation took place. During the time that they were undecided respecting a further agreement, they were suffered to do as they pleased, without small faults (which were generally severely punished) being inquired into; such as getting in debt, remaining out all night, getting drunk, &c. Several suffered themselves to be seduced by this bait, and took the bounty; they were then allowed a week or a fortnight's liberty, and led a merry life: they ornamented their schakos with ribbons, drove about the city in carriages, and had two or three women constantly with than. At night, Bacchanalian festivities were kept up, and excesses of all kinds were indulged in, sanctioned in some degree by the officers, who frequently took part in them. But no sooner were these golden days over, than the usual regulations were again put in force, and after this indulgence in lawless liberty, were the more severely felt. Many, relaxed by indulgence, could not at once accustom themselves to subordination, and were severely punished; they were placed under arrest, or were kept in motion five or six hours in the day, loaded with their arms and knapsacks, without being allowed to rest for a moment; this punishment was called drilling.

Upon returning from these pleasant walks, they were immediately shut up in their quarters; several also were .obliged to attend at the place of exercise, carrying a chain and padlock about them. In foreign regiments like our's, the discipline was not so severe; but even in our's, the method to tame the obstinate and insubordinate was well understood, and many a one, tired out, and thinking himself no longer able to bear this severity, committed suicide. Of this I have seen several instances; nevertheless I must say, that in many respects the English service is preferable to any other: the soldier is well and regularly paid; no one dares cheat him of any part of his pay: I have seen many instances of attempts of this kind being punished by dismissal, without the offender having the slightest chance of ever being reinstated: and examples of this sort deterred others from attempting the like.

The English equipment is complete and good: the soldier, indeed, is obliged to pay for some of the smaller articles out of his own purse; but under a better regulation these articles might not be considered requisite; or, if so, the soldier might be allowed to purchase them himself, and not be compelled to take those brought from England, where every thing is so dear. An English soldier, to be sure, cannot amass a fortune; but, in comparison with soldiers of other nations, he appears like a lord; and altogether his lot is far preferable. Every orderly and brave man is likewise remarked and esteemed by his officers; and the English service may be considered as the best school for order and neatness. Every soldier is obliged to change his linen twice a week; in summer, during fine weather, all are obliged to bathe, and each division is marched down to the bathing-place, under the command of an officer.

Once, while bathing on the beach at Palermo, I nearly lost my life; however, I escaped with the fright. It was one Saturday afternoon; the wind blew from the sea, and the waves broke heavily on the shore, so that but few ventured in. Owing to a glass of wine which I had been drinking, I was very courageous, and trusted to my skill in swimming. Together with some of my comrades, I plunged into the foaming waves; and after we had made our way through the surf, we found it very pleasant; for the sea being rough, made it less laborious to swim. After amusing ourselves for about half an hour, the bugle was blown, to recall us. We made for the shore, expecting to find it as easy to come out as to go in; but we were mistaken: the waves breaking on the beach threw us like corks upon the sands; but the following ones carried us directly back again. This happened to me five times: every time I grasped the beach as tightly as I could, until the blood ran from my fingers, but I could not retain my hold; one wave threw me ashore, and the next carried me back along with the sand I had grasped. I had, as yet, swallowed no water, but was so exhausted by my extraordinary efforts, as to be unable to make any farther attempts to save myself, and gave myself up to the direction of the waves. Presently one of the largest threw me with such force upon the shore, that I lost my senses. While in this state, a soldier of the 10th Regiment, and one of my comrades, hastened to the spot, and at the risk of their lives carried me out of the reach of the waves. In this manner I was saved: but two seconds later, both myself and my two preservers would have been carried into the sea.

When I came to my senses again, I found myself in the hands of my comrades, who had been placing me upon my head, in order to allow the water to run out which I might have swallowed. My companions likewise all succeeded in getting out, though not without endangering their lives. After the accident, which did not affect my health in any way, I took such an aversion to the water, that it was a long while before I could make up my mind to go into the sea again; and it was just the same with my companions.

Owing to different circumstances, some situations became vacant, and I was made corporal. This procured me some advantages not enjoyed by the privates, but at the captain's request I continued in the same company.

Disputes frequently arose between our soldiers and the Sicilians; partly owing to love intrigues and points of honour, but principally to the English having always money in their pockets, and the Sicilians scarcely a *bajocco*. On the 7th of February, 1814, in one night, at the time of the carnival, seventeen persons, mostly natives, were murdered: but among the slain was a Neapolitan horse-chasseur, upon whose death I shall make a remark. Our battalion on this day had been marched up into the country, which was often done to exercise us; and we returned very late, hungry and thirsty. I went, accompanied by another corporal, named Friedrick, and five privates of our company, to a tavern, the proprietor of which was a Swiss; here we got the meat we had brought with us fried in oil, and to this we added a salad and a good glass of wine.

When the time for our departure had arrived, we got up, and upon going out at the door, heard the words: "*Attend, Coquin!*" We hastened to the place from whence the sound proceeded, but found the deed already done—a Neapolitan chasseur was weltering in his blood. He had received a thrust from a sword in the left side. The cause of this occurrence was as follows:— A soldier of our company had formed an acquaintance with a waiter's daughter, who had previously been upon intimate terms with this dying Neapolitan, but had preferred the German to the Italian. By this dismissal, and the preference shown by the girl, his jealousy and revenge became so strongly excited, that he had for some time past been watching for an opportunity to assassinate his rival, but hitherto had been unable to put his design in execution.

This evening, upon the soldier stepping out of the house, arm in arm with his beloved, the jealous rival, unable to contain his resentment any longer, rushed upon him with his stiletto, and he would inevitably have been sacrificed, if the trumpeter of our company had not happened to be standing behind the Neapolitan; and before he could complete his purpose, plunged his sword between his ribs. The wounded man was stabbed through the liver; he attempted once or twice to rise, and then remained perfectly still. We thought he was dead, and went home. Soon afterwards he was brought into our quarters, still alive; but instead of fetching a surgeon, to render him assistance and dress his wound, the natives sent to the church, had the holy vessels brought, and invoked all the saints they could think of to heal him. They, however, rendered him no assistance, and he very shortly breathed his last. A strict inquiry was set on foot respecting this occurrence, but the perpetrator was never discovered, or he would most likely have been punished, notwithstanding the murder was an act of necessity, to save the life of a comrade.

I had here likewise an opportunity of seeing the punishment

of hanging in the Sicilian manner, which was attended with very little ceremony. The criminal was a man named Peter, the servant of a captain of grenadiers. The battalion formed a square in the place appointed for the execution; the criminal was brought in a cart from the prison, escorted by a detachment; the executioner and the galley-slaves who were to assist him were placed around him, and until their arrival on the spot, all chained together. Upon reaching this their bonds were loosened, the executioner came without saying a word, placed a rope round the delinquent's neck, and led him up the ladder. He then made the rope fast, and without any further ceremony threw him from the ladder; the galley-slaves seized him by the legs, and pulled until he was dead. I was particularly struck with the costume of the executioner, which resembled that of a Jack-pudding at a fair, and was also surprised at the singular mode of expression in the English sentence;—"he shall suffer death, and be hanged with a rope about his neck."

CHAPTER 9

Sicily

On board the ships lying in the harbour, some punishments were inflicted which I had not yet seen; for instance, a sailor had to pass through the fleet. This punishment is usually awarded by the sentence of a court-martial, which also fixes the number of lashes to be received by the delinquent. He is then carried round to all the ships of war present, and in each receives a certain number of lashes on his naked back, so that when he shall have passed all the ships, he will have received the appointed number. The punishment of keel-hauling, which consists in the criminal being fastened to a rope, and being drawn once or oftener under the ship, is no longer practised. at least I have never seen it, so often as I have been on board of ships and in sea-ports. The punishment of hanging was not unusual; this I have several times seen. Once I saw two sailors, one of whom was a black, drawn up at the same time to the main-yard.

During my present stay I had plenty of leisure and opportunity to make myself intimately acquainted with Palermo and its inhabitants. The city is built in a beautiful situation; it lies in a large plain, spreading out on both sides, with a fine chain of mountains in the back ground. On the right is Mount Pelegrino, with the chapel of St. Rosalia, who concealed herself for I know not how many years in a cave on the mountain, to escape from her pursuers, until she was at last discovered, and since that time she has been very devoutly worshipped in Palermo, and throughout all Sicily.

The path leading to the chapel of Saint Rosalia is very steep, but here and there improved and rendered more passable by means of art; the ascent is, nevertheless, very laborious, but the view on reaching the top is one of the finest imaginable: at the foot of the mountain lies the city, on the left the sea, on the right the beautiful valley with the bordering mountains, and Etna with its cap of snow in the background. This affords ample enjoyment to the eye; and in contemplating the lovely prospect, all the difficulties of the ascent are forgotten: on the extreme point of the mountain stands the telegraph. The whole mountain is rocky and barren; only a few tufts of grass being here and there visible.

The city itself has only two main streets, the beauty of which is universally acknowledged, the Via Macqueda and the Via Cassero.[1] The other streets are mere lanes running in different directions through the four quarters. From the central point, that is, where the two main streets cross, the four gates of the city may be seen at the same time, and from this spot the view is very fine. The Royal palace is well situated at the end of the Via Cassero, and somewhat resembles a fort, being fortified nearly all round, and provided with batteries. In the tower of this palace is the only clock in Palermo which strikes in the German manner, that is, from one to twelve; all the others are repeaters, and strike in the Italian fashion, from one to twenty-four, So that upon asking what o'clock it is at nine at night, you receive for answer, it is one at night. In the same building was the establishment for making bread, and the telegraph for the Sicilian troops, and close by, the barracks of the Royal guard; behind this is a palace formerly inhabited by the Duke of Orleans, with a fine garden, laid out in the English style; this was afterwards inhabited by Lieutenant-General MacFarlane.

Among the buildings dedicated to religious devices, the cathedral is particularly remarkable; the number of other churches is very considerable, and there are upwards of ninety convents

---

1. These two streets cross each other in the centre of the city, and form the *quatro cantoni*.

and monasteries. Of the palaces belonging to the nobility, that of Prince Buteras is the most worthy of attention; it is situated on the beautiful promenade by the sea-side; the owner, one of the richest individuals in Sicily, died while I was here, and was buried with extraordinary pomp; his daughter afterwards married a lieutenant in the English service, a Hanoverian by birth. The mole may likewise be reckoned one of the curiosities of Palermo, it stretches a considerable distance into the sea, and forms a commodious harbour for a number of vessels.

The Castello di Mare is a fort of no very considerable importance, which protects the harbour, but has no great influence upon the city, not lying high enough to command it; it is, however, furnished on the land side with ditches and outworks. In this citadel were a number of state prisoners, who were distinguished by fetters, exactly resembling in form those of the galley-slaves, but so slight as scarcely to be perceivable. Once, upon the arrival from Malta of a large sum of money, amounting to some millions of dollars, destined for the payment of the English troops in Sicily and Spain, no safer place of deposit could be thought of than the Castello di Mare. The money was washed with vinegar, on account of the plague raging at Malta, and then disembarked: this occupied fourteen days: it was deposited in one of the casemates, where it was secured as well as possible. On the doors were several locks, the keys of which were in possession of different persons in the paymaster-general's department, so that three persons were obliged to be present whenever the door was opened. In addition to these precautions, an English guard was posted at the magazine, and it was considered impossible for any thief to gain admission.

One morning, upon the paymaster and his assistants opening the door, they saw, with astonishment, that a hole had been made in the wall from above. With astonishing labour, stones weighing from four to six hundred weight had been broken out and removed on one side, without the sentries having heard any thing of it, so that all must have been done without the slightest noise. In spite of all their pains, the plan had not succeeded; for these skilful miners had broken into the room adjoining the treasury, into which the empty sacks and casks had been thrown, and here they found the doors so strongly guarded with iron, as to render it impossible to be forced without a noise, which would have alarmed the guard; they therefore retreated without any booty.

The Vicaria, the principal prison for criminals, situated in the Via Cassero, is also, remarkable for its massiveness. The prisoners, in spite of the strength of the building, endeavoured several times to break out, but their plans were always frustrated. In the vicinity of Quatro Venti, the English had erected a chapel for the Protestant mode of worship, where upon all Sundays and fast-days service was regularly performed, and all Protestants were obliged to attend; the sacrament was also administered twice during the year; religious duties are strictly adhered to in the English military service, every soldier being obliged to attend, oh pain of imprisonment or fine, unless prevented by military duties.

In general each brigade has its chaplain; in the absence of a church, the most convenient open space is selected, and the drums are piled to form an altar; the band supply the place of an organ; a hymn is sung, the chaplain then delivers a plain discourse, suited to the capacity of his audience; and I have frequently been as much edified under the canopy of Heaven, as in the most splendid church. The Sicilians were astonished at first at beholding our mode of worship, but with all their ignorance and bigotry, I never observed them cast the slightest ridicule upon it.

Near Quatro Venti was the burial-ground belonging to the English garrison, which, after the departure of the English from Sicily, I understood was fresh consecrated by the priests, owing, as they said, to the ground being contaminated by the bodies of heretics, as we were called.

I may as well here mention a circumstance, respecting which I never could obtain any correct information. Not far from the before-mentioned burial-ground there is a very fine convent, which I often passed with my comrades, in going out for a ramble in the environs. There is in this convent, on a level with the ground, a small cell, the windows of which are strongly guarded with iron bars; not sufficiently close, however, to prevent the inside being plainly seen. In this cell are placed the mummies of a monk and a nun, in the full dress of their order, holding a child in their arms. Respecting this I was informed that the monk had carried on a secret intrigue with the nun, the consequence of which soon became apparent in the birth of a child. They were both, according to the laws of the church, sentenced to be walled up alive. After their decease they were taken out and placed here to serve as a warning to others.

In the environs of the city are several establishments worthy of remark; among others, the garden of Flora, with some fine buildings for botanical purposes: further on the Campo Santo, where the inhabitants of Palermo, who have no burial-places in the churches, are interred. This is a large space, surrounded by walls, and planted with tall cypresses: here, I was told, all bodies are thrown into large pits, but that the bones of those persons are preserved, whose relations or friends wish it, in a building, the interior of which resembles a museum of natural history; receptacles being formed in the walls, where the bones are placed, under which the names, ages, rank, days of birth and death of those to whom they belonged.

During this time, I found the remarks I had made, during my former stay in Palermo and Sicily, upon the inhabitants, fully confirmed, and to these, therefore, I will add nothing. The Sicilians are of small stature, brown complexions, and well made: the women are remarkable for beauty and a particular partiality for foreigners, of which many of our men received proofs. They live very temperately, drink scarcely any spirits, and but very little of a light wine; animal food the lower orders are unaccustomed to; they live upon fish, fruit, and different preparations of flour, particularly macaroni. The Sicilian character does not admit of much praise; of their thirst for revenge, usually ending in assassination, I have already given several examples, and in the course of my narrative shall have to relate more: they are likewise very cunning, and among the lower orders accomplished thieves; this they often convinced us of.

For instance, the major, whose orderly I was, came down one morning to the battalion, standing on the parade, ready to march out to exercise, and said to the officers who were assembled; "Gentlemen, it is impossible I can go out with you today, I have no uniform; this great coat is all the thieves have left me. Last night when I was lying in bed, the window was opened, and before I could get up, two rascals with drawn knives stood at my bedside, and commanded me not to stir. Unarmed and amazed as I was, I was obliged to obey. In the meanwhile these fellows had been followed by others, who made themselves masters of my clothes, writing-case, arms, in short of every thing of any value that was to be found in my room. When they had packed up their booty, they very politely wished me a good night, and retired. I jumped up immediately, and gave the alarm; my orderly, coachman, groom, and the other servants who slept on the story above, and had heard nothing of the occurrence, hastened to my assistance; but in spite of every inquiry, we have not been able to discover the slightest traces of the robbers."

Lieutenant-General MacFarlane, on account of his approaching nuptials, had procured twelve sheep from Africa, which were kept at his quarters. One day, when I was upon guard there, which duty our battalion usually had to perform, the general made a violent outcry; one of his sheep, he said, had been stolen. He insisted upon it that some of us had conveyed it away by stealth, and threatened to have us all hanged; but in spite of all his researches and threats, the sheep was nowhere to be heard of.

A short time afterwards, two priests called and wished to speak with the general. As he was everyday constantly annoyed by troublesome visitors, he would not see them, but they would not go away, and when he came out of his room, not being able to escape them, he was obliged to grant them a hearing. One of the priests then informed him, that a communicant of his, who was employed in the general's stable, had stolen the sheep, and now wished to return it; but in spite of the general's pressing entreaties he would not name the thief. The sheep was brought back again, but so much reduced by hunger that it very soon died, and was thrown to the dogs. The general, very naturally, did not like to keep such people in his service, and in order to be sure of his man, turned away all the Sicilians in his employment. A ship lying in the harbour caught fire, owing to the carelessness of the people on board. The crew were obliged to make their escape in the boats as quickly as they could, for the wind being strong, the fire burned so fiercely, that there was no chance of extinguishing it.

To prevent any danger of the other vessels catching fire, which were lying near, the cables were cut, and the ship was towed out to sea. She ran ashore close to the Castello di Mare, and was burning the whole of the night, so that half the city was illuminated; she was even not entirely consumed till towards the middle of the next day. The Sicilians came down immediately, and surrounded the vessel with their boats, in order to get what they could out of the lower part of her, and also to steal the copper sheathing. To prevent these thefts, a guard was posted on the beach, but they were so eager as to endeavour to make their way by force to the burning vessel, and we could deter them by no other means than by letting a ball occasionally whistle over their heads.

They are also very dexterous in counterfeiting the coin; and notwithstanding every endeavour, the government is unable to prevent this trade being carried on. When I was in Palermo, the government, in order to prevent the circulation of this base coin, in the place of the *bajoccos*, which at times were made of a composition of brass, without any impression, and of a square shape, issued pieces of from one to five *bajoccos* in value, handsomely stamped; but these had been scarcely a fortnight in circulation, when it was discovered that they were already imitated.

The Sicilians are also extremely clever in talking by signs; they will discourse together in this manner for hours, without a single word being uttered. I often remarked this when I was on guard in the place of Saint Dominico, where a lady almost every day about noon had an interview with a gentleman; they had probably matters to converse about, not interesting to a third party; this I concluded from the nature of the signs made use of.

One of the most remarkable and enlivening festivals of the populace is the carnival, at which time every one forgets all his troubles, and gives himself up to the liveliest joy. During the first days of this festival, the drollest groups of figures possible are to be seen about from morning till night, with harlequins and *punchinellos* in abundance, who crack jokes upon every passer by. They are usually provided with syringes filled with water, with which they amuse themselves, by squirting at every one within their reach. They likewise pelt each other with pease, beans, &c.; and without any notice being taken, or the slightest offence being given, they amuse themselves, with a thousand antics. The bagpipers, mostly inhabiting the most distant parts of the city, also make their appearance, and delight the Sicilians, who are accustomed to this instrument, with their melody.

Insurrections were several times attempted by the lower orders, but these were always successfully quelled without bloodshed; once only there appeared to be any danger, the galley-slaves being concerned in it; however, it was discovered in time, and some cannons being planted in front of the prison, and fired often times, soon restored order. Several of the ringleaders were beheaded, and their heads exposed in baskets over the gates of the prison: these afforded a most disgusting sight, particularly when the sun shone hot, and the fat dropped from them. Once it was said, that several persons of consideration were concerned in a plot which did not at all coincide with the politics of the English government, but that it was discovered in time, and defeated. Very soon after, the Queen embarked on board of an English frigate, and returned to Austria, her native country.

To the instances already mentioned of the blood-thirstiness of the Sicilians, I will add a few more, which I myself witnessed.

I was one day on duty in the place of Saint Dominico, and just after dinner was standing with several of my comrades at the corner leading to the Via Cassero, amusing ourselves with seeing the motley crowd pass by, when a dispute arose between two apparently well-dressed men; after a short, but very animated conversation, in which, after the Italian fashion, the hands were made great use of, one of them drew his stiletto from under his coat, plunged it in the other's side, and then escaped into the church of Saint Dominico. The wounded man was carried away, and but little farther notice was taken of the occurrence; two officers of police, indeed, came, and inquired after the murderer, but upon being told he was in the church, they went quietly away: and I would myself not have advise any one to have laid hands on a criminal, who had betaken himself to the protection of the priesthood.

Murderers of this kind were to be found in the churches, regularly domesticated: I was shown one in the cloisters of Saint Dominico, who had lived there for four years. He was a saddler by profession, and carried on his work here quite as well as in his shop; his relations brought him food, and no one dared to molest him, so great is the respect for the priesthood. Once only, upon an occurrence similar to this, an English officer dared to enter the cathedral, and I cannot even yet comprehend why the priests and the populace suffered it to be done without any opposition. The circumstance was as follows:—A soldier of our company, named Maifisch, a Netherlander, was stabbed in a tavern of bad reputation through the neck by a Neapolitan soldier of the guard; the dagger passed close to the windpipe, and the man received at the same time a severe wound in the hand. He was carried immediately to an English barrack, his wounds were dressed, and he happily recovered; losing the use, however, of his right hand.

The perpetrator escaped as usual, and an English patrol going to the house to make inquiries found that the landlord was flown, and that a girl, the cause of the quarrel, had taken refuge in the cathedral close by. The officer commanding the patrol proceeded instantly without any ceremony to the church, found the girl kneeling before the altar, commanded the soldiers to seize her, and carried her off. She confessed that she knew, the perpetrator of the deed, and upon being conveyed to the regiment of guards, pointed him out directly. He was taken into custody, and his whole punishment consisted in a few months' imprisonment; but upon his being released, the major of our battalion took the matter up again, and insisted upon a severer punishment being inflicted, upon which, the criminal was sentenced for twelve years to the galleys.

When the weather was fine, and we had nothing to do, I used to walk out in the environs of the city, and frequently in the morning visited the Capuchin convent, not far from the gates, where there was a great quantity of mummies placed upright against the walls, and also the bones of the deceased brethren. Belonging to the convent was a beautiful shady garden, in the centre of which was a fountain, surrounded by trees; in the back-ground was a neat hermitage, inhabited by a real hermit. I and my comrades used often to seat ourselves at this fountain, and refresh ourselves with its cool water; after which, we generally went to take a glass of wine at a tavern hard by. Here, upon one occasion, we fell in with some of the Neapolitan guards. Among them was a sergeant, who, a short time previously, had had a dispute with the trumpeter of our company, who also happened to be with, us at the time. We understood too little Italian to know what the Neapolitans were talking about; but their gestures evinced that they meant us no good; we were, therefore, upon our guard, and awaited quietly what was to happen. We could do this without apprehensions, as there were six of us, all armed; for in Sicily we never went about without our sabres. Our trumpeter, who paid most attention to their movements, presently got up, and said to us: "Two of you go directly to the door, and the other three do exactly as I tell you."

As soon as the door was guarded,, he cried out: "Now draw!" In an instant the sabres were out of the scabbards, and he approached the table of the guards, with these words: "Gentlemen, produce your daggers!" and although he could speak but little Italian, he contrived to make them understand him. The guards did not feel disposed to obey his orders, and made a show of resistance: but we were upon them like lightning, and took away their daggers, which we broke to pieces; we then seized the guards, turned them out of the house, and would not suffer them to come in again. It now became time for us to be gone, for a mob was beginning to assemble, which would not have failed to take their part against us, and we should scarcely have escaped with a whole skin. This, however, we did not wait for, but went off, and reached our quarters without molestation. Disputes of this kind occurred almost every day between the English and Sicilian troops, on which account the latter were prohibited from carrying their side-arms when off duty: this occasioned them to have recourse to their stilettos. These dangerous instruments they generally carried concealed in their sleeves, holding the handle in their hand, or in a sheath, placed on the right side, near the hip.

We foreigners, on the contrary, agreed very well together, and amused ourselves in a variety of ways. In fine weather we took walks into the country; during calms we went out to sea, and caught turtles, of which there are here such quantities, that on market-days they are brought in, twenty or thirty together, for sale. We placed ourselves in a boat, approached these animals softly, who were sleeping cm the surface of the water, seized them by the feet, and threw them upon their backs into the boat. They afforded us delicious meals and most excellent soup.

Another of our favourite amusements was the acting of plays, which were composed by the second trumpeter of the company. This man, a real genius, but without any education, sketched and took likenesses very well, although he had never received any instruction; was a musician, composed and arranged our theatrical pieces extempore, not being able either to read or write. I was Vater's secretary (this was our poet's name); to me he dictated the parts. During the representation I was prompter; but I sometimes performed myself, whenever I could find any one who could take the other office. Some of the younger soldiers, whose voices were tolerably soft, dressed in clothes borrowed from the soldiers' wives, performed the female characters admirably: the getting up of the remainder of the wardrobe was managed by Vater, who was not only poet, but also manager, composer, and tailor to the theatre—the *factotum*, in short, which gave animation to the whole.

We had chosen a chapel for our theatre, built up a stage of boards, and ornamented it with bed-coverings. Our scenery was often composed of boughs of trees: these Nature afforded us, and were superior to any artificial decorations. Of spectators there was no scarcity; our officers, and those of the other English regiments, frequently came to witness our representation; and we often received many a dollar entrance-money; so that our finances were benefited, in addition to the pleasure we derived from our representations. In teaching the parts, I had a hard piece of work, as I was obliged to read them over and over again to those actors and actresses (in *formá,* if not in *genere*) who were not able to read, until they had got them perfectly by heart. This method of teaching parts is certainly of all others the most laborious; but it afforded me no small pleasure, when I found them able to repeat every thing perfectly, and without hesitation. Vater not only distinguished himself on this occasion, but he had a peculiar talent of making himself serviceable, and of extracting amusement from every occurrence.

I will only relate one of his jokes, which afforded us all considerable amusement. The mess-man,[2] who had provided our officers' meals, had a very handsome daughter, whom one of the men of our company fell so desperately in love with, that his whole mind was absorbed in the idea, and he sometimes wandered about like a man in his sleep, without knowing where he went. The cunning Vater had for some time perceived this; and one day said to the man, seeing him look so sorrowful: "Well, comrade, what's the matter?"

"Oh, no one can help me."

"How so?" replied Vater, "no one should talk so. Tell me only what is the matter with you. I know a great many things; and if it is possible, I am sure I shall be able to assist you."

---

2. In all English regiments the officers dine together; and the superintendent, or provider of the meals, is called the mess-man.

The soldier, upon this, confidently told how matters were; how much he was attached to this girl; and that his utmost wish was for once only to hold her in his arms.

"Oh! if it is nothing more than that, I shall be able to serve you."

Upon this he began to tell him a story of the same kind, which he said had happened to himself, in which he had been assisted by an old soldier, who had likewise taught him the art of compelling any girl to appear with whom a person was enamoured. The soldier rejoiced at this discovery, and happy already in the idea of seeing and embracing his beloved Mary, pressed him strongly to make no delay, but to commence his incantations immediately.

"Oh, for my part," said Vater, "I care not if it takes place this evening; but you must be careful to do exactly as I tell you, otherwise I cannot be answerable for the consequences." The man, in the joy of his heart, promised punctually to obey, and they parted with mutual promises of meeting in the evening.

Towards night Vater came into our room, the whole of us (eighteen in number) who slept there being present, saying: "Comrades, tonight we shall have some excellent sport together! I only have to beg of you to take no notice, and not to laugh, whatever may happen: lie down in your beds, and pretend to be asleep."

Upon this, under a promise of secrecy, he told us as much as it was necessary for us to know, and we promised to follow his directions. Towards eleven o'clock, when we were all lying down full of expectations, Vater and the soldier came in, the latter in his drawers and sleeping jacket, the former with a mask over his face. The magician muttered, a few unintelligible words, drew a circle with a piece of chalk, then muttered another mysterious sentence, and then commanded the soldier to seat himself in the circle, and to look steadfastly towards the door; he also forbade him to make the slightest movement; and promised him, if he fulfilled these conditions, that, sooner or later, the wished-for object would make its appearance.

He added: "be cautious to do nothing which may awaken your sleeping comrades, else everything will be in vain; I also must not be present: my stay would only render the appearance of your beloved more difficult. I have now done my part, and shall get into bed." Vater then retired, and left the soldier full of expectation. It struck eleven, then twelve. From sitting so long on the paved floor, the soldier's teeth began to chatter. When the clock struck one, he could bear the cold no longer, in his light clothing, and called out aloud: "Vater, will she not soon come?"

"Be still, you fool!" was the answer.

We could now contain ourselves no longer, but burst out into a loud fit of laughter. The poor dupe at first could not tell what it meant; but he soon found out he had been cheated, and jumped into bed to escape our jokes. The next morning the whole story was made known; it was even told to the girl; and the incantation afforded her no small amusement. She afterwards married a lieutenant in our corps, and returned to Germany in the same vessel with us. During that time, at any rate, her former admirer could satisfy himself by gazing upon this really handsome young woman, without exposing himself to the night air, or making use of enchantments.

In Palermo I had also the opportunity of witnessing the singular English custom of the sale of wives. A soldier of the 10th Regiment of Infantry, sold his wife to a drummer for two pounds sterling; he, however, did not keep her long, but parted with her to the armourer of the regiment, for two Spanish dollars. The woman did not appear to be at all annoyed at these dealings, but rather to be pleased with the change.

Soon after the peace of Paris, we had a sight of some French vessels, bearing the white flag; and shortly alter a whole squadron came into the harbour of Palermo, where it remained a considerable time. Many of our soldiers, who were, native Frenchmen, deserted at this time, and took the opportunity of returning to their own country.

To my great joy, the splendid annual festival, in honour of St. Rosalia, took place during my abode here. It lasts three days, and is celebrated with the utmost solemnity by the whole population of Palermo. At the sea-side a large machine is erected, somewhat resembling a ship, and covered with tinsel and all sorts of gaudy ornaments. On the top is a statue, representing St. Rosalia; behind her sits an old woman biting her fingers; this woman the natives of Palermo call *Bruga*, which means, witch. In the body of this machine are placed musicians, and to it are harnessed forty or fifty oxen with gilded horns, who drag it upon its ponderous wheels slowly up the Via Cassero, as far as the Royal Palace.

During this journey the people behave as if they were mad, the cry of "*Viva la Sante Rosalia*," is heard without ceasing, while the old witch behind the saint is saluted with all manner of execrations. The balconies along the whole street are hung with handsome carpets, and adorned with all kinds of flowers; and the windows in the street through which the procession passes, are filled with the *beau monde* of Palermo. All the vessels are ornamented with flags, all the bells are in motion, and from time to time a salvo, is fired from the artillery; before every church a quantity of petards are placed, which are fired in honour of the saint. At night the whole city is illuminated, and hundreds of handsome equipages parade up and down the Via Cassero, while the foot passengers walk on each side.

The crowd is immense, and it is necessary to be upon one's guard to prevent being rode over; the cry of *guarda,* to the foot passengers, is incessantly heard from the coachmen. Booths with refreshments for person's of all ranks are placed in every direction; in one place may be seen the Lazzaroni, eating his boiled or roasted beans, while close to him sits his richer neighbour, refreshing himself with ice or confectionery. Lemonade, fresh water, lemons, oranges, and all kinds of fruits which the season affords, are offered about for sale, and the whole presents a most animated scene; every one apparently occupied with his own engagement, and caring little for his neighbours.

Later in the night splendid fireworks are let off, and this, life lasts for three whole nights until daybreak, from which time until about eleven o'clock the streets are tolerably quiet, with the exception of the fish-women and dealers in fruit, who are busied in crying their wares. In this street there are likewise on these three days public horse races, which afford the populace considerable amusement. The horses are handsomely ornamented with gold and silver stuff; upon their backs are hung balls filled with spikes, which spur them on during the race. I am sorry that I cannot give a more minute and lively description of this festival, which is certainly one of the most splendid in Europe; but every description must necessarily fall short of the reality, and only a person who has been present can form any correct idea of the scene.

My residence in Palermo, which upon the whole was exceedingly agreeable, was rendered uncomfortable for a time by an unpleasant occurrence, which likewise occasioned a fit of illness. I had been guilty of an act contrary to discipline, and as a punishment, was deprived of my rank as corporal for four weeks: this had such an effect upon me, that it produced a fit of the jaundice. This complaint was quite new to me, and I could not conceive what was the matter, when I found my nails getting yellow, soon after yellow spots began to appear on my skin, and at last the whites of my eyes were discoloured: my comrades then told me I had the jaundice. I did not like to go into the hospital; this I had a great aversion to, and always avoided it as long as possible. I made use of different remedies which had been of service to others, but after doctoring myself for some time, without producing any beneficial result, I went to a Sicilian doctor, with whom I was acquainted, and requested him to cure me. I then took his prescriptions, which, however, were of no avail. I was constantly in hopes of getting better, but in vain. I lost all my appetite, and crawled about with the greatest difficulty; at last I was so weak as to be scarcely able to stand.

While in this situation, I was one day on guard in the place of St. Dominico; the sub-officer who placed the guards gave me, on account of my weakness, one of the easiest posts in the interior of the convent, before a magazine of leather, where the shoe-makers belonging to several regiments worked during the day. The magazine had formerly been a chapel, but for want of room had been applied to this purpose; not far from hence, in the court of the convent, a soldier of our regiment had shot himself a few days before. Exactly at eleven o'clock I came upon duty, and the solitude and stillness of the night produced in me a variety of sensations. I thought upon my youthful days, my home, relations, and friends; upon my fate, which had led me through so many countries. I began also to reflect upon the future; whether I should ever be permitted to return in health to my native country.

Deeply occupied with these reflections, I had not remarked that the lamp, which dimly lighted the place where I was posted, was extinguished, and upon looking round, I perceived that I was almost in total darkness. The only light which came in was afforded by a door in the middle of the passage, but this merely allowed me to perceive objects, without being able to distinguish what they were. All at once, I thought I discerned a figure with two long horns coming in at the door, leading from the before-mentioned court, and ill as I was, my fancy was the easier excited. I will not deny that I was exceedingly alarmed, at this unexpected appearance, and the more so from the loneliness of the place and the hour of the night. However, fear overcame me for only a few moments: I then called out—"Who goes there?" and rushed towards the figure with my drawn sabre.

"Be still," was the answer; "I only wished to see if you were awake and well, in order that nothing might happen to you when the posts are visited."

The apparition was one of my friends, who knew how ill I was, and wished to rouse me up (in case I should have fallen asleep) before the officer went his rounds. His feather, which was in a case, and the rifle hanging from his shoulder by the strap, had formed the two horns. In my present state, this occurrence affected me a good deal, and I was truly rejoiced when I was relieved. I threw myself down upon the hard bed in the guard-room, and slept sound till morning, when I got up, very weak, but yet much better than I had been for some days previously.

My appetite was also somewhat keener; but by way of precaution, I only took a little tea and some bread, and in spite of the hunger I afterwards felt, I abstained from eating until dinnertime, when I made a better meal than I had done for some time. After this, I felt myself well enough to attempt putting my things in order; I exerted myself a good deal, and perspired considerably; presently I felt myself very unwell, and brought up a quantity of bile. From this time I was relieved, my strength began to return, and I was soon quite well. What means produced my cure—whether it was the fright, as I have some reason to suspect, I leave to the doctors to decide: for my own part I will only say, that fright is not the most pleasant method of cure for the jaundice.

I was scarcely recovered from this, when I was attacked with another complaint, at that time very common among the English soldiers, namely, the ophthalmia. Owing to the great number of patients, an hospital was especially fitted up for those afflicted with this disorder. I laboured under this complaint for three months; at last I was cured, but to this day the sight of my right eye is so much impaired, that I cannot distinguish small print or writing without a glass. Numbers of the regiment were so unfortunate as to lose their sight, but for these the government comfortably provided; in this respect the English soldier has no cause for complaint. When he becomes unfit for service, he receives a pension; upon this he can subsist, not very handsomely, it is true, but he has this advantage, that he can spend his money wherever he pleases.

A report had for some time been prevalent that Napoleon had escaped from the Island of Elba, and that King Murat had declared war; suddenly an order arrived for six thousand English and Sicilian troops to be assembled at Milazzo, and, accompanied by the King of Sicily, to proceed to Naples. The rifle company was ordered upon this expedition; and in the beginning of April, 1815, we embarked at Palermo, to which place we did not again return.

The next morning we reached Milazzo, where we found a

part of the troops already assembled. Here we remained some weeks, and had nothing to do but to be daily exercised, and then to go out walking. Milazzo is beautifully situated, and produces excellent wine: the town is old and very irregularly built, but well fortified; the bay in which it lies is protected from the winds, and capable of containing a number of vessels. There is likewise here an old castle, but this was not in the best state of defence. At last we were again embarked, and proceeded immediately to sea; the King joined us with his whole family; he was on board of a Sicilian frigate, which hoisted the English and Sicilian colours. On the arrival of this frigate, the troops saluted the King with three cheers; the ships fired a salute, and displayed their colours.

Owing to a calm, the fleet was detained for three days in the neighbourhood of Stromboli; and I had the pleasure of enjoying the sight of a burning mountain tolerably close. The mountain is circular, and from nearly the summit on the side towards Italy the fire and lava flows down.

It vomited a considerable quantity of fire just at this time, and the majestic, and at the same time tremendous appearance of streams of burning lava flowing into the sea, was to me particularly interesting. The other side of the mountain, as far up as possible, was planted with vines. Close to the sea-shore were a number of dwellings, and also several batteries.

A favourable wind soon sprung up, and we sailed to the Island of Capri, which is in front of the Bay of Naples. We supposed it to be still occupied by the troops of Murat, which was the case; but before we reached the harbour they had capitulated. We next passed the Island of Procida, and about six o'clock in the morning ran into the Bay of Naples, where hundreds of boats, handsomely decorated and filled with ladies and gentlemen, came out to meet us. Cries of "Long live the King, the English, the Austrians, down with Joachim!" were heard on every side, and the crowd was so great that our sailors had the utmost difficulty in keeping the boats out of the ship's way, so as to prevent mischief. I admired above every thing the beautiful bay, and the enchanting situation of the city of Naples. At the entrance, are situated the small islands of Ischia and Procida; next appears the extreme point of the mainland, covered with splendid palaces, country-houses, and gardens, with here and there batteries. After this, Naples presents itself, one of the finest cities in the world, built in the form of an amphitheatre, with its spacious white palaces rising out of the deep green of the plantations. Next is seen Vesuvius, and its neighbour the Monte Sommo; then the other side of the bay, with its mountains reaching towards the Island of Capri, presenting altogether a picture so enchanting, that neither pen nor pencil is able to describe it; only those who have seen it can form any correct idea of its splendour and beauty.

The wind blew so strong from the shore that we were not able to land on the day of our arrival, although we were lying close to the shore. On the King's approach all the ships saluted with cannon, and the like was done by the batteries on shore; multitudes had assembled on the beach, and there was no end to the shouts. The windows of all the houses, as far as we could see, were decorated with carpets and flowers; in the evening an illumination took place, and there was no peace during the whole night.

The next day the troops were landed at the arsenal; here the populace received us with acclamations, and broke into our ranks and embraced us.[3]

Accompanied by an immense crowd, we marched up to the Royal palace, upon the balcony of which were assembled the whole of the Austrian staff, and among them Leopold. Prince of the Two Sicilies; The King was not yet in the city, and had appointed a future day for his formal entrance. We defiled past, three cheers were given, the bands struck up the English national melody—"God save the King," and we were then marched

---

3. The first lieutenant of our company, whose name was Von Sebisch, was embraced by an old woman, whom he repulsed with abhorrence. We had scarcely been an hour ashore, when we became aware of the Sicilian character. Upon going to a tavern to get a glass of wine, the landlord endeavoured to cheat us of half a dollar, and but just before the populace would have carried us on their shoulders.

to our separate quarters. The rifle battalion was lodged at the farther end of the city, on the road leading to Vesuvius, in the quarter of St Magdalena. We were placed in a building capable of holding six thousand men; in the lower part were a number of galley-slaves, who were in hopes of obtaining their liberty by the change in the state of affairs; they several times threatened to break out, but by proper representations were always deterred from their purpose. Vesuvius, distant about twelve Italian miles, was very plainly to be seen, it was constantly smoking, and during the night we frequently perceived flames issuing forth.

Chapter 10

Italy & Homewards

The day now appeared on which the rightful King of Naples, after so long an absence, was about to make his entry into his capital city. The Austrian troops, quartered in the neighbourhood, and the whole garrison of the city, consisting of English, Austrian, and Neapolitan regiments, were under arms, and formed in four ranks on each side of the street by which the King was to pass, reaching from the quarter of St. Magdalena to the Royal residence. Discharges of artillery announced the approach of the King and his suite. The populace had assembled in vast multitudes, and every instant threatened to break through the ranks of the military: the houses were filled with well-dressed people; the roofs even were covered with awnings, to afford more room, and every place was occupied.

The procession advanced, the troops presented arms, and we saw the old man pass by who had been so long an exile from his native city. He was on horseback, dressed in a plain blue coat, and wore but few orders; by his side rode the two Princes, and behind him the staff belonging to the different forces. Before him ran a crowd of people of the lowest class, with branches of trees in their hands, vociferating with all their might—"*Viva il Re Ferdinando quatro.*" As soon as the King, his attendants, and the guards had passed, the whole of the troops followed in parade order. Amidst the sound of cannon and martial music, we defiled before the King, who had descended at his palace, and then returned to our quarters.

We were now removed from the quarter of St. Magdalena to the Jesuit Convent of St. Apostoli, not far from the Porta di Capua. From hence we had a view of nearly the whole city, the surrounding country, with its villas and Mount Vesuvius. As we were not much occupied with military duty, we filled up our time by rambling about the vicinity, in order to see what we could during our stay. Our first excursion was to Mount Vesuvius; we ascended as far as the hermitage, where we obtained some sour wine and hard cheese. The road hither is delightful, passing by pleasant country-houses, and through vineyards; the inhabitants of this mountain appearing as easy and careless as if nothing had ever happened, or could happen, although an eruption could at any instant occasion their destruction.

We passed several places over which the lava of the late eruptions had passed, but everything was restored so that the mischief appeared to have been caused ages ago. The view from the height we reached is magnificent, commanding the whole bay, the interior of the harbour, and the city; it is in short beyond description, and no one who has any taste for the beauties of nature, would depart from hence without ample gratification.

I often visited the Via Reale, a very delightful promenade along the sea-shore, ornamented with a number of antique statues. This was my favourite place of resort, although at some distance from my quarters, and whenever I came here I took the opportunity of bathing in the sea.

I also paid a visit to the tomb of Virgil, situated at the entrance of the grotto of Pausilippo. This extraordinary subterraneous passage is said by the lower orders of the Neapolitans to be a work of his Satanic majesty, but at what time, or for what purpose he performed this feat, I never was able to learn. The passage is about a mile and a quarter in length, according to my calculation,[1] for at the time I passed through I had no watch. It is cut through the mountain, upon which Fort St; Elmo is situated, so wide that two carriages may easily pass each other, and

---

1. I lighted my pipe at the entrance, which burned exactly half an hour, and it was out just as I reached the end.

from thirty to forty feet in height; on each side are accommodations for foot-passengers, so that they may pass without any danger from the carriages. At each end, and in the centre, images of saints are placed, and every passer-by usually throws a trifle into the box placed underneath. Although there is a shaft in the centre, it is so dark that in cloudy weather lighted lanterns are necessary day and night; these are placed before the images, and at different distances, either on iron posts or suspended from the centre. The road is excellently paved, and kept tolerably clean.

Among the curiosities of Naples may be reckoned the White Horse, (*cavallo bianco*) a colossal statue standing under cover before a church, in the centre of the city; and likewise the beautiful fountains in the Strada Reale. In the delightful gardens round the city I have passed many a pleasant morning, particularly in one where I used to drink milk presented by a pretty Swiss girl. The owner, whose name I have forgotten, had fitted up the place in the Swiss fashion; and for this purpose had procured a whole family from Switzerland.

The Neapolitans differ but little, either morally or physically, from their neighbours the Sicilians, being just as passionate and revengeful; and there are here quite as many Lazzaroni as in Palermo, if not more. The vigilance of the police, which, under the government of Murat was much more strict, prevented a number of crimes which otherwise would have been committed: and this was one reason of the great joy of the populace, for they were in hopes that the king would restore all their old privileges, and thus make way for the return of all the abuses which Murat had so wisely put an end to. The better orders of the inhabitants were not at all dissatisfied with Murat's government, and many of them have confidentially told me, that they would much rather have kept King Joachim, but that they were obliged to put a good face on the matter, and cry "*Viva el Re*" as well as the rest.

During my stay, I had an opportunity of becoming acquainted with the Austrian troops, which were here in great numbers: the head-quarters were likewise fixed here under Generals

Bianchi and Neiperg. Their artillery pleased me very much, as did likewise their cavalry, consisting chiefly of Hungarian Hussar regiments. The Tyrolese riflemen and the infantry did not look much amiss; but there was one volunteer corps, dressed in brown, which I did not like at all. Some of them were quartered in Naples, and looked so dirty and filthy, that it was quite sufficient to see them at a distance. They were covered with vermin; and when we relieved them on duty at the police establishment, which was frequently the case, we found them in a detached place, where they were obliged to remain during the whole time of their being on guard; for the national guards, who did the duty jointly, and who consisted entirely of decent citizens, would not suffer them to be along with them, On the contrary, when we mounted guard, they received us very civilly, and often invited us to dine with them at their houses.

The Neapolitans in general disliked the Austrians, and gave us by far the preference. The Austrian troops were likewise not so well off as we were; their pay, for what reason I know not, was kept back, so that they received, together with their rations, not quite two *kreutzers* per day, while we received ten, and much larger and better rations. The bread-contractor once endeavoured to put us off with Austrian bread; some was delivered out to us, but we refused to receive it: a complaint was lodged against the baker, and he was rewarded for his roguery with a handsome flogging. In all cases of this sort the English discipline was very strict, and to the advantage of the soldiers. The purveyor of the grenadier company of the 61st Infantry Regiment, on board a transport, once kept back four ounces from each ration of biscuit, furnished to every six men; the fraud was discovered, and the man received three hundred lashes.

On the 2nd of July, 1815, we were embarked on board the Neptune, to proceed to the fortress of Gaeta, which had not yet surrendered, and where most of the adherents of Murat were collected. It had for some time been besieged and hard-pressed by the Austrians; but they had hitherto not been able to compel the garrison to surrender.

We passed between Procida, Ischia, and the main land, and soon reached Gaeta. Upon approaching so near as to be within range of the guns of the fortress, a brig of war came alongside of us, and brought us orders to proceed to the island of Ponca, where two companies of our battalion were stationed. These were embarked, and we then, sailed to Genoa, whither the remainder of our battalion had proceeded before. We passed Terracina, coasted along the island of Elba, where the brig which convoyed us captured a French privateer; and on the 28th of July ran into the harbour of Genoa, and cast anchor before the Molo Nuovo.

There is certainly nothing more delightful than a coasting voyage, and I know of none to compare with that from Naples to Genoa. We sailed along generally from thirty to forty miles distant from the coast, and the land resembled a half-faded picture, in which the objects are not plainly to be distinguished. The extreme distance appeared enveloped in blue mist; the nearer objects were rather plainer to be seen, but still indistinct. The beach ran along like a thread, and the sea always had the appearance of being higher than the land. Upon nearing the shore, the effect produced was that of a picture, from before which the curtain is withdrawn; objects appeared plainer, and groves of trees, houses, villages, and small towns, became by degrees visible. On approaching still nearer, human beings, cattle, and in short all that the eye could reach, appeared distinct. In the same manner, on stretching out to sea, every object appears by degrees to retreat, until at last the land entirely disappears.

We were soon disembarked, and lodged in the quarters of St. Thomas, near the gate of St. Thomas. Here we found the manners and customs of the inhabitants half German, which, even to us who were Germans, appeared strange. The inns and taverns were exactly after the fashion of our native country; tobacco was smoked out of pipes; we got beer to drink, and potatoes to eat; the people were more friendly and communicative than in the other parts of Italy: we observed, in short, evident symptoms of being at no great distance from the German territory. We were also much pleased at being able to write letters to our friends at home, which could be safely forwarded, an opportunity which we had for a length of time been deprived of.

Genoa is an old fortified city; the buildings are not amiss, but much crowded together, and the inhabitants are said to be possessed of considerable wealth. It possesses only one handsome street, the Strada Balbi; all the others are narrow and crooked. Upon the mountain which surrounds the town, a number of forts are built; among others the Fort Diamanti, situated so high as in misty weather not to be visible from the city. The harbour is commodious and roomy, and ships of all trading nations may be seen here.

Among the Piedmontese artillery of the guard lying here, I found a number of my countrymen, which afforded me much pleasure; they could, however, give me no intelligence from home, having been taken prisoners in Spain, in 1810, and afterwards enlisted into the Sardinian service.

We remained here for six months, during which time the King of Sardinia with the whole family, made a visit of several weeks to the city. The English troops had the honour of guarding him, and I was several times sentinel at the door of his apartment; the guard consisted of two of his *gardes du corps,* and two English corporals.

The Genoese were not much pleased with their ruler; they would rather have become a republic, as before; or if they must have had a sovereign for their master, would have preferred the King of England; their own they usually called the "*Roi des Marmottes.*"

While the Royal Family remained here, the Genoese gave several fêtes in honour of their visit; among others, the whole of the Strada Balbi was upon one occasion splendidly decorated; young trees were planted at regular distances, and between each of them were erected pillars of a pyramidical form, made of transparent canvas, which at night were illuminated. A fountain at the upper end of the street was covered over, and figures of Neptune and other deities placed upon it. At night all the houses were illuminated, and the whole of the Royal Family with their suite proceeded to the Doria palace, outside of the gate of St. Thomas, which, as well as the other palaces in the city, was handsomely illuminated. In the garden, of the palace, the fountains (of which there are several) were ornamented with large mirrors, so disposed, that in some every thing was reflected exactly, and in others the spectator appeared standing on his head; there were also a number of wax-figures, placed in different parts of the garden, which were, by some sort of mechanism, kept constantly in motion. A brilliant display of fireworks was last of all exhibited; and during the whole entertainment, I did not remark the slightest disturbance. The cry of "*Viva il re de Marmotte*," was now and then heard; but to this the police, though generally speaking very strict, paid no attention whatever. The Genoese are throughout a steady, industrious race, completely free from the blood-thirsty, revengeful disposition of the Sicilians and Neapolitans, and unassuming and obliging towards strangers. I remarked here that the mules were shod in a very singular manner, namely, with round shoes; the reason of this is said to be, that when shod in this way, the mules, in passing the mountains, tread safer, and are less liable to meet with accidents. I have likewise never seen so fine a breed of these animals as here.

Upon the receipt of intelligence that Murat, the ex-King of Naples, had fled to Corsica, we were embarked in pursuit of him; but before we had quitted the harbour he was taken prisoner on his expedition to Pizzo, and we were disembarked again immediately.

There were likewise here a great number of galley slaves; and although these unhappy wretches are miserable enough every where, yet in Genoa their fate is harder than in other places. When they are not employed in the galleys, they are kept in the arsenal, where they are lodged in subterraneous chambers, loaded with chains, and fastened together in pairs, with nothing but the hard boards to lie on. In the country they are employed upon the hardest, most dangerous, and dirtiest labours, with no other allowance than every day two pounds of black bread, and a few horse-beans mixed with bad oil.

It is, in my opinion, very wrong that criminals of all description should be mingled, without any distinction being made between greater and lesser offences. Murderers, thieves, smugglers, coiners, and deserters, are all kept together; so that those who may be possessed of any relic of virtue or honesty, are sure to become utterly depraved. I found among these unfortunates ten Germans, who deeply excited my compassion; they had belonged to a Savoy regiment in garrison at Turin, had endeavoured to procure their liberty by desertion, but were taken in the attempt. They were brought to trial; the two ringleaders condemned to the galleys for life, and the others for the term of ten years. At the sight of these unhappy prisoners I keenly felt the value of liberty, and their distressed condition affected me even to tears I did what I could to serve them; I begged for them of several soldiers in the regiment. and many of my comrades were charitable enough to give them a trifle, so that during our stay they were somewhat better off, and this excited the envy of their Italian fellow-prisoners.

When they are on board the galleys to cruise against the Corsairs, they are chained two and two to the benches, and only released on coming to close quarters during a fight, when they are supplied with weapons to defend themselves and the galleys. When they are fortunate enough in this manner to contribute to any victory, the least criminal obtain their liberty, and the others have at least a part of their punishment remitted. On this account the galley-slaves were always pleased to go on board; for in addition to their hopes of obtaining their liberty, they are better fed and less severely treated than when on shore. I often saw galleys proceed to sea, and heard as frequently of ships being taken by the Corsairs, and even of landings which they had made; but during the six months we remained here, I never saw a Corsair brought in by a galley.

Every company in the English service has a cook, who is a soldier of the company, and receives for this employment a monthly pay, and some few trifling privileges. The cook of the fourth company was one day busied in preparing dinner, when suddenly the large kettle, filled with boiling water, fell down, and almost buried the unfortunate man under the meat, which weighed nearly a hundred pounds. He was taken up immediately, still alive, although severely scalded all over, and carried to the hospital, where in a few weeks he was considerably recovered, the surgeons taking all possible pains, and using every method they could think of in order to save him. Excessive use of wine, and other heating liquors, however, destroyed what the skill of the physicians had restored, and in spite of all their endeavours, he died. This was in one respect a good thing for him; for had he survived, he would have been a cripple for life.

We celebrated a wedding here, under such comical circumstances that I cannot help thinking they may be interesting enough to amuse my readers. A corporal of our company had for some time been upon a very intimate footing with the daughter of a non-commissioned officer of another battalion, and had promised her marriage; but the parents, from what cause I know not, would not give their consent. The corporal made application in the usual way to his captain, and received permission to marry; he then applied once more in form to the parents, but they, as before, positively refused their consent. Upon this, he applied for advice to the chaplain, who told him, "if it is really and truly your wish, and you have the proper permission from the regiment, I will perform the ceremony for you, without inquiring any farther."

The parents, who probably had some suspicion of what the suitor would attempt, kept very strict watch over the girl. However, one day, when the battalion to which the father belonged was on parade, and the mother as usual was keeping watch at the front door, the corporal seized the opportunity, took his bride under his arm, and proceeded to the back door. Upon finding this locked, he instantly, without reflecting on the consequences, snatched up a carpenter's axe lying near, and soon cleared this impediment; in doing which, he cut his hand very severely: this, however, did not stop him, but binding a handkerchief round the wound, he hurried off with his prize to the chaplain, and in a very short time the ceremony was performed.

From hence he returned with his wife to the house where the mother was, who, upon seeing her daughter, endeavoured to take her away from the corporal, who said, "No, she is now mine, the chaplain has this instant married us, and here is the certificate!"

The mother foamed with rage; by degrees the whole company assembled, and carried the married pair in triumph to our apartment, which happened to be a very large one. The general cry now was, "Comrades, we must celebrate the wedding!" A collection was immediately made, for we were always ready to promote any thing which promised amusement, and each one willingly contributed according to his ability, when the cap was carried round. The subscription was ample enough to procure a sufficiency of wine; the musicians of the company came and played their liveliest tunes, and we were all joyful and merry, to the extreme vexation of the mother, who stood at the door, and wished us and the married couple any thing but good. Two of us stood at the door with drawn sabres, as a guard of honour, and at the same time to act as a protection against the parents; for upon being released from parade, the father had joined the mother, and both united used all their endeavours to take away their daughter from the happy bridegroom. The wine put us all in high spirits; we collected all the young women belonging to the regiment, and had a merry dance. Every one who heard the noise, inquired what festival was going on? "Oh!" the answer was directly, "the sharp-shooters are celebrating a wedding."

In our regiment there were many Catholics; several of them very bigoted. Among the number was a Bohemian, who, having been dangerously wounded by a soldier of the Italian Legion, was confined for a length of time to the hospital. Here he was often visited by a Capuchin friar, who, although he wore a religious dress, was neither religious nor moral in his conduct. He, however, by all sorts of unmeaning arguments, endeavoured to inspire the wounded man with courage. No one of the least sense could forbear laughing at his ridiculous speeches. We, however, entertained so much respect for his clothing, that we never gave him the slightest interruption.

One day, during a festival in honour of some renowned saint, we went into a tavern, where we, owing to our frequent visits, were well known; and whom should we fall in with in this temple of Bacchus but our worthy friar, the apparently devout servant of God, so drunk as scarcely to be able to stand, sitting upon a chair, and preaching the gospel in a tavern. We drank our wine, and with the second bottle we began to get more lively; the friar came again across our minds; and, in the exuberance of our spirits, we resolved to set him upon one of the large wine-casks, which were lying in the court-yard of the house—a post at that time, at least, well befitting him. We proceeded instantly to work; took hold of him, and, in spite of all his endeavours, seated him upon his new throne, where we were obliged to hold him, to prevent his falling off. All laughed heartily at the friar; even the Catholics who were present, for he was known to be a good-for-nothing fellow; and it was soon after discovered that he was not a priest, but only a menial servant, who had formerly been employed in a monastery, from whence he had absconded, owing to some offences he had committed. He was apprehended, and sent back to his masters.

During our stay in Genoa our discharge had often been spoken of, but our hopes were again disappointed. We embarked on the 10th of February, 1816, once more, and on the 13th left the harbour in a strong gale of wind. From the place where we were lying at anchor, we could not sail direct out of the harbour, but were obliged to be towed towards the opposite shore. This required a great deal of labour to effect, and in addition we were nearly wrecked on the coast.

We had such rough weather, that very soon after our departure we lost sight of every ship in the convoy, consisting of thirteen sail. It was with the utmost difficulty (and carrying only a single sail) that the vessel could be managed; and for several days we were tossed about, without knowing where we were. I had hitherto never been sea-sick, but during this voyage I was for the first time; I lay quite stupefied, with five of my comrades in the hold, and was scarcely able to get up once during the day to procure a little refreshment, or a drink of water, which even then my stomach was unable to retain. The waves dashing constantly against the vessel sounded like the firing of cannon; the side passengers groaned, and the women screamed whenever a wave broke over the deck.

Suddenly, about four o'clock in the morning, there was a tremendous noise upon deck, followed by a heavy rolling for about a minute. Everyone was up in an instant, rushing towards the ladder, for we all thought the ship was wrecked. Fortunately, this proved not to be the case; but the long-boat had got loose from its fastenings and rolled overboard, carrying with it the caboose, all the spare masts, and everything lying in its way. The ship had sustained no farther damage than the railing on one side being partly broken away, so that it was dangerous to be on the deck. In spite of the weather, the carpenters were instantly set to work, and this damage was soon repaired. In the hold, about a dozen hammocks had given way, and those lying in them were thrown forcibly down: this occasioned a violent dispute between those who had fallen and those upon whom they had fallen, which almost proceeded to blows.

We imagined that we had long passed the Balearic Islands, but upon the weather clearing a little we got sight of the coast of Corsica; from this time the weather cleared up, although for some days there was a considerable roll in the sea, and all our vessels reached Gibraltar separately, but in good condition. Here we were obliged to perform a strict quarantine, and no person was allowed to leave the ship. Our officers were anxious to procure some fresh meat and a few other things, and at their request, four sheep, some oranges, and about one hundred cigars, were brought alongside; for these the owners had the conscience to ask twenty-seven dollars: this price being by far too high, the officers sent the pickpockets back again.

After a short stay, we took the same course we had formerly pursued, passed Cadiz, the coast of Portugal, Cape St. Vincent, the heights of Lisbon, and Cape Finisterre. We then entered the Bay of Biscay, passed through it in safety, and soon got sight of the coast of France and the Lizard Point, We soon passed Falmouth and Plymouth, and at last entered the port of Lymington. Here we got too near the shore, and grounded on the sand; all sails were immediately taken in, a number of pilot-boats came off to our assistance, and with their help we got. afloat without sustaining the slightest damage. We then sailed past Yarmouth, in the Isle of Wight, and ran into Portsmouth with the quarantine flag flying as we came from the Mediterranean.

As soon as we had anchored at the place of quarantine, which is opposite to Portsmouth, the quarantine-officer came alongside, but not on board; inquired from whence we came, if we had any, and how many sick on-board, and required a written report from the captain, to be signed also by the officers and the surgeon. To receive this report, he handed up a small box, fastened to. the end of a pole, into which the report was put. The officer himself was dressed in a linen frock and trousers, covered with pitch; his boatmen were also dressed in the same manner. Our imprisonment lasted for fourteen days, and every day this visit was repeated. However, here we were supplied with fresh meat, bread, and vegetables; but no one, on pain of death, was allowed to leave the ship. At last, when the fortnight was expired, the officer made his appearance in his usual dress, advanced half way up the ship's ladder, and handed the captain a Bible, upon which he was to take the oath. It is not the custom in England to take an oath with the fingers held up; but the form of the oath is repeated with the hand placed upon a Bible or Testament. As soon as this ceremony was over, the officer came on board, his men followed, compliments were exchanged, and a few glasses of wine were emptied in celebration of our safe arrival. The anchor was now weighed again, we came close in towards Portsmouth, and by chance were laid alongside of the man-of-war in which Nelson had fallen at the battle of Trafalgar. From the harbour we could very plainly see a pillar which had been erected in honour of this naval hero; but never having been near it, I am unable to give any description of it.

While in the harbour a dispute arose on board our ship. The

sailors had been engaged until the arrival of the vessel at the place of destination, namely, in a German port; they were, however, fearful of the ice in the Elbe and Weser, which at this time of the year usually floats down, and one and all refused to make the voyage to Germany. The captain insisted upon the fulfilment of their contract; but a fresh crew soon offered, who were willing to go, and even with lower wages than our men, a number of ships having been lately laid up and the sailors discharged. This our men were not aware of, and their object was to compel the captain to give them higher wages. They then gave in, and would willingly have remained, but the captain's turn was now come, and he discharged them one and all from the ship.

We were now at last on our way to Germany. Deal soon lay before us, but owing to contrary winds we could not proceed, and were tacking about for three days without making the least way. At last we got to anchor in Deal-roads, and waited for a wind, which soon sprung up and carried us up the channel.

At Harwich we cast anchor again, to wait for orders and an agent, who had to give us our regular discharge.

Everything at last was in order, we set sail; in thirty-six hours we saw the Dutch coast, and not long after we got sight of our beloved country. The joy which this caused us can only be felt by one who has been absent as long as we had from his native land. We sailed in safety past the sand-banks, and entered the harbour of Embden, where we were disembarked on the following day. Numbers had not patience to wait until the boats reached the landing-place, but sprang into the water up to their knees to reach the shore the sooner.

Amidst shouts, huzzas, and the music of our band, we marched into Embden, where we were for the last time quartered in the barracks lying close to the wall. Although the inhabitants speak a bad mixture of Dutch and German, still we could understand them tolerably well, and entered into conversation with any one who would talk with us, so glad we were to hear once more the German language.

As our hopes had been deceived so often, we still could not

entirely convince ourselves that we were to be discharged; but I am firmly convinced, that if orders had been received to embark again, but very few would have followed the colours, as we were all so much rejoiced at finding ourselves once more upon the Continent; and since our last voyage, had contracted such an aversion to the water-houses, as we in sport called the ships. But, thank God, no new orders arrived, and by order of our commander, the Duke of Cambridge, Viceroy of Hanover, we were discharged; each one first receiving his arrears of pay to the last farthing, We were allowed to keep all our clothing, and received besides a few dollars for those things which we had worn beyond the time, so that every soldier had from five to six *louis d'ors* in his pocket, and had not the slightest cause of complaint against the English government.

On the 13th of May, 1816, I received my discharge. I was now free, released from my military profession; I was once more a peaceable citizen, and began seriously to consider in what manner I should contrive to earn a subsistence, as a useful member of society. As an inexperienced lad I had left my native country, had passed nearly ten years chiefly in the field, and among rough warriors, had contracted, perhaps, many bad habits; but had now returned, thank God, not completely depraved, and still possessing a feeling of honour and honesty. The property I had to expect in my native-place was very inconsiderable, and I was uncertain likewise whether, owing to my having been absent at the time of the conscription, it had not been confiscated. At any rate, I knew that this trifle would not be sufficient to support me for the future, and without some addition would very soon be consumed. I might have entered the Hanoverian service, but I was tired of a soldier's life, and could not make up my mind to this. I thought to myself, you are still young and strong, and as long as Heaven grants you health, you will not fail, if you seek after it, to get employment; and hitherto these thoughts have not deceived me.

On the morning of the 13th of May, 1816, with my knapsack at my back, and a stout staff in my hand, I joyfully quitted Embden, and set out with. two of my best friends on my journey towards home. We halted no where, and without meeting any interruption, we travelled by way of Oldenburg, Delmenhorst, Bremen, Nieuburg, Hanover, Göttingen, Heiligenstadt, and Langensalza, to Gotha, which place we reached on the 21st of May, 1816, where about noon I entered the house of my married sister, who, notwithstanding the alteration in my complexion, browned by the sun, knew me instantly, and during the time of my stay here, treated me with the most sisterly affection. I made inquiries immediately about my other relations, and found to my great joy that all were well, with the exception of my eldest sister, who had been happily married, but was since deceased.

I did not remain long here; I was anxious to reach the place of my destination—my native town; for although I had been born in the country, still, from having passed the whole of my youthful days in it, I called it my native town. I scarce know how to describe my sensations, when upon reaching the last height I obtained a view of it. Tears, which I had not shed for a length of time, rolled down my cheeks; I recollected well how ten years before I had proceeded along the same road to meet my fate, and in what manner, young and inexperienced, I had wandered forth into the world without considering what might happen. I was now again in the same spot from whence I had departed in good health and condition; but when I considered how uncertain it was, whether I should recover any of my little property, and what means I should resort to to support myself, I felt a sinking at my heart, and often stood still for several minutes absorbed in reflections on the future: but with every step my courage increased, and at last I found myself at the gates of the town.

I wandered through the streets, but everything was changed. I met no-one I knew, I felt as if in a new world; at last I sought out my sister, and found her as much changed as everything else. I now looked for employment in various ways, but nothing succeeded; the little money I received, and which a greedy guardian endeavoured to make less, was gradually consumed, and I found myself in a melancholy condition.

At last I obtained the situation I at present occupy. If I do not here live exactly at my ease, still I am not in want. I can lay myself down every night quietly on my bed, without any apprehension of being awakened too soon by a drum or a bugle. Sometimes, when in my solitary hours I give way to reflection, and see many who were brought up with me now living in comfort and affluence, and scarcely deigning to cast a look upon me, I experience a bitter feeling of repentance, and I often feel vexed and sorrowful when I consider in what way I destroyed all my brightest prospects. But when, on the other hand, I remember that I have often been in situations, compared to which my present condition is a blessing, I become resigned and cheerful. However, in conclusion, I would advise everyone never to act without reflection, in order that he may avoid repentance, such as I have felt

Although I do not consider myself possessed of more courage than the generality of men, yet in all dangers and difficulties I have constantly retained a kind of self-possession. If I was to say, that where there was real danger I felt no sort of trepidation, I should say that which was not true: for every man, even the bravest, feels a sort of shuddering when he goes to encounter death, even if his hour should not be come. But this natural abhorrence is of a very different description from that felt by a criminal on his way to the place of execution. Everyone who gives out that he knows not what fear is, I call a boaster; for this feeling is a part of our nature. I have often heard old veteran soldiers speak upon this subject, before I had myself experienced it.

No sooner does a man find himself in the heat of action, and enveloped with smoke, than all reflection is lost, and he is only occupied with himself and his business, without paying any attention to his neighbours. If obliged to remain a quiet spectator—to stand under fire, and be shot at like a dog—then this feeling of abhorrence is doubly felt. In this manner I once saw the 10th and 11th French Dragoon Regiments dreadfully thinned near Astorga, without the men ever having the opportunity of drawing their sabres, they having been placed as a support, in case of the besieged attempting a sortie. I could relate many instances of this kind. Upon young soldiers facing the enemy, perhaps for the first time, the sight of the wounded carried by makes a most decided impression: these often describe matters as a much worse than they are in reality, in order to impress their comrades with a higher opinion of their courage. Every soldier takes his chance; and if exposed to danger, a bullet is as likely to strike the commander as the commonest man: there is therefore no great proof of merit in being wounded; for, if the man who is wounded only knew that a ball, which would injure him, was about to come that way, would he not, unless actually compelled by circumstances to remain, change his position without hesitation?

Among the many thousands who may be present in an action, no one believes that he himself will fall; because he is impressed with a sort of confidence in his own safety, although he may not be able to repress a dread at the idea of exposing himself to death.

What many a one relates upon his return from his campaigns, is frequently more than one-half untrue: on one occasion, for instance, "the men were over their shoes in blood;" in another, "the dead have been piled twelve deep on one another, &c." When such a one meets with a person well acquainted with such matters, he is unquestionably ashamed of himself. That much blood has often been shed upon the same spot cannot be denied; but that it ever is so deep as to be waded through, is a decided falsehood: that upon some occasions, ten, twelve, or even more men have been struck at the same time, is true enough; but is it ever the case that all those who fall are killed upon the spot? No; certainly not. I well know that at Astorga eighteen men of my company were struck down by one shot; but only two were killed; the others, more or less wounded, were taken away immediately to be assisted by the surgeons, and they did not all meet with their fate in a mass like herrings. I would therefore recommend to all great talkers not to excite such a feeling of horror in those inexperienced in these matters, because they themselves happen to have been present at such occurrences, and have most probably seen double.

www.ingramcontent.com/pod-product-compliance
Lightning Source LLC
Chambersburg PA
CBHW032043080426
42733CB00006B/181